Navigating Japan's Business Culture

A Practical Guide to Succeeding in the Japanese Market

by Robert Charles Azar

Write Way Publishing Company, LLC

Navigating Japan's Business Culture
A Practical Guide to Succeeding in the Japanese Market

Printed in the United States of America
ISBN: 978-0-997607628

Library of Congress: 2016945525

Front cover concept by Robert Charles Azar
Cover created by CSinclaire Write-Design
Book design by CSinclaire Write-Design

Published by Write Way Publishing Company

What Readers Are Saying

"It has been my distinct privilege to work with Robert Azar on many different projects and in many different capacities off and on over the past 30 years. The depth and breadth of Mr. Azar's experience in doing business in Asia is truly staggering. I cannot think of any non-Japanese person who understands the language and culture of Japan better than Mr. Azar. It is this …unique and thorough understanding of culture that enables Mr. Azar to help his clients and business partners to succeed in Japan and other Asian markets."

Paul Taylor, Esq.
Vice President & General Counsel
Ajinomoto North America, Inc.

"The depth of understanding in *Navigating Japan's Business Culture* is unprecedented. As a Japanese reader, I was surprised to learn the cultural dynamics that govern management and communication in Japanese business. Azar's book is informative, practical, and strategic, and will help you achieve your goals in Japan via effective strategies and correct cultural understanding. I recommend this book to everyone who engages in Japanese business, even to Japanese businessmen."

Koyama Tomohisa
Executive Advisor to the President, Nagoya University
Former Deputy Director, New and Renewable Energy Division,
Ministry of Economy, Trade and Industry of Japan

"Robert Azar's book is essential reading for foreign businessmen looking for success in the Japanese market. He has had over 35 years practical experience in Japanese business, academic training about Japan, and is fluent in Japanese, a rare and invaluable combination. You will profit from reading this book."

Prof. Gerald Curtis
Burgess Professor Emeritus of Japanese Government,
Columbia University

"*Navigating Japan's Business Culture* consists of tons of useful tips as well as actual examples in the Japanese business world. I was most impressed by Robert Azar's understanding of Japan's historical background as well as the intricacies of Japan's actual business practices. (He sometimes knows Japanese culture more than I do!) This book provides deep insight based on his broad business experience and his scholarly study. I highly recommend this book as a practical guide to those who want to really understand and overcome the cultural gap and succeed in the Japanese market."

Matsuo Takashi
Director, Sumitomo Electric Lightwave Corporation

"My architectural/engineering firm has navigated the intricacies and challenges of doing business with Japanese companies since 1985. I only wish Robert Azar's book had been available when we started this journey. Azar provides keen insight into the business culture of Japanese companies and describes strategies and tactics to be successful. If one is doing business with Japanese this is required reading."

John L. Atkins, III
Honorary General Consul of Japan in
Raleigh, North Carolina 2009–2014

"Robert Azar is a gifted global communicator with astounding insight into the enigmatic and opaque business practices of the Japanese executive. Whether you are looking to invest in Japan or develop an import relationship with a Japanese company, Robert's insights will be instrumental to your success."

Rick Van Sant, Ph.D.
Executive Director, Center for International Understanding
Chapel Hill, North Carolina

"Robert Azar is an accomplished businessman, consultant and commentator with vast experience in Asia—and particularly in Japan. His fluency in Japanese, his deep understanding of the culture and how it shapes Japanese business practices and his academic training in East Asian political, economic and cultural affairs make his insights a valuable resource for those doing business with this valued strategic and economic partner."

James T. Fain III
Former North Carolina Commerce Secretary, 2001–2009

"Knowing 'what' is good, but knowing 'why' is critical. Robert Azar's 35 years of living and doing business in Japan sheds valuable insight into why some companies succeed and others fail in Japan. His business experiences combined with his deep cultural understandings make this book an essential tool."

Elaine Marshall
North Carolina Secretary of State, 1997–present

"This book is a must read by all who engage in international economic development. The North Carolina and Japanese economies are hugely important to each other. Understanding each other better; understanding how to better collaborate; …honoring each other's culture—all extremely important. Robert Azar understands… all this better than most. Read his book; enjoy his depth and most importantly LEARN from him. He's made it all work."

Norris Tolson
Former North Carolina Commerce Secretary

DEDICATION

This book is dedicated to the following individuals who have inspired, mentored, and made possible what has turned out to be a lifelong passion and journey with business and culture in Asia.

Prof. Sonoda Koji, Prof. Moss Roberts, and Prof. Patricia Eichenbaum-Karetzky who encouraged my early interest in Asian studies when I was an undergraduate student at New York University.

Prof. Hugh Patrick, Prof. Gerald Curtis, Prof. Paul Anderer, Prof. Carol Gluck, Prof. Yasuko Watt, Prof. Herbert Passin, Prof. Wm. Theodore de Barry, Prof. Donald Keene, and Prof. Richard Rubinger at Columbia University where I studied East Asian political, economic, and cultural affairs as a graduate student.

To my U.S., European, South American, and Asian clients over the years who by affording me the opportunity to work on their business ventures in Asia enabled my intercultural and international business experience to come to life.

Paul Taylor, Yamada Mitsuo, Dr. Shirakabe Yukio, Melvin Williams, Yamane Toshimi, Ii Naoaki – individuals for whose steadfast friendship and encouragement I am equally as indebted as I am appreciative.

Dr. Ohmori Kitaro and the numerous executives and other professionals throughout Asia with whom I have had the pleasure of collaborating over the past three-and-a-half decades.

目次

TABLE OF CONTENTS

Chapter 3:
The Challenges of Japanese Communication 99

Chapter 4:
Sales the Japanese Way 139

LIST OF TABLES

まえがき

This book is a hands-on manual for foreign companies wishing to succeed in the Japanese market. It is designed to serve as a practical guide for understanding and successfully navigating the numerous obstacles that foreign executives confront in Japan.

Those generic challenges that companies face when conducting business in any foreign market—such as government regulation, size of the country's economy, size of the market for a product, competitive environment, purchasing power of consumers, import duties, and the like—are not covered in this book. Those issues are already well known and understood by American executives. Instead, this book focuses exclusively on the difficulties of doing business in Japan that arise from culture-based differences in business practices. In contrast to the known generic challenges, foreign executives generally are not aware of culture-based challenges, how they hinder the success of foreign companies, or what to do about them. This book will resolve much of this handicap by raising awareness and providing solutions that are practical and proven.

That Japan should have business practice differences that arise from its distinct culture is not surprising. Dr. Peter Drucker (1909-2005), the founder of modern management in the West, viewed the need of a country to successfully combine capitalism with its indigenous social values and cultural practices as a critical step for capitalism to succeed in that country. He expressed this specifically when he wrote:

> *Management...is deeply imbedded in culture. What managers do in West Germany, in the United Kingdom, in the United States, in Japan, or in Brazil is exactly the same. How they do it may be quite different. Thus one of the basic challenges managers in a developing country face is to find and identify those parts of their own tradition, history, and culture that can be used as management building blocks. The difference between Japan's economic success and India's relative backwardness is largely explained by the fact the Japanese managers were able to plant imported management concepts in their own cultural soil and make them grow.* — **Peter F. Drucker,** *The Essential Drucker* **(New York: Harper Collins, 2001), p. 11.**

What is that native "cultural soil" that Drucker refers to in the case of Japan? This book will elucidate this in a major, far-reaching manner. When Japan imported and adopted capitalism from the West in the later part of the nineteenth century, it succeeded in becoming a powerful capitalist economy precisely because Japanese business leaders of that day were successful in combining capitalism with their country's indigenous cultural values and social customs.

The well-recognized business success Japan was able to achieve—becoming the largest economy in Asia and the second largest in the world after the U.S. until it was recently surpassed by China—is a clear indication of the degree to which Japan's leaders were able to combine indigenous culture and capitalism. Japan is a country with a two thousand year history and a homogeneous society. Its culture is extremely well formed and distinct even within Asia. As a result, both the cultural framework within and the cultural foundation upon which Japan engages in business are fundamentally different from America's cultural framework.

This book illuminates those cultural values and social customs so entwined in Japanese capitalism. What are they? How do they impact the way business is conducted in Japan? How do they challenge foreign companies in the Japanese market? How can American companies effectively deal with them to thereby level the playing field and attain greater levels of success?

To clarify, by culture, I do not mean music, literature, theater, art, and other areas of the humanities. In this book, I define culture as the sensibilities of the people; the preferences of the society; and the customary norms by which the people live, view the world, make decisions, relate to each other, engage each other within groups, and interact between groups. These sensibilities, preferences, and norms bring with them their own complex web of cultural nuances, unspoken expectations, and built-in requirements that are unique to each society. This is especially true for Japan's cultural context. This book identifies those sensibilities, preferences, and norms in Japan explaining their cultural roots, how they inform the way Japanese manage and engage in business, the resulting challenges they present to foreign companies, and how American executives can most effectively navigate them.

Ten years of formal academic training in Asian culture and

field research; fluency in the Japanese language; seven years of living in the Far East; thirty-five years of hands-on, executive-level experience in U.S. business in Japan and eight other Asian countries, and a lifetime of study have made it abundantly clear to me that there is one overwhelming reason why American companies either do not achieve their maximum potential or outright fail in Japan. That reason is ultimately failure to understand and effectively deal with culture-based differences in Japanese management and business practices. Fail to recognize and successfully deal with these indigenous practices and a foreign company's business will never fully get on track in the Japanese market.

With their far-reaching impact, why then are culture-based obstacles so underestimated and even ignored by foreign executives targeting the Japanese market? Even when recognized, they often are treated as trivial when the reality is quite the opposite. The influence of cultural factors on business in Japan is as primary as it is profound.

If the generic challenges in international business that are readily understood by international business men and women are akin to the tip of an iceberg that is seen and recognized, then the culture-based obstacles are the part of the iceberg below the surface. That part of the iceberg is not seen, not known, and certainly not understood. Just as the submerged part of the iceberg is much larger and has significantly greater weight than the part above the surface, culture-based factors are a major determinant impacting the level of success for foreign companies doing business in Japan—often even more influential than the recognized generic challenges.

In most cases, these culture-based factors never even appear on the radar of foreign executives—either before they engage in business in Japan, during the time they do, or even after they complete their work in Japan and leave for assignments elsewhere. Over the course of three-and-a-half decades, a significant majority of companies I have worked with had no realization they needed to consider the possibility that products, management methods, sales approaches, and other business practices might need to be adjusted to accommodate Japanese cultural differences.

Let's get specific. The following is a quick look at fifteen representative areas of business where cultural factors have a direct impact on a foreign company's bottom line business in Japan. Most of these factors will apply broadly to other Asian markets as well.

- **Product Selection:** Culture has a major influence on which products from your company's product line will sell well in overseas markets. Your best-selling product in America may not be the one that sells well abroad. There are cases where your best selling product abroad may not yet exist in your domestic market and will only be developed as you adapt your product line to local market preferences abroad.

- **Product Features:** The cultural preferences of the target country will decide what features the products must have if they are to be accepted and gain meaningful market share.

- **Product Packaging:** Both the type of packaging and packaging colors to use (or to avoid) will need to be considered carefully. For example, consumer products packaged in unadorned black, while sleek in the U.S., will not sell well in Japan. And the reason is entirely cultural.

- **Product Advertising:** Advertising styles differ across cultures. Should your advertising directly promote your product as advertising does in the States or should it be more subtle and indirect as is customary in Europe?

- **Product Marketing:** The "hot buttons" that will lead overseas customers to decide to purchase your product will be influenced by the social norms and cultural preferences those customers embrace. Your company must determine what aspects of the product or product line should be emphasized in order to gain meaningful market share.

- **Product Size:** American products are nicely sized for our "bigger is better" society. However, larger sized products are often undesirable in land-starved Japan. Entire categories of American products have never been sold in Japan simply because the products are not scaled for living conditions there.

- **Negotiating:** Cultural values and business styles have a profound effect on business negotiation. Correctly understanding and navigating Japan's negotiation dynamics is vital to successfully negotiating your corporate interests and building strong relationships, which drive business success in Japan.

- **Managing:** Both corporate and employee management are quite different in Japan based on deeply held and intrinsic cultural values. Failure to take this into consideration will negatively impact the sales results of your business or joint venture there.

- **Human Resources:** Putting the right executives in place to run your Japan operation is critical. Assuming this means executives who have been most successful in America can bring an unwelcome surprise.

- **Business Partner Relationships:** It is important for

your company to recognize that business relationships in Asian markets, Japan in particular, have a different framework and significance than in your domestic market.

- **Business Motivation:** It is necessary to determine what motivations (besides profit) drive an Asian company to want to work with your company and to be certain those driving factors are in your corporate best interest.

- **Perception of Time:** Understanding the cultural perception of time is vital. This impacts business agreements, project planning, the development of your overseas business, and your relationships with your partners there.

- **Sales and Marketing:** Cultural values, practices, and national preferences are essential considerations in determining your sales and marketing approaches.

- **Manufacturing:** Your company must understand and account for cultural differences that will directly and indirectly affect how you perceive, plan for, and execute manufacturing in Japan.

- **Communication:** Even something as basic as "communication" is strongly affected by cultural difference, especially in Japan. Dealing with a communication culture where even "yes" can mean "no" has a serious effect on business negotiations, agreements, expectations, relationship building, and sales performance.

This representative list of fundamental business areas hints at the impact cultural differences create. The questions now are how do you recognize those differences and then how do you deal with them effectively so as to enable your company to attain optimal success in the Japanese market.

A survey of the books available in America on the subject of doing business in Japan shows that they almost exclusively deal with Japanese etiquette. They discuss, for example, how to exchange business cards, the importance of gift giving, and the need to have drinks in the evening or play golf together with Japanese executives. The problem is that these are rules of social etiquette; they are not core aspects of business. While these rules of etiquette are important to know, they do not enable foreign executives to even enter the batter's box, let alone enable them to hit a home run in conducting business in the Japanese market.

I have found that books on cultural intelligence (CQ) tend to focus on cultural competence theory—namely, paradigms regarding how to describe the traits of a foreign culture. For example, is communication high or low context? Or is decision-making top down or bottom up? While theories and paradigms of cultural intelligence are helpful by providing *adjectives*, this book provides for *action*. Going far beyond theory and cultural descriptions, this book provides real, actionable intelligence. In other words, while CQ books describe how peoples and cultures might differ from each other, this book is unique in that it helps you know what to do about those differences from a management perspective in order to maximize your business success in Japan.

I refer to this as intercultural management in that it identifies differences in culture, how those differences impact business, and what executives can do to most effectively manage their business in light of those differences. The goal is for cultural variations to no longer be obstacles to companies working to achieve their business goals in foreign markets. Furthermore, once aware of these cultural dynamics, foreign executives can for the first time strategically leverage them to attain even greater levels of success. Specific areas of actionable intelligence covered in this book include negotiating, planning, product research and development, production, marketing, sales, distribution, human resources, customer service, management, operations, communication, relationship building, and leadership.

This book was written to shed new light on how business is actually approached, planned for, and conducted in the world's third largest economy. Besides dealing with the important fundamental aspects of business from both company and executive views, it helps foreign companies understand Japanese employees and Japanese workplaces by explaining how employees view their employer and their work positions, what motivates them, and why Japanese are so dedicated to their work. It addresses consumer preferences and expectations, why product distribution can be problematic, and numerous other salient areas foreign companies do not address sufficiently if at all.

The first section of this book identifies the challenges that are caused by Japan's culture-based differences in business practices within individual areas of business that challenge foreign executives on the micro level, such as in sales, management, and customer service.

The second section addresses macro level management challenges that more broadly impact a foreign company's business in Japan. This section also includes mini case studies of the experiences of several former clients. Both sections provide practical and proven steps for foreign executives to effectively navigate Japan's cultural challenges so that foreign executives can maximize their success in the Japanese market.

The book, then, has three major objectives:

- Identifying Japan's culture-based differences in management and business practices so foreign executives can be aware of them

- Explaining and clearly linking these practices to their cultural roots so that they may be understood in their correct cultural context

- Serving as a practical guide to successfully deal with culture-based differences in business practices so that foreign companies can optimize their business success in Japan

The information contained in this book is factual and was learned through personal experience engaging in U.S.-Japan business over the past thirty-five years. The names of companies, employees, and products of American and Japanese firms that I worked with have been changed out of respect for their privacy; however, the names of historical Japanese companies and individuals have not been changed. The names of Japanese individuals are written family name first, followed by their first name in accord with Japanese tradition. Citations in this book quoted from Japanese language sources have been translated into English by this author unless otherwise specified.

The content of this book deals with modern Japan's mainstream management and business practices. It is acknowledged that in Japan, as in most countries in the world, not all companies and individuals swim in the mainstream.

While the focus of this book is Japan, the principles of how to approach a foreign market can be applied broadly to engaging in business in many international markets; what issues to look for will be similar but how to effectively deal with them will vary culture to culture.

This book will be of interest to and benefit three groups of readers. In the first group are individuals with professional interests in Japan, such as those in business and government. The second is comprised of those with an academic interest in Japan, such as teachers and students of both Japanese business and culture. The third group constitutes the culturally curious and globally minded who are interested in the many diverse cultures that enrich our world, as well as those seeking greater cross-cultural competence. It is my hope that this book will help improve U.S.-Japan business and cultural understanding, thereby promoting greater stability, cooperation, and prosperity in the 21st century.

Robert Charles Azar
July 2016

Navigating Japan's Business Culture

PART ONE

THE JAPANESE
APPROACH TO BUSINESS

*How Business Is
Conducted Differently &
How To Do It Right*

交渉術

CHAPTER 1

Approach To Business & Negotiating In Japan

I. APPROACH TO BUSINESS & NEGOTIATING

In America, the goal of negotiating is to gain as many of your company's business interests as possible, while ceding as few as possible. Negotiations—and business in general—are approached as a zero-sum game whereby it is commonplace for one company's objectives to be obtained at the other party's expense.

In Japan, however, negotiating and doing business are approached with a very different viewpoint. The Japanese focus is on the mutual benefit of both companies. They see negotiating and business as a process of give and take in which both companies recognize and try to accommodate each other's business interests while endeavoring to secure the long-term success of the joint project and their mutual relationship.

For them, the objective of negotiating is to identify and, to the extent possible, agree on what is in the best interest of the mutual business project and the steps to achieve project success. Doing this, they believe, will allow for each side to achieve the greatest number of their respective business interests over time. This holistic approach to negotiating and business wherein securing the mutual interests of the companies' relationship and the specific business project is the best way to secure the business interests of each company for the long term is quite different from a zero-sum game view.

Why is the approach to business and negotiating so radically different between the two countries? The reason is that there is a dichotomy between the dynamics that govern business in Japanese culture and what drives business in American culture.

In America, business is *transaction driven*. That is, two or more companies agree to collaborate to achieve the specific business objectives of a mutual project. Typically those goals are clearly delineated in the business agreement the companies sign at the outset of a project. These agreements spell out the specific roles and responsibilities of each party in great detail, and by signing the agreement, the companies commit themselves to performing those specified tasks. They are not responsible for or obligated to provide any work or services beyond what the agreement specifically calls for them to do.

In contrast, business in Japan is *relationship driven*. Business is engaged in based on the foundation of the relationship between the companies involved. So while it is possible in America for companies previously unknown to each other to start conducting business together by simply putting in place a clearly defined business agreement, that would not happen in Japan. Japanese companies do not work together without a relationship.

As a consequence of this preference, negotiating in Japan takes place on two distinct levels:

- Working out the business specifics of the joint venture

- Creating a sense of partnership and mutual benefit between the two firms by building a trust relationship for long-term cooperation

Japanese pursue these two objectives simultaneously and in parallel. This dual pursuit is the reason Japanese engage in so much relationship building activity during the course of the negotiations. This also is one of the reasons why negotiations proceed more slowly and take longer in Japan than in other countries.

American executives are well acquainted with this first part of negotiating—working out the specifics of the joint business venture. However, the second aspect of relationship building is not given much importance in American business culture. In Japan, the two aspects have equal significance. In many cases, Japanese companies consider the relationship to be even more important than the individual project itself.

Why is that? In the States, once the purpose of the joint business project is completed, the parties wish each other well and go their separate ways. In Japan, the mutual relationship is expected to outlast any individual business project. Through negotiating project specifics and building a business relationship, both companies become committed to work together to enhance their mutual interests and well-being long term—through the initial business project and then any subsequent ones.

In addition, Japanese culture has long placed great importance and priority on relationships. They are highly valued and taken very seriously. This is why Japanese are quite formal and polite in relating to others. In America, by contrast, we tend to take relationships much more lightly. We are comfortable with being casual even with those we are meeting for the first time. This is not the case in Japan. Japanese remain formal and respectful in most relationships, especially in business.

For example, while Americans are quick to relate to each other on a first name basis, Japanese do not use first names in business; they only use first names with close social friends and relatives. Even when employees have worked together for decades, they still call each other by family name, not by their given name. This is done out of respect for the relationship as well as respect for the individual.

It is imperative that Americans realize how important relationships are to Japanese and give relationships the attention they require. Failure to do so inevitably limits, if not destroys, one's chances of success in Japan.

Think of these two parts of negotiating as the two rail tracks of a railroad. A train can only move forward if both tracks are laid in parallel and at the same time. Likewise, negotiations with Japanese companies will only move forward when progress in both project planning and relationship building occur in tandem. That is, the Japanese must reach a comfort level with both the specifics of the proposed business venture and the relationship development simultaneously. Japanese companies rarely embark on a business venture with a new partner without a sufficient comfort level in both areas.

Another difference in the way Americans and Japanese approach negotiating and doing business is that Japanese take a long-term approach while Americans are more oriented toward the short term. Consequently, Japanese need to see that the American company they are negotiating with is committed to working together for the long term and is willing to make decisions based on what is in the long-term—not just short-term—interests of the project.

While American companies tend to emphasize maximizing profit in the short term, Japanese companies prefer stable profit over the long term even if it means a smaller profit initially. Long-term profit stability means long-term stability for the company and for all of its business interests. During negotiations, American executives need to demonstrate to Japanese executives that they also have a long-term view of the joint business. Without it, Japanese typically do not form a sufficient comfort level to want to work together or even to continue negotiations.

With this long-term, relationship-oriented approach, it is expected that both parties will make compromises; Japanese negotiations generally do not utilize a zero-sum game approach or other techniques that force the other party into agreement.

The Japanese want to see that you are genuinely interested in the mutual benefit of both parties—not just in your own company's best interest. Willingness to compromise is one way this is done. In the sensibilities of Japanese, to compromise in negotiating is not seen as a weakness but rather a strength. Compromising is a strong indication that your relationship with them is a priority to you—you are willing to put your money where your mouth is. Compromise is an important way in which American executives can demonstrate to Japanese that your relationship with them is important to your company. With this in mind, it is advisable to start negotiations with several "give away" items that you have prepared in advance that are likely to be of interest to the Japanese company.

The Japanese negotiating dynamic of compromising, together with its commitment to the mutual relationship and the long-term success of the project, often causes foreign executives to feel bewildered. Just how much do you need to compromise during negotiations? It is not necessary to compromise on or agree to every proposal Japanese put forth. It is, after all, a negotiation, not a give away.

So then what degree of flexibility and compromise should American executives demonstrate when negotiating in order to show "sincerity" (genuineness of purpose in Western culture) and not alienate their Japanese counterparts? There is no hard and fast rule. It will vary from industry to industry and company to company. As a general guideline, what I have found is that flexibility expectations rise the more important the matter is. In the end, striking a sensible balance between the needs of the long-term project and the realities of your company is always a reasonable—and sustainable—approach. This can only be decided on a case-by-case basis.

Given the Japanese tendency to press for compromises both during the negotiations and even after the project begins, the issue becomes how can American companies put off agreeing to a given request for a compromise without alienating Japanese partners. The "we are not contractually obligated to do that" response that is commonplace in the States is counterproductive in Japan and should be avoided. It makes your company come across as inflexible and, rather than thinking about the needs of the mutual project, focused only on your company. Simply put, the notion of "not being contractually obligated" does not translate well culturally in Japan. Being a good business partner, having a good relationship, is defined in part by giving priority to both the needs of the project as well as one's own needs.

The following are ways to avoid agreeing to proposals or requests from Japanese both during the negotiations and once the project has begun that I have developed and found work well:

- If applicable, take the position that a proposal goes against the established corporate policies of your company. Japanese respect that and realize nothing can be done about that. This reason translates well culturally.

- Reply by saying that your company has thought about that option before but never came to a decision about it. Report that the matter can be discussed further in your company. This is an effective way of deflecting the issue.

- Respond by saying that your company has never considered that before, but your company will look into it. When all else fails, this catchall reply is generally favorably received.

As mentioned above, the objective of negotiating for Japanese companies is to identify and agree on what is in the best interest of the mutual business project for the long term and how to achieve that. In this holistic negotiating focus, the goals and needs of the group project are discussed at great length, sometimes even more than the interests of the individual companies. Japanese often do not specify the responsibilities of each party in the detail that Americans do. Of course, roles and general areas of responsibility are covered in a broad stroke manner, but typically they are not delineated with the degree of detail and specificity that Americans prefer having in business agreements. There are two reasons for this.

First, realizing that the challenges any business project faces will, of course, change over time as market and competitive conditions evolve, the Japanese focus is on the interests of and mutual commitment to the total project instead of on individual company tasks.

Second, as a result of both parties being committed to their mutual relationship, it is expected that each party will act in good faith to engage in tasks that become required over time to meet each new challenge and advance the success of the project.

So while American negotiations and business focus on specific roles and tasks of the companies involved, the Japanese focus is on commitment to the long-term success of the business project as well as to the mutual relationship. The American business agreement excels in making sure that the participants engage in the specific roles and tasks delineated in it. The Japanese approach excels in making sure each participant is committed to performing the changing roles and tasks the joint project requires over time. The Japanese approach affords the companies involved greater flexibility to meet the needs of the project as those needs evolve over the long term.

The American approach locks each company into specified roles and tasks that they are contractually obligated to provide as delineated in the business agreement. At the same time, it gives the company a way to avoid engaging in any additional tasks. An American company can decline any requests to engage in any roles or tasks it did not agree to in the negotiated business agreement. This can be a valuable safeguard in the event the project is not going well and the company wishes to cut its losses and move on.

In contrast, while not bearing the same level of contractual focus on specific tasks as American companies, Japanese companies are committed to carrying out project tasks that can be reasonably expected of them over time because they are committed to the long-term success of the joint venture as well as the mutual relationship of the parties involved. Through their relationships and business agreements, Japanese companies are on the hook for a lot more than American companies are.

> While the American approach to negotiating and conducting business puts companies in a position to be *contractually* obligated, the Japanese approach leaves companies *relationally* obligated.

In other words, while the American approach to negotiating and conducting business puts companies in a position to be *contractually* obligated, the Japanese approach leaves companies *relationally* obligated—that is, companies are obligated to act due to the expectations of the relationship and the joint project.

Being obligated to a joint business project for the long term reinforces even further the Japanese natural preference for wanting to establish a sufficient comfort level and strong relationship before they decide to commence doing business with a new business partner.

From the Japanese perspective, the importance (and priority) of building that favorable working relationship has practical value. Namely, that the favorable working relationship will outlive any individual business project. Since Japanese companies typically maintain the relationship even after the business venture itself has ended, it is very easy to start subsequent projects together as the relationship is already in place.

As a result of these factors, negotiating in Japan requires more time than negotiating in other countries. These factors are also why Japanese companies are slow to sign a business agreement.

II. COMMUNICATION IN NEGOTIATIONS

A. APPROPRIATE TIME, VENUE & TYPE OF COMMUNICATION

As business is relationship driven for them, Japanese prefer face-to-face meetings rather than e-mail or telephone communication. This is especially true for discussions of substantive matters. In the case of negotiating, face-to-face is imperative.

Americans place high priority on expediency and convenience, so we are comfortable communicating via e-mail and even using e-mail in negotiating. Japanese, on the other hand, see taking the time, expense, and effort to travel to meet face-to-face as a measure of a company's relationship sincerity and a reflection of how important the matter is to both parties.

Typically the frequency of face-to-face communication is the greatest during the early stages of collaboration, starting with the "becoming acquainted" stage and on through the negotiation process, the signing of the business agreement, the official launch of the project, and an appropriate lead-in time. After that, the frequency of face-to-face meetings tends to decrease though they still remain an essential part of maintaining both your relationship and your business interest with your Japanese partner. This is true for as long as you engage in business together.

Japanese will continue to require face-to-face communication even after your business has started in Japan in the event of major developments or problems. Examples of these circumstances would include:

- **Regulatory issues:** When your product being sold in Japan experiences regulatory problems or questioning, for instance

- **Consumer use problems:** In the event harm comes to a customer as a result of using your product

- **Problems with third party collaborators in Japan:** On occasions when difficulties arise with parties other than your sales partner

- **New product launches:** At the launch of any new products you are selling in Japan

There are other times face-to-face communication and meetings are necessary after project commencement:

- **Sales training for your Japanese business partner:** Sales training will be needed both before and after launching your business in Japan. Any foreign company seeking to maximize its success in the Japanese market should plan to provide training in new product developments and sales on a regular basis for the duration of its business efforts in Japan. The more you keep your partner company focused on selling your products, the more they will keep their salespeople and marketing efforts focused on selling your products.

- **Product usage training for product retailers and users:** For example, you sell medical products to your Japanese partner (your customer) who sells your products to hospitals or clinics (retailers). The clinic then uses your product to treat their patients (product users). The training for your retailers (hospitals, clinics, etc.) and product users needs to be done jointly by your company and your Japanese sales partner.

Given the time and expense of traveling to Japan, it is not only fair but also reasonable and appropriate for some of the negotiation meetings to take place in the States. The perfect time for American executives to suggest that the next meeting be in the U.S. is at the conclusion of a meeting in Japan. Inviting the Japanese company to meet at your U.S. corporate headquarters signals to them that you are serious about wanting to build a strong working relationship with them.

As your company endeavors to engage in business in Japan, it is common for more meetings to take place there than in America as you will want to make firsthand decisions about the Japanese market by visiting factories, warehouses, distributors, and retail sales channels. However, if the Japanese company hesitates or does not agree to your invitation to come to the States for meetings, that is a major red flag. It is a clear sign that their interest in working with your company is weak. It likewise demonstrates an insufficient commitment to your business project. In that case, it would be better to move on and seek another business partner for the Japanese market. Accepting or declining to meet at your corporate headquarters may be a subtle action on their part but nonetheless it is one that speaks volumes.

American executives often suggest Hawaii as a location for face-to-face meetings with Japanese companies as a sensible way to deal with meeting venue. While Hawaii is a good midpoint location for American-Japanese meetings, having initial meetings there does not carry the same significance as meeting at your company's corporate headquarters unless, of course, your headquarters is in Hawaii.

Should your U.S. company request an initial meeting in Hawaii and not at your corporate headquarters, Japanese will interpret this as a weak interest in them as your partner. They will assume you must be having similar discussions with other potential Japanese partners and have not yet narrowed the field.

When the Japanese firm suggests a Hawaii rendezvous early on instead of meeting at your corporate headquarters that likewise is a red flag. They may be more interested in the opportunity to travel to Hawaii to enjoy a few days in the sun and on the golf course than in pursuing business with your company.

Where meetings take place has an additional significance in Japan that is not found in the U.S. Namely, the more important the topic of the discussion, the more "appropriate" the venue must be. Japanese are rarely flexible on this point.

By way of example, I was facilitating a negotiation between an American company—let's call them the GHI Company—and a Japanese firm (referred to here as Mori Inc.). The two companies were interested in working together on a very large project that would bring to Japan a product line that was the world's leader in its product area. Mori Inc. was one of the leaders in Japan for selling products in that category and being able to sell GHI's product would not only significantly increase their sales and profitability but also would establish them as the clear leader in their industry in Japan.

During the second day of negotiations, Mori Inc.'s sales director, Mr. Shizuno, mentioned that they were organizing a special sales team comprised of the company's best salesmen who would be dedicated to selling only GHI's products. The international sales director for GHI, Henry Thompson, asked how many people were on that sales team. Mr. Shizuno responded that there were twelve. Mr. Thompson was surprised by that reply.

After the meetings finished for the day, we walked from Mori's corporate headquarters to a restaurant that was a short distance away. While we were waiting at an intersection for the traffic light to change, Mr. Thompson suddenly turned to Mr. Shizuno and said, "This is a very important business opportunity that our company takes very seriously, and Japan is a huge market for our products. How in the world can you possibly hope to cover the entire Japanese market with only twelve salesmen?" Mr. Shizuno froze. The traffic light changed to green and the rest of the group crossed the street and continued to the restaurant. Mr. Shizuno, however, did not move. He remained in place momentarily, with Mr. Thompson waiting there for a reply.

Mr. Thompson was irritated by Mr. Shizuno's total lack of response and repeated the question two more times. It was a simple, straightforward question, and Mr. Thompson could not understand why Mr. Shizuno was not responding. Mr. Shizuno turned to me and suggested that Mr. Thompson and I catch up with the rest of the group. We did and Mr. Shizuno joined us shortly thereafter. However, he would neither talk to nor even look at Mr. Thompson the rest of the evening. Later that night after I had returned to my hotel room, there was a telephone message waiting that asked me to call Mori Inc.'s president immediately. In that call, the president expressed what he termed as the anger and disappointment his whole company felt as a result of Mr. Thompson's actions on the way to the restaurant.

While Mr. Thompson was correct in thinking it was a simple, straightforward question, what he did not realize was that in Japan a question of that importance should only be discussed at an appropriate time and in an appropriate venue. The more important the topic, the more appropriate the venue needs to be. A street corner was definitely neither the correct place nor time for a discussion of that significance. The Japanese perceived his attempted street corner conversation as rude and unprofessional.

Here are common times and places that are appropriate to discuss topics important to you and your Japanese partner:

- During official business meetings at the offices or facilities of either company

- A formal meeting room in a hotel

- During a meal at a restaurant

- In the evening over dinner or drinks

- On the golf course

Places where substantive business subjects are never discussed include:

- In hallways

- In elevators

- On the street

- In taxis

- In rest rooms

- In the lobby of your hotel or company offices

- While walking

It is important to remember that Japanese have a very strong sense of propriety. In their culture, there is an appropriate time, place, and way to do and say just about everything. Abiding by those "appropriate" ways is how respect is shown to the other party. Following the prescribed protocol is how each party demonstrates its level of interest in the mutual business. It is how harmony is promoted. And it is how misunderstanding and friction are avoided in Japanese society.

B. Saying No & Counter-proposing

Another fundamental part of communicating in negotiations is what to say and, more importantly in the case of negotiating in Japan, what *not* to say. When negotiating in Japan, never say "no." There are two major reasons for this.

First, saying "no" indicates you are not concerned about your partner's interests. By saying "no" you are not only rejecting the specific idea proposed but you also are rejecting outright the larger corporate interest your partner is attempting to discuss with you. This makes you appear inflexible, which is not a desirable trait in a business partner. A direct "no" demonstrates in the Japanese business cultural context that you are not negotiating with "sincerity" (in good faith). Mutual compromise is a sign of mutual respect and mutual commitment to the long-term mutual relationship as well as to the success of the business project. Given this cultural framework, it is clear why a zero-sum game approach is not appropriate for negotiating and business in Japan.

The second reason Japanese avoid saying "no" is related to the broader cultural orientation of valuing group harmony. As discussed in chapter three of this book, Japanese go to great lengths to avoid being too clear or direct when communicating. Keeping things vague and not saying "no" prevents parties from having to either agree or disagree and take sides. This promotes the cohesion of the group. As a result, "keeping things vague" (*aimai ni suru* 曖昧にする) is common practice in the art of Japanese communication.

How then do you say "no" in a culture that avoids direct disagreement—especially when negotiating and trying to come to terms on so many points of importance to both companies?

Rest assured negotiating in Japan is not simply a give away fest with everyone agreeing to everything. Japanese are very shrewd and tough negotiators. How then do they communicate disagreement and say "no" in a way that is culturally acceptable?

So important is this cultural dynamic of promoting social harmony through vague and non-direct communication that Japanese have numerous expressions for saying "no." I have heard linguists state that there are more than two dozen ways to say "no" in the Japanese language, which is indicative of how important the cultural value of group harmony is in Japan and illustrates the culture provides many ways to disagree while still supporting harmony.

Many of the ways to indirectly say "no" are either non-committal or are even outright positive in their literal meaning. For example, the word *chotto* (ちょっと) literally means "a little." It is a very good example of a word that is non-committal in that the literal meaning indicates neither agreement nor disagreement. However, when used as a reply to a proposal or request, it is universally understood by Japanese to mean a clear "no." It can be used as a single word or in the phrase *Sore wa chotto* (それはちょっと), which literally means "That is a little." Despite it being a very vague phrase in its literal meaning, its actual meaning is crystal clear culturally— definitely "no"!

It is interesting to note that in the ways to disagree you

will find not only the word "no" but also the word "yes"! That is correct, the word "yes" can also mean "no." This begs a question for every foreign company conducting business in Japan. How on track, really, are your understandings and agreements with your Japanese partners? When they reply "yes," do they really mean "yes"? Do they mean "no"? Or do they mean something in between?

The following is a list of twenty-two terms that I am familiar with commonly used to express non-agreement or to indicate "no." Notice that the majority of them have a literal meaning that has nothing to do with meaning "no."

1. *Iie* (いいえ): No.
2. *Hai* (はい): Yes.
3. *Chotto* (ちょっと): A little.
4. *Sore wa chotto.* (それはちょっと...): That is a little...
5. *Iya* (イヤ): Not really.
6. *Sore wa.* (それは): That is...
7. *Dou deshou* (どうでしょう): How about that?
8. *Saa* (さあ): Well...
9. *Jitsu wa* (実は): Actually...
10. *Honto wa* (本当は...): In truth...
11. *Wakarimashita* (分かりました): I understand.
12. *Wakarimasen* (分かりません): I do not know.
13. *Kentou shimasu* (検討します): It is worth our consideration.
14. *Zenshou shimasu* (善処します): I will do my utmost best for that.
15. *Suimasen* (すいません): I am sorry.
16. *Moshi wake nai desu* (申し訳ないです): I apologize.
17. *Moshika shitara* (もしかしたら): It could be such that...
18. *Muzukashii desu* (難しいです): That is difficult.
19. *Nanno koto* (何の事): What is that?
20. *Ittai nanno koto deshou* (一体何のことでしょう): What in the world?

21. Replying with silence.
22. Sucking in air through one's teeth.

These communication dynamics affect all areas of Japanese society, not just business. It is noteworthy to point out their effect in the political arena—especially in regard to Japan's diplomatic relations with the U.S.

When a new prime minister takes office in Japan, he visits America to meet with our president. At the conclusion of their meeting, they invariably hold a joint press conference in the Rose Garden of the White House. Our president explains how fruitful the meeting was and then lists all of the items America successfully negotiated. Next, the Japanese prime minister, speaking in Japanese, typically echoes that the meeting was fruitful. Regarding the list of items the president requested of him, he says that he will *zenshou shimasu* (善処 します)—translated literally into English as "I will do my utmost best for that." U.S. government officials are pleased, believing that Japan has agreed to the items America demanded. It was mission accomplished. However, in Japan a different conclusion is drawn.

Upon returning to Japan, the prime minister meets with the Japanese press and recounts that the president requested Japan to agree to several items and that he replied with *zenshou shimasu*. When writing their articles for Japan's newspapers, the press acknowledges the good job their prime minister did in *not* giving in to U.S. pressure.

How is it possible for the American government, including the president, to think that Japan agreed to their requests while the Japanese government and people understand that their country in fact did not agree to them? While the literal meaning of *zenshou shimasu* is "I will do my utmost best for that," the actual cultural meaning is "thanks, but no thanks." While the correct literal translation connotes agreement, the correct cultural interpretation is diametrically opposite.

When Japan fails to implement any of the meeting items, America concludes Japan was disingenuous. Japan, however, has a clean conscious because, according to their cultural norms and communication dynamics, they very politely replied at the meeting that they did not agree to those items.

Foreigners almost always rely on Japanese to provide the translator when meeting. This puts Americans at a great tactical and strategic disadvantage. Because of Japan's code of respect, foreigners will only receive polite, literal translations. To understand the actual cultural meaning, foreigners must have a translator *on their team* who is in a position to provide accurate cultural interpretation. This is the focus of chapter seven of this book.

The encounter between the U.S. president and the Japanese prime minister is an example at the highest level of political power demonstrating how Japan's communication dynamics can easily lead to inaccurate communication in negotiating and business. This difference between the literal meaning and the actual cultural meaning is also an example of the Japanese communication dynamic of *tatemae* (建前) and *honne* (本音)—that is, what is ostensibly the case versus what is the actual situation. The communication dynamic of *tatemae* and *honne* is discussed further in chapter three.

So what then is the best way for you, speaking in English, to say "no" without offending your potential business partners in a culture that avoids direct disagreement? In mediating between these two cultures and languages, I have found two methods that work very well.

The first option is instead of replying with "no," respond

with "That might be difficult." It translates well into Japanese—*sore ga muzukashii deshou* (それが難しいでしょう). While you are not saying "no," in a very Zen-like manner, you are saying you are not in a position to agree, at least not at this point in time, but may be able to in the future. With this reply, you do not come across as being inflexible or disinterested in the interests of the other party, but neither have you committed to anything.

The second way to indicate politely that your answer is "no" without alienating the Japanese is to reply with a counterproposal. In other words, if the Japanese company is discussing a point that you cannot agree to, do not reply about that point. Instead answer by saying, "That certainly is one option for achieving that, but would another option be XYZ?" Then go on to describe your counterproposal.

By replying to their point in this way, you avoid saying "no" all together. The beauty of this response is that you come across as being open-minded, not inflexible. The strategic advantage of this negotiating tactic is that instead of replying "no," you use the opportunity to advance one of your own interests or goals in the negotiations. And you do so in a way that comes across as an effort on your part to advance the interest of your partner or potential partner as you offered the idea as a way to achieve what the Japanese company just requested.

If they agree to the alternative option you put forth, then this becomes a classic example of how both companies are keeping in mind each other's interests in the negotiating efforts. You helped them get a point they were negotiating for with an option that also was acceptable to you.

Notice my suggestion to reply with: "That certainly is one option for achieving that, but *would another option be* XYZ?" When

Americans offer a counterproposal, we typically phrase it "*I have* an alternative option." By saying "I have," the alternative becomes the idea of the person saying it—the American executive. In that case, accepting it means the Japanese idea was shot down and they instead are being asked to agree with the American position in that matter. This can cause them to lose face within their company, especially when they later report back to other executives.

I recommend American executives use the words "*would another option be*" instead of "*I have* an alternative" because that leaves ownership of the idea up for grabs. You can graciously allow the Japanese executives to take ownership of the idea in the event they like it. That makes it easier for them to accept the idea, easier to lobby for that idea with other executives within their company, and simultaneously advances both companies' interests. Also, it is a powerful demonstration on your part of your company's willingness to keep their interests in mind. It goes a long way in giving them the comfort level they need for determining that they would like to conduct business with you on a long-term basis.

Japanese often use another interesting method for communicating disagreement. They say "no" through a trusted third party. Japanese may be vague and non-committal during a meeting, or even reply to proposals saying "yes," then have a third party directly convey their non-agreement after the meeting. The use of third parties in business negotiations is widespread to avoid disagreement or conflict, thereby maintaining good relations (harmony) between the parties. Foreign executives, however, often take this communication dynamic to mean that the Japanese were not honest. This, however, is not the case. The reason Japanese utilize this dynamic is that to disagree directly with someone would be deemed disrespectful and impolite.

Foreign executives should not view a Japanese company's

use of a third party as a negative sign regarding their interest. On the contrary, it is an indication that their interest in your business is so strong that they took the additional step of bringing in that third party.

C. The Meaning & Use of Silence

Silence is another part of communication when negotiating with Japanese that foreigners find not only difficult to understand but also outright awkward. In Japan, silence is actually a common part of communication not only in business but in society in general as well.

Silence is used in communicating in Japan much more than in other countries. The most common use is as a pause to think about and digest what has just been said. We sometimes use silence for this reason in America, but not to the extent Japanese do. Not only do Japanese use it more frequently but the pause in discussion they take is much longer than Americans are accustomed to experiencing. As a result, Americans typically feel very uncomfortable and are not sure what the silence means.

Often this silence is viewed by foreigners as a breakdown in communication or even in the negotiations themselves. However, that is a misinterpretation. The meaning of the Japanese use of silence is usually lost in cultural translation.

Japanese use silence in ways other than as a moment of reflection on what has just been said. It also may be utilized as a way to strongly object to what is being discussed or proposed. Remember, it is not appropriate to disagree directly in Japanese communication. So if the listener is greatly put off by what they are hearing, rather than using some polite, indirect way of saying they disagree, they use silence as a way to express strong disagreement.

Given that silence makes many foreigners uncomfortable, Japanese occasionally use it as a negotiating tool to frustrate the other party. Americans typically respond to silence by rushing to fill it. In a social conversation, we fill silence with social chitchat. In a negotiation, we typically rush in and fill it with something that has business significance. What happens all too often is that Americans fill the silence by softening the point they are negotiating. Mistakenly thinking that the silence represents a blowout that could end the negotiation, American negotiators commonly back off what they had been pushing for and reply to the silence by filling it with a less demanding position. When this happens, Japanese negotiators have used silence to improve the Japanese position and win concessions. This is a good example of the Japanese notion of gaining more by saying less in negotiating.

What should American companies do when they are confronted with silence? I recommend making it a Zen moment—sit back in your chair, take deep breaths, and relax. Allow the Japanese to take as much time as they like and let them see that their silence does not cause you any discomfort or concern.

During the silence, do not stare at the Japanese, look at your watch, check your e-mails, dabble with your smart phone, or chat with colleagues from your company. Instead, stay silent to respect the need of the Japanese to reflect. Keep yourself occupied by reviewing your notes for the next points you want to cover, by jotting down any points you may want to discuss further, or by taking that Zen moment to catch your breath and rest.

Allow the Japanese to break the silence. When they are ready—that is, when they have had sufficient time to reflect on what has just been discussed or when they realize that using silence as a negotiating tool will not work with you—they will resume the discussion.

During these silences, Japanese break off all eye contact. Given the importance of constantly maintaining good eye contact when communicating in our culture, this deliberate and long break in eye contact by Japanese is another reason why the Japanese use of silence causes American executives to feel so uncomfortable. In our culture, deliberately breaking and avoiding eye contact is a way to communicate dissatisfaction or the outright end of communication. So it is common for American executives to misinterpret not only the lack of dialogue but also the lack of eye contact during silence from Japanese.

What is the best way to navigate this Japanese negotiating tactic? Hold your ground—that is, do not soften your negotiating position. And take the silence in stride. If they engaged in silence to express strong disagreement with your last point, when they end the silence, they will offer a counterproposal or move on to another topic without responding to your previous statement.

III. TIME IN NEGOTIATING

A. PACE OF NEGOTIATING

From the very first negotiating session with Japanese, it becomes clear that they engage in negotiating at a much slower pace than Americans do. This stems from the fact that Americans and Japanese view both the purpose and process of negotiating very differently.

To reiterate, typically Americans have a list of objectives that are fundamental to the business opportunity that we want to discuss and come to agreement on—that is the primary focus of the negotiation. We expect the negotiations to proceed in a straightforward and timely manner. If they do not, that is an indication that something is off target—the other party is not really interested or possibly has ulterior motives.

For Japanese, we have already identified that the negotiation process takes place on two distinct levels: project and relationship. While Americans approach negotiating with the one primary objective of coming to agreement on the major points of the business deal, Japanese pursue three major objectives through the negotiating process. And they pursue them simultaneously. As a result, the Japanese negotiating process is far more involved and requires significantly more time than the American approach.

Specifically, the three major business objectives Japanese simultaneously pursue through the negotiating process are:

- Becoming well informed about the project and products

- Building a constructive, long-term working relationship with the other party

- Coming to agreement on the particulars of the business deal not only with the company they are negotiating with but also simultaneously arriving at a consensus on these points within their own company

Let's look at each of these three facets of Japanese negotiating in detail.

Japanese conduct negotiations in a meticulous fashion. This is part of their exact, detail-oriented approach known in Japanese as *komakai* (細かい). This is most commonly seen in the level of detail Japanese request on the business project during the course of negotiating.

The detail they typically ask for is far more than Americans require or even consider reasonable. From an American perspective, it often seems like information overkill. I have witnessed numerous cases where American executives wondered if the Japanese were simply seeking all this detailed information for the purpose of "knocking off" the American product. However, as a general rule, this is not what is taking place.

Japanese require this enormous amount of detail in negotiating because they want to be extremely thorough in their work. They prefer to know as much as possible up front during the negotiating process in order to avoid surprises down the road. Finding out after the business commences that they were not sufficiently informed or that they outright made a mistake causes embarrassment and loss of face in Japan—the worst possible outcome in Japanese social and business culture. For them, it is better to err on the side of being overly cautious by being overly informed than risk having themselves and their company experience loss of face because of a failure to gather enough information.

Loss of face and dishonoring one's company in Japan is equivalent to having your credibility, integrity, and standing in society called into question or destroyed in American culture. Japanese will go to great lengths to avoid that. In pre-modern Japan, the samurai values of *Bushido* would call on a samurai who lost his honor to commit *seppuku* (切腹 ceremonial disembowelment). In modern Japan, an executive's loss of face or dishonor requires the executive to take responsibility by resigning his position and leaving the company. That is why executive resignations are commonly seen in Japan in the aftermath of corporate scandals or crises.

In the Japanese perspective, the amount of information exchanged is an indicator of how serious parties are about working together. It is an indicator of how sincere both parties are to collaborate, and it is an indicator of how much both parties trust each other.

American companies typically do not have pre-existing relationships with Japanese companies so the important process of relationship building must take place during the negotiations. This adds a whole other unfamiliar dimension to the negotiating process for the foreign company; one that requires considerable time, effort, and attention in addition to the time, effort, and attention being spent on negotiating the specific points of the business.

As will be discussed in detail in the next chapter, Japanese utilize a bottom-up decision-making process. Known as *ringi* (稟議), this decision process requires each department that will be impacted by a business decision to be involved in the discussion and negotiation of the details of that decision. Each department must approve the decision before it becomes final. The process of bottom-up internal consensus building within the Japanese company requires significantly more time than the typical American top-down approach to decision making. This process of *ringi* must also take place during the period of the negotiations, adding depth to that third objective to the Japanese negotiating process.

While this internal company consensus making must take place during the negotiating process, it cannot take place during the negotiation meetings with foreign companies. Rather it takes place between meetings with potential business partners. This factor is another reason why Japanese companies proceed in negotiating at a speed considerably slower than American companies. To compare the speed of American and Japanese negotiating styles, if American negotiations move forward at the speed of trickling water then Japanese negotiators advance at the speed of poured molasses.

I have encountered American executives who have found the longer and more involved negotiating process with Japanese to be daunting. Is it worth it to be patient and go through the much longer negotiating process with Japanese companies?

The most obvious point is that being unwilling to accommodate the need for the negotiating time that Japanese require will preclude your company from completing a business agreement for their market. Simply put, not allowing for the necessary time for negotiating in Japan would be to fail in the Japanese market even before you had the opportunity to start your business there.

When we step back and strategically analyze this longer and more involved negotiating process of Japanese companies, it is clear that the process offers American companies distinct advantages that are well worth the extra time. I have found the following three fundamental advantages for American companies to be especially noteworthy:

- As a result of needing to be so meticulous, detailed, and well informed during the negotiation process, your Japanese partners are in a very strong position to sell and service your products in the Japanese market from day one of project launch. I have been involved in countless projects in which Japanese actually ended up knowing the business or product even better than the foreign company.

- Japanese companies are committed to the project for the long term and, as a result, typically have greater staying power than partners in other countries. Since business in Japan is conducted based on the long-term relationship between the two parties, the bottom line benefit to you of this cultural trait is that Japanese typically will continue to promote your products even if sales turn out to be slower than anticipated.

- As a result of the *ringi* decision-making process, all parts of the Japanese company that will be involved in your business in Japan are already quite familiar with your product and business and what will be required of them; they are already on board, geared up at the start line, and ready to move forward on a long-term trajectory from the date your business agreement is signed. This provides American executives the following three invaluable tactical advantages:

o   Your partner will require a shorter ramp up time to prepare for the start of your business in Japan.

o   Your company's launch in the Japanese market will be more informed, effective, and professional given your partner's in-depth knowledge of your products and business gained *before* your business is launched.

o   When your product faces challenges in the Japanese market, your partner is in a position to quickly formulate effective hands-on solutions in the field. While your staff will certainly know the products very well, they will not understand the Japanese market and the actual challenges your products face there over time. The Japanese company will not only be well informed about your product but also will be intimately familiar with the market challenges. As a result, they are able to contribute real time solutions in a quick and effective manner to a greater degree than you would find in other international markets.

Briefly returning to the first of these three advantages, I noted that as a result of needing to be so meticulous, detail oriented, and well informed about a product, Japanese can actually end up knowing them even better than the American entity does. Management expert Peter Drucker experienced this himself through his work with Mr. Ueda Atsuo, who translated and edited the Japanese language editions of Drucker's books over the years. As he noted:

> *"He (Ueda Atsuo) has actually translated many of my books several times as they went into new Japanese editions. He is thus thoroughly familiar with my work—in fact, he knows it better than I do."* — Peter F. Drucker, **The Essential Drucker** (New York: Harper Collins, 2001), p. vii.

In summary regarding Japanese negotiating, I have always found that while the negotiating process may be long, so is the resulting business relationship between American firms and their Japanese partners. In short, the courtship is long, but so too is resulting marriage.

B. TIME AS A NEGOTIATING TOOL

Some Japanese companies use time as a negotiating tactic. While not the norm in Japan, it is important that American companies are aware of this possibility.

In most cases, the initial negotiating meetings take place in Japan. Typically the U.S. executive arrives and is there for a few busy days of meetings. No matter how seasoned the executive might be, he or she invariably is fatigued due to the long journey and the jet lag. On top of that, the body clocks of American executives are off during their initial days in Japan, given the fourteen to seventeen hour time difference between mainland U.S.A. and Japan—fourteen hours from the east coast and seventeen hours from the west coast.

Having approximately forty-eight to seventy-two hours in Japan to negotiate is a very short window of opportunity. Not only do foreign executives operate on a short time horizon because of the limited time they are in Japan, they are used to negotiations moving forward at straightforward pace. In the foreign executive's mind, there is an expectation of meaningful progress within a short period of time. On top of that, he or she would like to return to the States and report positive news about the negotiations. I have often experienced U.S. executives showing me their company's sales agreement before meeting with Japanese and stating that their goal is to have it signed before they leave in a day or two. This is simply not realistic given the dynamics of Japanese business and negotiating.

As a result of these factors, the U.S. executive is weighed down with several challenges even before walking into the meeting room to conduct the negotiations. Some of these challenges are:

- **Logistical:** Fatigue from the long journey to Japan (twenty to twenty-two hours door-to-door from the east coast of America to your hotel in downtown Tokyo); jet lag from the fourteen to seventeen hour time difference between the continental U.S. and Japan; and the need to conduct as much business as possible during the short visit all put the American executive at an immediate disadvantage.

- **Cultural:** There are culture-based differences in business such as the much slower pace and more involved process of Japanese negotiating. In most cases, American executives are not aware of the cultural differences, their implications, and their challenges.

- **Expectancy:** There is pressure to report positive news about the negotiations when they return to the U.S. or even to have a signed agreement completed during that visit.

Japanese negotiators are well aware of the time restrictions and these other challenges that their American counterparts bring to the negotiating table. While Japanese approach negotiating at a much slower pace than Americans do to begin with, some may elect to deliberately slow down the negotiating process even further as a negotiating tactic to frustrate and wear down the other party.

Given the desire of the U.S. executive to make progress during the very short window of time for negotiating, Japanese executives may try to win concessions by dragging out the discussions. They are betting that as the American executive's stay nears its end, the urge to achieve progress in the limited amount of time he or she has in Japan will prompt the executive to make compromises and concessions to the advantage of the Japanese company.

You can avoid this negotiating tactic by stating at the outset of your initial discussion that you are not in a hurry to conclude an agreement or to report progress to your company headquarters. Instead, take the position that your company is simply exploring the possibility of doing business in Japan at this time. Report that you want both companies to get to know each other during your visit and that your company is taking a long-term approach to negotiating and to conducting business in Japan. Stating these points makes it known to the Japanese company that they cannot use time as a negotiating tool against you.

While it is not realistic to expect to have a business agreement signed during your initial visit to Japan, it still is prudent to bring your company's agreement with you. Why is that?

If the Japanese company is strongly interested in your company's business opportunity and if you are favorably inclined to work with them, you may want to present your business agreement to them at the conclusion of your last meeting for the purpose of allowing them to have it translated into Japanese so it can be discussed at a future meeting. You should only present the boilerplate version of the agreement, one without the specifics you will be negotiating.

Depending on the length of the agreement, the level of technical content included in it, and the prevalence of specialized terminology it may contain, a translation can take any where from a few days to one to two weeks. Having the boilerplate version of your document translated into Japanese allows the Japanese executives the opportunity to become more familiar with the general terms you have in mind before your next negotiating meeting. This often aids in shortening the amount of subsequent time you need to complete the negotiating process.

C. DIFFERENT NOTIONS OF TIME

In assisting American clients engaged in business in Japan and other Asian markets over the years, on numerous occasions I came across the following situation regarding notions of time.

A business agreement had been successfully negotiated between an American and a Japanese company. The two firms had developed a strong working relationship. Regulatory approvals to import and sell the products in Japan had all been obtained. The two companies launched the project and began sales and marketing as planned. Everything was proceeding smoothly.

Then after a month or two, the U.S. company would inquire about the progress of sales, asking the Japanese company why the sales numbers were not at the mutually agreed levels for the short-term phase of their business project. They were beginning to worry that the Japanese company was slacking off, or, worse yet, not capable of meeting expectations.

The Japanese company for its part was puzzled by this concern. They would reply by saying they were on track and doing just fine to reach those targets in the specified time frame. They began to think the American company was becoming impatient and was starting to push them.

Looking into this, it became apparent to me that the two companies were operating with two entirely different understandings of "agreed" time frames. For the American company, short term was a few months or a few quarters at most. For the Japanese firm, short term was considered eighteen to twenty-four months. What a huge disparity! Given how different the two time frames are, it is easy to see how misunderstandings could occur in the relationship and with evaluating progress in sales performance, marketing, advertising, and so many other areas of business.

To avoid these problems, it is important to understand the meaning of short term, mid term and long term in the cultures of both companies.

The frameworks for time common in America:

- **Short term:** Measured in weeks, months, or quarters; typically up to six to nine months

- **Mid term:** Nine to eighteen months

- **Long term:** Eighteen months or longer

In Japan, while the time frames vary in length from industry to industry, they are all considerably longer than in the States. The following time frames are an average of the time periods I have often encountered in Japan:

- **Short term:** One-and-a-half to two years

- **Mid term:** Three to four years

- **Long term:** Five years and beyond

As we can see, the time frames Japanese and Americans bring to the negotiating table are markedly different. The same terms are used, but their cultural meanings are significantly different. This is true even when Japanese negotiate in English; while they may use the same English term "short term," their cultural understanding and expectations are quite different.

This is another case of accurate literal translation, but inaccurate cultural interpretation. There are occasions when Japanese will negotiate in English so that both they and American negotiators are speaking the same language. Executives of both countries feel a sense of relief with this, believing that, as a result, misunderstandings are less likely since nothing can "get lost in translation." While it is true that there is less risk of the literal meaning being misunderstood when both sides are speaking in English, the actual cultural meaning and expectation still often get lost in translation. The result is that both sides are setting themselves up for misunderstandings, friction in their business relationship, and diminished business results. This is true not only with regard to understanding time frame terms but also with communication in general.

While common ideas and terms in international business that come up in business negotiations and subsequent management of the joint business venture may be the same, the cultural connotations quite often are very different. Because these cultural connotations are subconscious and taken for granted, negotiators and managers on both sides are usually unaware that differences exist between them.

The critical lesson for international business executives is that there is a monumental difference between having accurate language translation and achieving correct cultural interpretation both during the negotiating process and during the course of the joint business project.

This aspect of negotiating and communication—that is, having both accurate language translation and correct cultural understanding—is critical to the success of a foreign company's business in Japan, yet it is usually overlooked by management on both sides of the Pacific. I have experienced time and again how this gap in understanding can emerge at any point in the business project, even in year two or three of the business project.

> There is a monumental difference between accurate language translation and correct cultural interpretation.

The importance of obtaining correct cultural interpretation between America and Japan along with accurate language interpretation is covered in depth in chapter seven, "Critical Role of the Translator and the Cultural Facilitator."

To avoid this cultural miscommunication during negotiations, it is always preferable to quantify terms and concepts whenever possible. In the example in this chapter, for instance, the use of numerical time periods (such as twelve to eighteen months) instead of terms for time frames (such as short term, mid term or long term) would have resulted in clearer expectations for the companies. Other commonly used—and misunderstood—terms for time frames include: "in phase one," "in the initial stage," "for a while," and "in the interim." Business interests are always best served by quantifying and defining all terms and concepts whenever possible—even when discussed in English by both parties.

Not quantifying typically results in several unwelcome consequences. First, misunderstandings occur regarding completion dates and achievement of project milestones. Second, misunderstandings due to operating with different time assumptions cause friction in the relationship between the two companies. Not working with the same timetable can lead a company to think the other party is not carrying out its end of the bargain or, conversely, to feel the business partner is harassing them when they feel they are in compliance with the agreement. Commitment to and involvement in the business project suffer as a result, eroding sales performance. This is another example of how possessing or not possessing appropriate cultural understanding directly impacts the bottom line performance of international business operations.

D. RESPECT FOR TIME

In Japan, the value of time is greatly respected as is being punctual. This is true both in business and in society in general. As a result, being late is unacceptable. In America, we are a bit more relaxed about punctuality. Being "socially late" is quite common, and if we are a few minutes late, it is not usually a serious matter. Unpunctuality in the business world in Japan is out of the question. You are expected to be on time for all appointments and engagements.

Being late indicates that not only do you not respect the value of time but also that you do not respect the other party. In the business context, being late translates culturally as being unreliable—and therefore undesirable—as a potential business partner. Punctuality is that important. This is especially true during the courtship phase when American and Japanese companies are getting to know each other to decide whether or not to work together. Given this great respect for time and the importance of being on time, the common practice in Japan is to arrive for appointments fifteen to thirty minutes early and wait nearby the meeting venue until the appointed time.

But there is more. Respecting time means being on time—but being on time only! Arriving early at the meeting location is likewise not done. When Japanese have an appointment with a company and arrive early, they wait in the building's lobby or a nearby coffee shop until the meeting time approaches. They then proceed to the company's reception area exactly at the appointed time. To arrive at the reception area before the appointed meeting time is considered disrespectful of the other party and their time since the people you are meeting with certainly are busy taking care of other matters. To meet you early would interfere with their responsibilities and planned agenda for the day. As a result, Japanese arrive at the reception area just on time. This is part of the Japanese predilection for being exact and detail-oriented (*komakai* 細かい). In this way, this cultural value of "just in time" does not only apply to Japanese manufacturing and inventory practices, it also applies to meeting protocol!

Respect for time and for the other party's time is so important in Japan that people actually apologize for keeping you waiting *even though they are on time and, therefore, have not kept you waiting*! The ubiquitous Japanese expression is *o-matase-itashimashita* (お待たせいたしました) and means "Sorry to have kept you waiting." They will say this upon arriving for any engagement, including when entering a meeting room exactly at the appointed meeting time. My favorite example of the use of this phrase is when a train closes its doors and starts to pull out of a station *exactly on time*, the conductor invariably says over the intercom "Sorry to have kept you waiting"—despite the fact that the train is precisely on schedule.

Finally, this great respect for time is indicative of the Japanese people's strong group orientation that will be discussed throughout this book.

E. Importance of the Long Term

The last aspect of time that comes to play in the negotiating process and in business in general in Japan is the importance of the long term. Japanese approach business with a long-term view. They strategize and plan for the long term. They allocate resources, train employees, invest in research and development, and engage in customer service all with the long term in mind. In a nutshell, Japanese companies engage in business for the long term so all aspects of business have a long-term orientation. Given this cultural norm, it is very important to them that they can see that your commitment is likewise long term for both the joint business as well as for the mutual relationship.

Foreign companies typically do not share such a long-term orientation. This is one of the main reasons many Japanese companies hesitate to engage in business with foreign companies and why many do not. Their concern is that many foreign firms do not stay in the Japanese market long term. As one prominent Japanese executive expressed it to me when we were discussing this: "The graveyard of foreign companies in Japan is very crowded. We Japanese are not eager to be a part of that."

The concern that Japanese companies have is that foreign companies in Japan are "here today, gone tomorrow." If a foreign company is going to cease business in Japan because sales were below expectations for a few quarters, why bother even to start the business? It turns out to be a waste of time, effort, and investment for both companies. Furthermore, this is problematic and often causes the Japanese company "to lose face" on two levels:

- **In their industry among their peer companies:** Prestige and perceived standing among their competitors often suffer as a result of come and go associations.

- **In public society in general:** Why? The exit of the foreign company leaves the Japanese company in a difficult situation. Officially they are no longer engaged in that business and have shut down those operations. However, the Japanese company remains socially obligated to continue servicing any and all customers who have purchased those products, even though years may pass.

Unlike in America, this is socially expected of companies in Japan. With the foreign company no longer active in the Japanese market, it becomes highly problematic and costly to handle any customer inquiries, complaints, maintenance, warranty issues, after purchase product service needs, and repairs with no back up from the foreign manufacturer and no sales income from that project.

These concerns make it clear why Japanese negotiators want to see that your level of commitment to their market is for the long term. This can have a direct and significant impact on negotiations regarding the sales targets for your business.

Why is this so? When negotiating, American executives tend to push for sales targets that are as high as possible. The Japanese often resist and want sales targets that are lower. The reason for this is not that their commitment to the project is weak or that they see lower sales potential than their foreign counterparts see, or even that they simply tend to be more conservative than American executives, as it is commonly explained in the West. Rather, the reason is that the lower the target numbers, the more likely it is that they will be achieved and keep American executives satisfied. And, more importantly, reaching those targets will keep the American company wanting to continue its business in Japan longer.

Considering this, I highly recommend foreign companies pursuing business in Japan proactively bring up the topic of their commitment to the Japanese market. It is advantageous to initiate and openly discuss this commitment early on in the negotiations. This is especially true if your company is competing with other foreign or even domestic Japanese companies to work with your target company.

Given the importance of doing so, how can American companies effectively express to Japanese companies that their commitment to the Japanese market and to the mutual business relationship is both strong and long term? Here are five specific methods I have developed that have proven successful for my clients:

- **Geographic importance of the Japan market:** Discuss not only the additional sales you expect from your business in Japan but also cover the *geographic importance* of the Japanese market to your company. For example, explain how your firm sees Japan as the gateway to other Asian countries, so succeeding in Japan will enable your company to expand more easily into those other neighboring markets.

- **Strategic importance of the Japan market:** Explain to the Japanese the *strategic importance* of the Japanese market to your business. For example, discuss how Japan is a major market in the world for your product or service and, consequently, your succeeding there is an integral part of your company's strategy to be the global leader in its product category.

- **Your company's Japan team:** Point out how you are creating a whole team within your company to manage your business with the Japanese company in their market. Explain this team will not be comprised just of members from your international sales department. That is not compelling enough. Instead, the Japanese want to know that your Japan team will include senior executives and managers from the various departments of your company that will be involved in your company's business in Japan. This would include sales, marketing, regulatory affairs, customer service, human resources, procurement, quality control, research and development, etc. Indicate that all of these individuals will work to meet the needs of the Japanese market—not just the director of international sales and his department. This approach demonstrates that your effort in Japan will be company-wide and not just the work of part of your international sales department. From the Japanese perspective, the higher the level of the personnel you include on your Japan team, the more serious your commitment is to their market.

Taking this stance requires that company members from those various departments attend meetings with Japanese. They do not have to attend all the meetings held in Japan, but when the Japanese company visits your office for meetings, the senior-most executives from those various departments should attend. While this may take a few hours of their time, it will be well worth it. Their presence sends a powerful and clear message that the Japanese market is a priority for your company.

- **On-going business support:** Discuss details on how your company will continue to provide product training and support to the Japanese company on an on-going basis for the long term after the project commences. That support will include teams of appropriate professionals from your company visiting Japan several times a year (or other frequency appropriate to your company's resources and the needs of the business project) to work with the Japanese company and the customers they develop.

- **On-going executive level communication:** Explain how you and other senior executives will maintain direct, personal communication with the senior executives of the Japanese company on a regular basis going forward. That will include face-to-face meetings in Japan as well as in the United States, meetings via Skype and other similar technologies, as well as telephone conversations. Remember that for the Japanese your business with them is relationship driven. You should be proactive in demonstrating that your relationship with them is a long-term priority. This will go a long way to giving them the comfort level to want to work with your company.

All of these actions send the clear message that you and your company take the Japanese market and your relationship with your Japanese partner seriously. They clearly state that you and your firm are committed to the Japanese market and to your partner and they highlight that your commitment is for the long term. These messages will help give Japanese executives the comfort level to move forward with your company.

IV. INDICATORS OF JAPANESE INTEREST DURING NEGOTIATIONS

Next, let's look at what signs foreign executives can pick up from their Japanese counterparts in the negotiating process regarding the Japanese level of interest in working with your company. What actions are positive indicators that a Japanese company is seriously interested and would be a good partner for your company?

How can foreign executives better read where Japanese executives stand during negotiations? What are typical red flags?

A. WHO ATTENDS THE NEGOTIATIONS

The first indicator Japanese companies give of their level of interest in your business is who is selected by the company to represent them in the early discussions and the negotiations. There are several signs that foreign executives can look for. Specifically:

- **Rank of attendees:** How senior in the company are the participants? If high-level executives attend, this represents a high level of interest. Conversely, junior manager representatives are indicative of weaker or uncertain interest.

- **Number of attendees:** How many individuals are attending the negotiation meetings? Two or three representatives? Or, on the other hand, six or seven? The greater the number of representatives attending, the greater the interest their company has in doing business with you.

The number of company representatives can send a powerful message to a foreign party regarding the level of interest on the part of the Japanese company. By way of example, the greatest number of individuals representing a Japanese firm in a negotiation that I have experienced is fourteen. That included the company CEO, senior executives, the heads of the departments that would be involved in the business, and top salesmen. When two executives from my American client and I entered the meeting room and saw them all standing behind their chairs at the board room conference table, there was no doubt about their level of interest in our business.

- **Number of departments:** The number of departments in the Japanese company represented at the negotiating table is another good indicator of level of interest. The greater the company's interest, the greater the number of departments that will want to participate. There are two reasons for this.

First, pursuant to the Japanese *ringi* style of decision-making, all departments that will be involved in a new business endeavor actively participate in deciding whether the company should embark on the new business project. To make an informed decision, they need to be involved in the early discussions and negotiations. Japan's decision-making process is discussed in detail in chapter two.

Second, given that these various departments will be directly responsible for executing the business, they want to be as knowledgeable about it as possible, as early as possible in the process, so they can be best prepared.

Given these circumstances, the number of departments represented in negotiations is a solid indicator of how serious a Japanese company's interest is in your business.

- **Seating arrangement of attendees:** Japanese typically sit in one of two formations.

The first seating order is hierarchical with the senior most executive seated in the middle on his company's side of the table and the others seated on either side of him in descending rank within the company. Those sitting at the ends of the meeting table on the Japanese side will be the lowest ranking members of the Japanese company. This hierarchical seating order means your discussions are proceeding smoothly and the Japanese are on board with your business.

The second order is the departmental seating arrangement with the senior executive sitting in the middle but the other representatives are sitting grouped by their departments. This seating arrangement means that they have questions or points that they need to clarify before moving forward with your business. Therefore, expect Japanese to raise questions or points to go over in greater detail. They may opt to discuss your replies among their departments right then and there to ensure accuracy of understanding and allow for immediate and additional follow-up questions or clarifications.

B. FREQUENCY OF NEGOTIATION MEETINGS

The request for follow-up negotiation meetings is another indicator of Japanese interest in your business. Two weeks between rounds of negotiating is a good rule of thumb to keep in mind. If Japanese do not want to meet within two weeks of a concluding round of negotiation meetings that is a sign they have limited interest—a definite red flag for foreign executives to keep in mind.

Likewise, a Japanese request for a follow-up meeting during the current meeting is an indicator of stronger interest than if the request comes after the current meeting has already concluded and the foreign executives have departed Japan already.

C. LENGTH OF NEGOTIATION MEETINGS

In most cultures, the length of a meeting is indicative of the level of interest in what is being discussed. The same is true in Japan.

When Japanese meet for one or two hours, their interest level is still not strong; meeting for four or more hours in one day shows good interest. When a Japanese company wants to meet with you for two full days or more, that is a sign of very serious interest in your business.

D. LEVEL OF COMPANY RESOURCES COMMITTED

Given the Japanese penchant for detailed planning for every aspect of a business, the amount of corporate resources they are contemplating to commit to your business is a solid indicator of how seriously they view your business and their role in it. This includes not only the size and scope of their marketing and sales plan and the attending budget but also the size of the sales team they would utilize, the number of locations throughout Japan they would involve, whether they will market and sell the products just through their own company or utilize sub-distributors and partners, and the number of sales channels they will sell in (if applicable).

V. OTHER NEGOTIATION PROTOCOLS

A. GIFT GIVING

Japanese companies are world famous for exchanging gifts. Doing so is an expression of gratitude for the opportunity to work together. Gifts are also a token of appreciation and respect for the mutual business relationship.

Foreigners are often confused about the gift giving protocol, particularly how often and on what occasions gifts should be exchanged. For example, do they have to be exchanged at every meeting for as long as the companies engage in business together?

Typically, gifts are exchanged at the first negotiation

meeting that takes place in Japan as well as the first that occurs in the U.S. or other location outside Japan. I always recommend a third gift exchange on the occasion of signing the mutual business agreement. Once engaged in business together, gifts are typically no longer exchanged at a set frequency, but rather periodically. For example, gifts might be exchanged during meetings to celebrate the achieving of major milestones in the business project. It is also recommended that foreign companies send their Japanese partners greeting cards every year for New Year's. When engaging in business among themselves, Japanese companies exchange New Year's cards (*nenga-jou* 年賀状) by the fourth business day in January every year without fail.

B. Meeting Agendas

In Japan, agendas are necessary for all meetings and discussions, and they must be provided in advance of the meeting. If an agenda is not provided, Japanese will consider it unprofessional of you as well as an insult to them.

Japanese do not like surprises. They want to know in advance what will be discussed at the meeting so they can be prepared and will be comfortable with those topics. Keep in mind that, as discussed earlier in this chapter, Japanese are put in an awkward position if they have to say "no."

Being able to review the agenda before the meeting allows them to ascertain how they can best discuss your topics, and it allows them to feel comfortable and in control regarding the meeting. Further, Japanese want to be professional as well as helpful to you in meetings. With their preference for details, they want to make sure they are prepared to answer your questions in a meaningful way.

Americans, however, can feel locked in by the preestablished meeting topics. To avoid this and allow for flexibility regarding the topics discussed in the meeting, I recommend always adding "Other" as the last topic on the agenda. This will help American executives to maximize the value of the meeting without violating the Japanese custom of strictly following agenda topics.

In addition to an agenda, it is also a good practice to send along a brief profile for each attendee on your team ahead of meetings. Adding an accompanying headshot is also helpful and appreciated. This will assist the Japanese team in understanding each attendee's name and role in your company. This is especially helpful for those Japanese who do not speak English and would otherwise stumble through the initial introductions and name card exchanges with your team only to remain in the dark about with whom they are interacting. As you can imagine, that is not an ideal situation in a culture where establishing a mutual relationship is of paramount importance in business.

Providing the meeting agenda, a brief profile describing each person's role, and a headshot for each U.S. team member in advance goes a long way toward getting your prospective relationship off to a favorable start.

SUMMARY

By way of summary, we have seen in this chapter how Japanese executives approach business and negotiating from a very different perspective than American executives do. Rather than the zero-sum game dynamic common in America, Japanese companies see negotiating as a process of give and take where both companies strive to recognize and accommodate each other's business interests as much as is reasonably possible while endeavoring to secure the success of the joint project.

In addition to aiming for the greatest level of success in the mutual business, Japanese also give great importance to developing a favorable trust relationship with their partners. In Japan, the success of the mutual business relationship is viewed as just as important a goal as the success of the business project itself. By now you have learned that Japanese companies rarely engage in business with parties with whom they are unable to form a favorable relationship.

Finally, as noted frequently, Japanese executives commit to—and look for their partners to be likewise committed to—both the mutual business project and the mutual relationship *for the long term*. Recognition of, and agreement with, this long-term time horizon is essential for succeeding in the Japanese market. The insights and methods provided in this chapter are proven tools for maximizing foreign executives' success in navigating these areas of negotiating and relationship building.

Representative examples of fundamental differences between Japanese and Americans negotiating dynamics are highlighted in the table on the following page.

Table 1: Differences in Negotiating Dynamics

Aspect of Negotiating	U.S.A.	Japan
Approach	• Zero sum game—your company's gain is the other company's loss	• Seek the mutual benefit of both parties and their long-term relationship—advance the corporate interests of both parties
Goal	• Secure as many of your own company's business interests as possible	• Identify and agree on what is in the best interests of the project and the mutual relationship and how to achieve them
Amount of information required	• As much as reasonably needed to commit to the project • Typically a moderate amount	• An extreme amount of information • Perceived by Americans as far beyond what is reasonably needed
Attitude toward amount of information needed	• Obtain information as needed to understand and commence the business project; obtain any additional details as project moves forward	• Get as many of the details on the entire project as possible before commencing, as the best way to avoid surprises, disappointments and losing face in the future
Typical speed of negotiating	• Move forward at moderate to fast pace • If U.S. moves at speed of trickling water ...	• Proceed at a slow and meticulous pace • Then Japan moves at speed of poured molasses
Notion of time in business and negotiating	• Short-term: measured in weeks or quarters, typically 6–9 months • Mid-term: 9–18 months • Long-term: More than 18 mths	• Short-term: 1.5–2 years • Mid-term: 3–4 years • Long-term: 5 years and beyond
Common misunderstandings in negotiating:	*Americans think:*	*Japanese think:*
• Regarding amount of information sought	• Are the Japanese more interested in obtaining proprietary information than in working together?	• How serious are they about working together? Have the Americans engaged in sufficient due diligence? • Amount of information exchanged has relational significance; it is an indicator of how serious parties are to work together.
• Regarding length of time negotiations take	• Japanese are delaying. Have they lost interest? What's going on?	• Americans are impatient. If they are in a rush when dealing with the **opportunity** we are now negotiating, how will they handle **challenges**? Will they be a good business partner to work with when challenges arise?

Source: Robert Charles Azar

経営

CHAPTER 2

Japanese Style Management

Japanese and American management styles are 95 percent the same—and different in all important aspects. — **Honda Soichiro, Founder & CEO, Honda Motor Co., Ltd.**

That Japan should have management practices that are different from those in other countries is not surprising. Dr. Peter Drucker, notable for developing modern principles of Western management, explained that a country must combine capitalism with its own indigenous social values and cultural practices in order for capitalism to succeed in that country. He said:

Management…is deeply imbedded in culture. What managers do in West Germany, in the United Kingdom, in the United States, in Japan, or in Brazil is exactly the same. How they do it may be quite different. Thus one of the basic challenges managers in a developing country face is to find and identify those parts of their own tradition, history, and culture that can be used as management building blocks. The difference between Japan's economic success and India's relative backwardness is largely explained by the fact the Japanese managers were able to plant imported management concepts in their own cultural soil and make them grow. — **Peter F. Drucker, *The Essential Drucker* (New York: Harper Collins, 2001), p. 11.**

What are the ways Japan's management style differs from America's management style? How do Japan's different management practices act as obstacles for foreign businesses in the Japanese market? How can American executives effectively navigate them so their bottom line is not curtailed by these differences in management? This chapter answers these questions.

I. GROUP-ORIENTED MANAGEMENT

It was the day of very important meetings between my San Francisco-based client and the Japanese corporation I had introduced to them. Our initial meeting in Tokyo twelve days earlier had gone very well, and the subsequent dialogue had all parties involved feeling optimistic about the prospect of working together.

The Japanese executives were arriving to visit the company in San Francisco for a second round of face-to-face discussions. I met them at the airport and drove them to the American company's corporate headquarters. Guest parking was in front of the main entrance. As I was parking there, one of the executives pointed to a sign at the parking space closest to the building's main entrance. With great interest, he asked in Japanese, "What is that?" I read the sign: "Reserved for salesman of the month." After I translated the message into Japanese, all of the executives were quite surprised. One of them commented: "That would be inconceivable in Japan."

He is right. It's not inconceivable because of a shortage of space as one might hazard to guess, rather it is inconceivable that an individual would be singled out for anything in Japan, let alone be given recognition as prominent as their own parking spot right in front of the main entrance to the company's corporate headquarters. While American society is strongly individual-oriented, Japanese society is just as strongly group-oriented, and that has a profound impact on how Japanese society functions and on how every facet of business is conducted, including how one manages in Japan.

In America, management and human resource practices focus on the individual and are geared toward developing, coordinating, and motivating individuals. In Japan, the focus is on developing, coordinating, and motivating groups rather than the individual employee. As a consequence, Japanese management practices aim at enhancing group solidarity, loyalty, and performance.

For example, in the event of a sales competition in American companies, individual salespeople typically compete with each other. The winners are individuals—the individual in first place gets, for instance, the salesman of the month parking spot or a paid vacation. In Japanese companies, sales competitions are between groups—sales team A versus sales team B or the Tokyo sales team versus the Osaka sales team. The winning team is congratulated as a group for their superior performance. Individuals are never singled out.

A case in point, I had just started working with an American client as a consultant to oversee their business in Asia. On my first visit to their Tokyo offices, I was told about the new American manager there who had just tried to give an award to the top salesman of the month for the previous month's sales results, and it was disastrous. The manager had the salesman stand up during a sales meeting to be recognized and to receive a round of applause. The salesman was utterly mortified. His co-workers were at a loss in this situation that was completely alien to them. The manager, seeing that this management practice he had used so successfully in the States did not work in Japan, realized that he had a problem. Instead of resulting in a stronger relationship with the sales team he was sent to Japan to manage, he had become alienated from them. He was never able to get the relationship back on track, and the performance of the company's most able salesperson was never the same for the remainder of the American's stay in Japan.

Peter Drucker explained the benefits of group-oriented management and leadership that is the norm in Japan. Drucker wrote:

> *The leaders who work most effectively, it seems to me, never say "I." And that's not because they have trained themselves not to say "I." They don't think "I." They think "we"; they think "team." They understand their job to be to make the team function. They accept responsibility and don't sidestep it, but "we" gets the credit. This is what creates trust, what enables you to get the task done.* — Quoted from https://www.goodreads.com/author/quotes/12008.Peter_F_Drucker, p. 1.

Let's look at the cultural dynamics that underlie Japan's group-oriented management. In Japan, one does not want to stand out, let alone be singled out. The reason for this is that it is considered both immodest and impolite to standout. As a result, Japanese go to great lengths to blend in, to be part of the group, to not be different, and to not stand out.

For example, Western visitors to Japan often comment that Japanese businessmen do not dress with the same wardrobe variety as Western businessmen do. Japanese all seem to wear the same color suits, shirts, ties, and shoes. The typical business attire is a dark blue or black suit; white shirt (not blue, yellow, or pink); dark, conservative tie; and black shoes, rarely burgundy or brown. Why is business attire in Japan so uniform? To avoid standing out or being different.

The social and cultural importance of not standing out or being different is clearly seen in the word for different in the Japanese language. In Japanese, the word for different is *chigau* (違う); it means not only "to be different" but also "to be wrong." So, something that is different is, quite literally, also wrong in the context of Japanese culture. Conversely, if you want to be correct, you need to be the same. That is, to blend in and not draw attention to yourself.

> Management techniques that focus on the individual generally end up being counterproductive.

This deep rooted cultural value of not standing out or being different is also expressed well in the old Japanese proverb *deru kugi wa utareru* (出る釘は打たれる)—"The nail that sticks up gets hammered down." No translation necessary!

When managing in Japan, it is important for American executives to keep in mind the group orientation of the Japanese. Management techniques that focus on the individual generally end up being counterproductive. At a minimum, they make all parties involved feel awkward. In the worst case, they can alienate everyone involved.

I have often heard Western business executives downplay the importance of acknowledging and dealing with cultural differences, failing to recognize the impact they can have. Cultural differences are often considered fluff, third tier issues that have little bearing on a company's business results. However, management and human resource approaches that lack a group focus typically exacerbate, rather than reduce, the cultural divide between Americans and Japanese in the same organization or who are collaborating on a joint project. As a direct result, worker morale, motivation, focus, and commitment are adversely affected. The net-net result is diminished sales performance and bottom line profitability as a direct result of these cultural issues.

II. DECISION-MAKING IN JAPAN

This difference between American culture being individual oriented and Japanese culture being group oriented greatly impacts management practices in the area of decision-making as well. This difference also has a profound impact on negotiating, which was covered in chapter one.

In America, decision-making is conducted in a top-down fashion. The senior most person calls the shots and what is decided is communicated to those affected by it for implementation. It is not uncommon for those impacted by those decisions to hear about them for the first time after the decisions have already been made, and in some cases, they first hear about a decision at the time of implementation. Different options may be discussed; different approaches may be recommended by the heads of the various departments involved; other pros and cons may be interjected by other participants in the discussions; however, in the end, it is the senior most executive involved in the decision-making process who makes the decision for the company.

Once the decision is made, it is passed down to all relevant parties in the company for execution. So, decision-making takes place at the top of the organization and flows down to the rank and file in a top-down fashion in most American companies.

The Japanese approach decision-making in a quite different manner. They utilize a group-oriented, bottom-up method of decision-making. All parties involved with the decision and its ramifications are included in the discussions from the very beginning and throughout the entire decision-making process. Here is how it typically works.

A proposal will be circulated to all of those parties who will be affected as well as those who should be aware of it. Each party will take as much time as they need to thoroughly review the proposal, closely looking at three fundamental considerations:

- **Proposal's effectiveness:** Is the proposal the best way to achieve its stated objective and intended purpose from the perspective of each individual party? If not, ways to maximize the proposal's effectiveness and efficiencies are formulated and added by those parties concerned.

- **Proposal's requirements:** What will each department need to do to comply with the proposal? Each department will identify, define, and analyze the specifics of this as it considers the proposal.

- **Proposal's impact:** How will the proposal impact each individual party? What will be the impact on productivity rates, quality control, cost, workload, employee moral, sales, and the company's competitive standing in the market? Each department will offer ways to avoid, or at least minimize, negative impacts the proposal may have and also will offer ways to maximize its benefits. After that, each party will examine how the proposal will impact their interactions with other departments within their company.

After concluding this initial review of the proposal, each group affected by it will add the results of their review to the proposal. The revised proposal document will then be circulated again to all groups involved. Each group goes through subsequent reviews of the document as the additions of all the other groups are added, each time again checking the proposal's requirements, effectiveness, and impact. Once all parties have reviewed and revised the proposal to best take into consideration their situation, the content of the proposal becomes finalized. The head of each department involved in this process stamps the proposal with a seal with his name on it, signifying that the department has officially approved the proposal's content. The proposal must be approved in that way by each and every department involved for the decision to be adopted.

Decisions are thus made by consensus. This requires all departments to work together to ensure the needs and interests of each and every department involved. Just as we saw in chapter one that negotiating *between companies* involves taking into account the business interests of both companies, internal decision-making likewise requires allowing for the business interests of the other departments *within a company*. This decision-making dynamic is based upon—and further reinforces—the strong group orientation of Japan's business culture and management practices.

In Japan, this process of involving all parties affected by a proposal in the group decision-making process from the very start and throughout every step of the decision-making process is called *ringi* (稟議). The table at right illustrates the *ringi* decision-making process.

Table 2: Japanese Ringi (稟議) Method of Group Decision-Making

Steps	Senior Management	Middle Management	Lower Management & Staff
Step 1: Potential issues identified	Review issues ◁	Identify potential issues ◁	Identify potential issues
Step 2: Issues selected	Select & announce issues ▷	Directive to find solution received	
Step 3: Solutions identified		Jointly identify possible solutions	
Step 4: Solutions vetted & finalized		Analyze & recommend solution options	
Step 5: Internal decision-making	Solution selected ◁	**Inter**-department ◁ consensus	**Intra**-department consensus
Step 6: Solution authorized & announced	Solution mandated ▷	Solution decision received ▷	Solution decision received
Step 7: Solution enactment		Solution decision implemented	

Source: Robert Charles Azar

As you can easily imagine, this process is very tedious and requires considerable time. In the Japanese way of conducting business, however, the advantages of the *ringi* method of group decision-making outweigh the cons. Let's look at these advantages.

Because each group or department of the company affected by a proposal is continuously involved in the decision-making process from beginning to end, they are all fully aware of the proposal when it comes time to implement it. They all are keenly aware of what the proposal will require of them, how it will impact them, and what practical steps they will need to take to execute it. As a result, they are ready to implement the proposal as soon as the decision is finalized.

Since all the relevant parties include their recommendations in the decision and give it their approval, they have a sense of ownership and responsibility regarding the outcome of the decision. They have skin in the game, so to speak. Consequently, once it is time to implement the decision, each party in Japan has a vested interest in making sure the decision is implemented as successfully as possible. As a result, another benefit of *ringi* is that rarely is there any implementation resistance to new projects or changes.

> Decisions are made through the agreement of all parties concerned... another example of how management in Japan is group oriented.

In contrast, in a top-down decision making process, the affected parties start to examine what is required of them, how it will impact them, and what changes will be required after the decision has been made. This often causes a delay between the time a decision is made and when it can be implemented. In addition, as the affected parties were not involved in the decision, there are occasions when they resist implementing the decision because it may have detrimental effects on them.

In summary, while *ringi* decision-making in Japanese companies may take more time than decision-making in American companies, the implementation of the decision takes place in a manner that is quicker and smoother by having all parties affected by a decision fully engaged in the decision-making process.

The American top-down decision-making method allows for decisions to be made much faster; however, the decision's implementation can be slower and can be less effective for several reasons:

- The parties affected by a decision often only hear about the decision after it has been made, sometimes only at implementation time. As a result, they feel no ownership toward the decision and may not feel as responsible for or committed to implementing it.

- When parties affected by a decision only hear about it after the fact, they are unfamiliar with the proposal's expectations. They need time to understand the requirements, formulate steps for executing them, and then time to actually implement the decision.

- The parties may not have everything needed to implement the proposal readily available and may need time to source or prepare for implementation.

- In cases where the proposal is likely to have a negative impact on a department's performance, the department head can resist—or outright derail—implementation to avoid their department taking a performance hit. Such turf wars can be costly to a company in many ways.

As decisions are made through the collaboration and agreement of all of the parties concerned, the Japanese *ringi* method of decision-making is another example of how managing in Japan is group oriented and therefore fundamentally different from the American decision-making process.

III. GENERALISTS & THE ROTATION SYSTEM

In America, workers are hired by a company to fulfill a specific job function. The job title is specified. The job function and responsibilities are clearly defined. Companies will evaluate job applicants based on their level of experience and success with those specific job functions in the past and gauge how likely the candidate is to succeed with that job function in the company going forward. For example, a software programmer will be hired based on his/her familiarity and proven track record with the specific programming needs of the company as they are defined in the job description and discussed during the interview process. This is true for executive level positions all the way down to openings in the company's mailroom.

Following this approach, American companies hire specialists, individuals who are qualified and committed to performing the specific duties of their job function. Management and human resource practices are designed to facilitate workers performing their specific duties. When it comes to pay raises and promotions, workers are evaluated based on their level of performance regarding those specific job functions.

In Japan, companies hire specialists (*senmon shoku* 専門職) for those positions that require high levels of specialized knowledge or skills, such as scientific researchers, medical professionals, and software programmers. But unlike in America, most workers in Japan are hired as generalists (*sougou shoku* 総合職), and generalists have the more promising career path within the company than specialists do.

Instead of hiring only workers with an interest in a specific job function, Japanese companies hire generalists who are thought to be able to contribute to the company by fulfilling diverse job functions over the long term—that is, over the long career of the individual at that one company. As a result, the common practice is for new workers to be interviewed and accepted with no specific job functions being agreed upon and with no title. They are hired simply as generalists and called "new employees" (*shin shain* 新社員).

While the company certainly will ask during the interview process what type of work the individual thinks he or she would be interested in doing, the generalist employees are not hired because of any past experience with, preparation for, or track record or interest in that area of work. Japanese companies actually prefer new workers without experience because previous work experience can get in the way of an employee doing things the company's way. For the sake of productive relationships with co-workers and to avoid "confusion"—in other words, for the sake of group harmony and maximizing employee efficiency—companies like to hire workers without experience right out of high school or college as it is easier to train them in the way the company does things if the employee does not have to unlearn the ways learned in previous companies.

> Companies give priority to having workers feel that they share a common fate with management for the company's future.

In addition to that practical reason for hiring generalists, there is an underlying cultural reason why human resource management in Japan favors the hiring of generalists. As discussed later in this chapter, companies take a paternalistic approach to managing employees and view the company as a family. Functioning within the framework of this human resource management approach, companies give priority to having workers feel that they share a common fate with management for the company's future as a result of being members of the same company family. As Morita Akio, cofounder and president of the Sony Corporation, wrote:

> *(W)e think it is unwise and unnecessary to define individual responsibility too clearly, because everyone is taught to act like a family member ready to do what is necessary.* — **Morita Akio,** *Made In Japan* (New York: E.P. Dutton, 1986), p. 149.

The job rotation system is the most common management and human resource practice that Japanese companies use to train their generalist workers to contribute to the company over the long term in various job functions. Typically, management will rotate employees across job functions and company departments every few years. The goal is three-fold:

- Enable the company to identify the areas where workers can best contribute

- Help employees discover through first hand experience what job functions they do well in and enjoy

- Allow the employee to become familiar with and gain experience in as many different parts of the company's business operations as possible

It is understood that workers will not have an affinity for every area of the company's business or become effective in every position. That is not the point. The goal is to have the employee get to know as much of the company's business as possible and gain an overall understanding of the company's operations; in other words, to become a competent generalist.

In addition, by rotating employees, the company reduces worker burnout from performing the same type of work for many years, as can happen with specialists who typically work in the same job function for the length of their employment. It also greatly reduces the need for employees to leave the company to experience working in different areas or functions. As job rotations usually bring with them promotions and salary increases, the rotation system diminishes the need for employees to look for work elsewhere to obtain them. For these reasons, the job rotation management and human resource practice fosters employee loyalty to and longevity with the company.

Finally, senior management uses this technique to help identify which employees to put on the track for upper management by identifying workers who are more comfortable and successful moving from one department to another.

The focus of management and human resource practices in the U.S. is to enable a worker to develop expertise in their one chosen job function as a specialist. In Japan, on the other hand, the emphasis is on giving employees who are generalists a broad understanding of the company's operations. Having broad-based experience with many of the company's areas of operations enables them to make well-informed decisions when they rise to executive level, because they at least broadly understand how those decisions will effect the various parts of the company based on their personal experience working in those departments. In short, in Japan, the generalist executive is thought to be well-prepared to manage and operate the company. This is a significant contrast to the specialist executive approach in America.

IV. SENIORITY

In the United States, the average worker changes jobs numerous times over the course of their working life. Moving from one company to another is often seen as a positive development. It can be the opportunity to negotiate a higher salary or move into a higher position—in other words, it can be a way to advance one's career. In Japan, workers change jobs less frequently. Until recently, it was commonplace to work in one company for one's whole working life. In fact, changing jobs has generally been viewed negatively, implying that the worker has a problem fitting in.

Such employee longevity at one company has long been encouraged and sought after by Japanese management as they view a stable workforce as being necessary for advancing the company's business interests over the long term. As a result, seniority based on the length of employment is highly valued. In fact, in most Japanese companies, employees are promoted based more on seniority and less on job performance. Pay raises are likewise based on seniority more than performance. This seniority-based system of promotion is known as *nenkou jyoretsu* (年功序列).

These two management practices of basing both promotions and salary increases on seniority are designed to encourage and reward employee loyalty to the company—that is, longevity with the company.

Underlying this practice of seniority-based promotions is the strong cultural value of respecting one's seniors in Japan. Respecting those who have come before you and appreciating those who have "done the work" longer than you have is a fundamental teaching of Confucianism and Japan's native Shinto religion.

V. TO BE SHOWN THE WINDOW

While it is common practice for those who have attained seniority to be shown respect in Japan's companies, management may not necessarily want every long-term employee to continue working in the company. There can be many reasons for this. For example, the employee may not be able to keep up with the changes affecting the market, the company, or how it operates. The worker's productivity may have declined. It could be the worker is simply burned-out after putting in long hours decade after decade.

How then does management release long-time workers in a country where seniority is respected and where layoffs are frowned upon by society because they do not promote social stability? In

American corporations, unwanted workers often are dismissed or "shown the door." In Japanese companies, unwanted workers are shown the window!

Management signals to senior workers, especially executives and managers, that their continued employment is no longer desired by giving them a desk in front of a window located in a corner of the room with no desks for subordinates in front of it. The senior employee becomes known as "a person by the window" (*mado giwa zoku* 窓ぎわ族). This is management's way of telling the worker that it is time to think about the possibilities that lie outside the window. That is, the possibilities to be found outside of the company! Being assigned to a desk in front of a window in the corner of the room with no subordinates in front of you is not moving up in the company in Japan; it is moving out of the company.

How different this is in America, where to be given a desk in front of the window is always a reward for a job well done. This is another example of how the same action can have completely different meanings in Japan and America because of the different cultural connotation the action has in each country. In this case, the cultural meaning is not just very different, it is the exact opposite.

> In American corporations, unwanted workers are "shown the door." In Japanese companies, they are shown the window!

American executives need to keep this difference in mind when managing Japanese workers or managing joint business ventures with Japanese companies. It would be a significant failure in intercultural management and cross-cultural communication if an American manager attempted to acknowledge the importance of an employee's role by giving them a corner window desk by itself. Because of this potential and inadvertent miscommunication, it is important for executives managing in Japan to know beforehand what their words and actions will mean in Japan's cultural context.

VI. STAYING LATE

As noted in the section on seniority, the length of time an employee works in the company is very meaningful in Japan. It is important to point out that the amount of time one spends in the company is important not only in terms of the number of years a person is employed there but also in terms of how many hours a person spends in the office *every day*.

By way of example, I was employed in Japanese companies for the first ten years of my working career. One of the first things non-Japanese realize in working in Japanese companies is that most Japanese workers stay at the office until very late every day—way past the 5:00 or 6:00 p.m. end of the day typical for American workers. It is common for them to stay until 8:00, 9:00, or even 10:00 p.m.

With an hour and a half commute between home and office in New York City and needing to be back in the office early every morning, I wanted to leave the office every day by 5:30 or 6:00 p.m. to be home at a reasonable hour. Of course, I would not think twice about staying later in the event of a deadline or some situation that required me to be there. But in the normal course of events, I saw no reason to stay late. My Japanese colleagues would always frown and ask why I was leaving so early.

This situation raised the question in my mind as to what employees were doing during those extra four or five hours at the office every evening. I was very surprised to learn that the employees usually were not working at the same hectic pace as during normal business hours. They worked on a few tasks but were mostly passing the time. I witnessed this pattern in every Japanese company I was employed by or later worked with on behalf of clients.

In discussing this with my Japanese colleagues over the years, I would mention that employees did not seem to be really working during those later hours and asked why everyone stayed so late every night. I never forgot the reply or the insights into the cultural values that so strongly drive how managers manage and how employees work in Japan. My colleagues typically mentioned any or all of the following three reasons:

- First, a worker never leaves the office before his boss does. There are two reasons for this:
  - It would be disrespectful to your boss to do this.
  - It would be bad form to leave before your boss as it would look like you are not serious about your work.

- Second, you stay late for the sake of the group and group harmony. You belong to the group and so you act as a group. That means you all leave together when everyone has completed all their work for that day; that sometimes may even mean you help each other finish that day's work.

- Third, you stay late in case a request comes in from a client, another department within your company, a branch office in another part of the world, or especially from headquarters. Your department would not look good if no one was there and that caused someone to wait until the next day to get an answer.

Notice that the focus of both Japanese managers and rank

and file employees is on the interests of the group (that is, company clients or other departments in one's company) front and center and that leads them to stay late and be available. Once again, the group orientation at work.

VII. MANAGING FOR THE LONG TERM

During the late 1980's, I worked for four years as a financial analyst and political economist at Daiwa Securities, Inc. in their North American corporate headquarters located in the World Financial Center on Wall Street. At that time, Daiwa was Japan's— and also the world's—second largest brokerage house. It was located directly across the street from the World Trade Center. That experience afforded me an incredible opportunity to work directly with the leaders of finance and industry in Japan, interacting with them in their language and in accordance with their cultural norms.

Shortly after commencing employment there, I quickly came to see how the framework of time that the Japanese use in business is very different from the one used in America. This difference in time horizons influences all aspects of business: strategic planning, management choices, asset allocation, forecasts for sales and profitability, expected return on equity, investment decisions, negotiating (as we saw in chapter one), and so on.

In the U.S., the focus of management is profitability and shareholder value in the short term. This is especially true on Wall Street. For the companies issuing securities, their focus is providing a respectable return on investment to their investors from quarter to quarter. For the investors buying the stocks and bonds of those companies, their primary concern is how the value of their investments fluctuates from quarter to quarter. Likewise, for the investment professionals who track and analyze business developments in

America, their focus is on following quarterly results and making trillion dollar investment decisions based on their analysis of these short-term results. This modus operandi has served the American economy well.

Companies, investors, and investment professionals in Japan, however, operate with a different framework of time. Their focus is on business and investment performance over the long term, just as it is in most areas of business in Japan. To quantify that, as we've already learned, their long-term time horizon is typically out three to five years. This difference in time framework is another fundamental difference affecting American and Japanese investment practices and also impacting the management practices of both countries.

The advantage of this Japanese approach is that company management is not beholden to short-term returns or the interests of shareholders. As a result, management is able to focus on the long-term interests and performance of the company—and they can do so even at the expense of short-term profitability. The following example illustrates this seemingly contradictory management practice.

One business practice the world has seen Japanese companies utilize on many occasions is the selling of products in international markets at prices markedly lower than the competition. This was done not because Japan could produce those products at a considerably lower cost than the competition. In fact, the disconnect between production cost and selling price was apparent to the point that many countries, including the U.S., denounced the practice as "dumping." Namely, that Japanese corporations were selling products so cheaply, it was as if they were just dumping them in the market at prices that were below cost.

Why would Japanese companies utilize this strategy? The answer is because their focus would be on long-term strategic benefits rather than short-term higher profit. While they had lower profit margins over the short term because of reduced prices, they were able to gain a greater market share for their products in markets around the world. That greater market share made an excellent springboard for introducing new products to the market. Eventually, the greater sales volumes that this strategy produced, together with increased cost efficiencies and additional products to sell, enabled Japanese companies to capture greater levels of profit. What was lost in short-term price margins was made up over the long run by sales volume, efficiencies, and additional products. It also enabled Japanese companies to capture large market shares in various industries around the world.

In addition, controlling a greater market share brought with it another strategic benefit. Control of a greater market share afforded a greater degree of revenue stability that is not possible with a smaller market share. This, in turn, supports greater long-term investment in product research and development to further increase cost efficiencies and develop more advanced products. Together these developments allowed Japanese companies to be even more competitive in the market, thereby increasing sales and market share.

Another example of the contrast between short-term and long-term management practices is what American and Japanese companies do when quarterly sales and profit are lower than expected. American companies have no problem selling corporate assets, delaying projects, laying off employees, or taking other quick, stopgap measures to make up for lower business results. While satisfying Wall Street and investors, these actions typically do not strengthen a company.

Focused on the long term, Japanese companies rarely lay off workers or take extraordinary actions to make up for weaker than expected sales results in the short term.

From the perspective of Japanese management practices, selling corporate assets, delaying projects, laying off employees, or taking other one-time, stopgap measures to cover short-term revenue shortfalls do not promote the stability of the business nor are they in the long-term interests of the company. Letting workers go when revenues are down and rehiring when revenues are better hurts a business in their view. Likewise, releasing senior, high paid employees and replacing them with cheaper, less experienced workers simply to reduce company costs baffles Japanese executives. They cannot understand how the cost savings can be worth more than the experience, insights, and efficiencies senior staff bring to the table. In their view, a stable workforce promotes stable business operations and stable sales performance for the long term.

VIII. DIFFERENT TIME HORIZONS

As noted, Japanese companies take a long-term view in management and business, longer than is typical in America. Regarding time, however, not only do Japanese manage business with a different time horizon, the actual framework of time they use also differs from ours. Specifically, the meaning of short term, mid term and long term is different from the meaning we assign in our country. This is discussed much more fully in chapter one. Table 3 gives a summary reference for time horizon comparison.

Table 3: Different Time Horizons

	Short term	Mid term	Long term
America	3 to 9 months	9 to 18 months	18 months and beyond
Japan	1.5 to 2 years	3 to 4 years	5 years or more

Source: Robert Charles Azar

The time horizon differences quite often cause friction between American and Japanese companies in a joint business project. The best way to avoid this is to quantify the time frames to make sure all parties are talking about and have expectations for the same periods of time. This will help alleviate American concern about timely milestone achievement and will reduce Japanese concern that the American company is impatient for progress. Both companies can now recognize and honor the same quantified timeframe.

IX. DETAIL ORIENTATION

While the Japanese need to be comfortable with the big picture, they need to be equally comfortable with details. Before commencing a project, they want to understand as many of the particulars as possible. As a result, they take a very detail-oriented approach not only in their due diligence review stage or during negotiations but also in managing the day-to-day operations of business. They call that detail-oriented approach being "*komakai*" (細かい).

While foreigners of course pay attention to details, the Japanese do so to a far greater degree than Americans do. From our perspective, their preferred level of attention to detail is overkill; Americans typically feel that degree of detail is not necessary to make broad-based management decisions. And, to the dismay of Americans, the more significant the project, the greater the level of detail Japanese require up front to agree to participate.

Not only is the need to understand overall details greater in Japan than in America but also the Japanese management style itself is much more detail oriented. As a result, such things as creating employee reports, managing operations, managing projects, and carrying out events are conducted with a level of detail that is uncommon in America.

For example, a businessman's expense reimbursement request in the States requires a list of expenses, their date, and their purpose (with whom and for what). That information would be insufficient in Japanese companies. An accounting of one's activities for twenty-four hours of each day of the trip is also required.

When I was working on Wall Street as a financial analyst for Daiwa Securities, I traveled several times a month to visit the companies I was following. These visits were necessary to interview senior executives and obtain management level information on developments at the company. When preparing my Daiwa expense reimbursement request, part one of the form was a list of the expenses, their date, purpose, and who was there. Part two of the form consisted of pages to record the movements and activities we made for the entire day.

Likewise, in planning such things as meetings or events, it is common for timetables to cover every minute of the day of the event.

Honda Soichiro, founder and CEO of Honda Motor Co., Ltd., commented on the importance of Japan's *komakai* approach by stating:

> *"To achieve this <a company goal>, it must be supported by meticulous attention to detail and unremitting effort."* — **Honda Soichiro, Founder & CEO, Honda Motor Co., Ltd.**
>
> http://www.quoteswise.com/soichiro-honda-quotes-3.html

American managers need to keep in mind this penchant for details when managing Japanese workers or working in a joint business venture in Japan. It is necessary to provide a significantly greater amount of detail when conducting business in Japan than would be customary in the States. In addition, keep in mind that

Japanese will require more time to identify and investigate the details of interest. Without this extra detail, Japanese workers lack confidence to commit to or work on projects full-heartedly.

X. MANAGING CHANGE

Japan is often referred to as a country of paradox. While it has all of the trappings of an ultramodern, industrialized nation, it also holds on to cultural traditions and social customs that are centuries old. This same paradox applies to Japanese attitudes toward change.

Progress, innovation, and improvement in business are highly valued. For example, Japan is world famous for its practice of *kaizen* (改善) or continual improvement. Conversely, in Japanese society, there is a real aversion to change that upsets the status quo. This impacts Japan's style of management and affects how Japanese companies operate.

In America, we are receptive to change. We see it as an opportunity to welcome in something new, as a way to improve and do things better. This is not always the case in Japan. Being more conservative, Japanese respect and are comfortable with the status quo. After all, the status quo took an inordinate amount of time and effort to achieve through consensus building.

Furthermore, given their two thousand year history and geographical confines, there is considerable historical momentum behind cultural traditions and their resulting status quo for Japanese. With our very short history and wide population diversity, the historical momentum of cultural traditions does not carry the same weight for us in America. We do not feel as bound by tradition and instead are more focused on the possibilities of what the future can bring. And change is the gateway to those possibilities.

The Japanese have a proper way to do most things. Having these prescribed ways means everyone knows how to act in a way that is proper and respectful. And by following those ways, everyone interacts harmoniously. Change can disrupt those prescribed ways, resulting in confusion. This is another reason Japanese dislike sudden or unexpected change.

Change is unsettling for people who are firmly entrenched in the proper way a thing is to be done. The type of uncertainty engendered by sudden or unexpected change is detrimental to the group harmony that is a central value of Japanese society. It is seen as potentially being so disruptive that Japanese refer to it not as uncertainty but as *konran* (混乱), which means confusion, disorder, chaos, and mayhem. It will take time for a group consensus to be reached to restore normalcy after an unexpected change.

Having an aversion to sudden change results in Japanese often not welcoming to do things differently. Remember from chapter one that the Japanese word for different (*chigau* 違う) also means "to be wrong." In English, of course, the word "different" simply means "not the same" and does not connote being right or wrong.

In business, the aversion to change is often seen with regard to procedure. Japanese place great emphasis on procedure—that is, the customary and proper way to do things. Culturally, the proper way to do something is the way it should be done. Doing something the way it is supposed to be done can be more important than how best to do it. From an American perspective, Japanese emphasize procedure more than content: form or procedure will often take precedence over content. Things need to be done in the prescribed way even though that may not be the best or most efficient way to do it.

Considering all this, Japan may appear to be a place where

it is difficult to introduce and affect change, and, indeed, there are several cultural dynamics that impede the introduction of change.

- It is not polite to disagree or do things differently.

- Maintaining the status quo is central to group harmony.

- Younger employees are obligated to be deferential to those with seniority.

Doing things in the prescribed manner (that is, in accordance with established procedure) is more important than doing it the best way.

How then did Japan become the world's second largest economy for so many years? What enabled Japan to originate and perfect the now globally accepted business practice of continual improvement or *kaizen*?

As is so often true in Japan, proper time and place must be considered. The culturally accepted venue and opportunity to discuss change and improvement is the "evaluation meeting" known as *hanseikai* (反省会).

During these meetings, employees discuss at great length how to do things better—how to do them more efficiently, more cost effectively, more successfully. Employees are encouraged to speak freely and openly. The customary cultural dynamics of not disagreeing and of being deferential to those more senior are relaxed in the *hanseikai* meeting.

In the States, we utilize brainstorming sessions to achieve the same goals of the *hanseikai*. The difference between the two is that Japan's evaluation meetings last longer and are held with much greater frequency. Japanese spend hours at each meeting discussing potential ways to improve business operations. While American brainstorming meetings tend to occur in a sporadic fashion, hanseikai meetings are regularly scheduled occurrences that take place with great frequency. For example, they can be held at the end of shifts, the end of production cycles, the end of the day, the end of the month, the end of the quarter, and the end of the year.

How can foreign executives best manage their business interests in Japan in light of Japanese attitudes toward change?

First, utilizing the *hanseikai* meeting is imperative. It is the best opportunity to find out what issues are affecting your workers as well as your business. It is the best place to constructively discuss the options for best navigating those issues. *Hanseikai* meetings may produce suggestions that enhance your intended change or are superior to it. While the Japanese penchant for being extremely detail-oriented can make attending these meetings nerve racking for foreigners, it is well worth it in the end.

> The culturally accepted venue and opportunity to discuss change and improvement is the "evaluation meeting."

Second, keeping in mind that decision-making is done as a group, meet with appropriate managers who will be involved with the decision-making and implementation ahead of time to plant seeds for the upcoming change. The goal is to inform them about what may be involved and get them on board before the need for change is officially announced in the company. In Japan, this practice of advanced, behind-the-scenes stage setting is referred to as *nemawashi* (根回し)—literally meaning to "turn the roots."

Third, whenever possible utilize the Japanese *ringi* group

method of decision-making. This will make acceptance and implementation of the change smoother. It could also lead to alternative options that are more effective than what you originally intended to implement.

Sometimes, for one reason or another, it is not possible to use any of these three Japanese methods. In that case, the following methods I developed have served clients well over the years:

- When at all possible, avoid abruptly announcing changes that are to take effect immediately. An effective way to introduce change is to inform your Japanese partners ahead of time of anticipated changes. In the event that the details of the change are not finalized or are still unknown, informing your Japanese associates that at-this-point-unspecified change is expected goes a long way. This removes the element of surprise and alerts them so they are now prepared to expect changes to the status quo.

  Avoiding sudden change reduces Japanese concern that the change is a response to an unanticipated problem with your product or business or that the alterations are an afterthought on your part, something you overlooked previously and only now realized needed to be included.

  By providing advance notice before the implementation date, you give Japanese the time they need to build consensus suggestions among themselves regarding how best to incorporate the change.

- Do not refer to alterations as change. Call them by the positive benefit(s) they will bring about. If the change is in the area of the timeliness of customer service, for example, then refer to it as "an even quicker response time." If the change refers to major product functions or features, then identify the change as "the next generation" of your product. Framing change as a positive benefit translates well culturally in Japan.

- Finally, show how the changes will result in your product or business operations being more in line with best global business practices. Being on the cutting edge and up to date with leading international business norms resonates well with Japanese as a reason for initiating change. In addition, since you are positioning the alterations as being in line with best global business practices—and not with American business ways of doing things—the changes become more comfortable for your Japanese partners. You are not asking them to give up their Japanese ways and replace them with American practices.

The above approaches to introducing and managing change will make change more palatable to your Japanese partners and will help enable smooth and effective implementation.

XI. INTRA-COMPANY RELATIONSHIP BUILDING

As discussed in depth in the chapter on negotiating, relationships play a significant role in business in Japan, much more so than in America where business is transaction driven.

In the Japanese style of management, relationship building and maintenance are important not only between companies engaged in mutual business but also *within* any given company. As different departments within the same company strive to work together with smooth relationships—harmony at the corporate level—it is important for American managers to realize that Japanese executives deliberately work hard at keeping up congenial relationships with other department heads. The most typical ways for doing this include going out for lunch or dinner together, enjoying drinks in the evening, playing golf, and socializing together.

In addition, during the *ringi* decision-making process discussed earlier in this chapter, department heads will meet with counterparts frequently. This type of intra-company relationship management occurs not only among executives but also among the staff of different departments at all levels of the company.

There is another dynamic that fosters the building of strong intra-company relationships among executives as well as rank and file employees in different parts of the organization. Japanese employees identify with those who commenced working at the company in the same year. Just as graduates of a school will identify with and be referred to by the year of their graduation, employees in Japanese companies identify with and are referred to by the year their employment started. For example, all those employees who started working at a company in 2016 will be called 2016 *nen nyusha-in* (2016 年入社員)—or "2016 hired employees" As a result, a special bond with others in one's employment year is formed from the outset and carries through the length of the employee's career in that company.

In managing Japanese employees or ventures with Japanese business partners, it is important that foreign executives keep in mind the importance of intra-company relationships and strive to build and maintain them. Doing this not only allows an executive to keep abreast of what is going on in other departments but also helps ensure smoother and quicker collaboration over time.

XII. COMPANY AS SOCIETY

We have seen that Japanese companies typically do not lay

off workers during difficult business times, as they are mindful that the experience and loyalty of their employees bring value and harmony to the company. There also is another reason why Japanese companies rarely layoff workers in Japan. And it has nothing to do with the interests of the company.

It is commonplace in Japan for companies to be thought of as having a responsibility to society at large. A major part of that responsibility is to provide stable employment not only for the welfare of the individual employees and their families but also for the sake of maintaining and promoting the social stability of the nation. For this reason, companies in Japan are thought of as having a much greater role in society than is the case for companies in other countries. In the States, for example, companies are viewed as existing primarily for the benefit of management and shareholders.

> A company is thought of as a worker's community or mini society.

Another part of the role that companies play in Japanese society goes well beyond simply affording a workplace. A company is thought of as a worker's community or mini society, a place where needs normally fulfilled by society at large can be met, at least in part, within the company. Examples of this include:

- The company becomes a central part of the workers' social lives, as employees typically socialize with co-workers during lunch, after business hours, and on weekends.

- Companies provide below cost housing for employees by renting them rooms in company-owned apartment buildings or dormitories.

- In addition to making a social network there, it is not uncommon for workers to look for and find their spouses in their workplace.

- Employees in Japan typically hesitate to take vacations even though they have plenty of vacation time. As a result, companies often arrange and even pay for company vacations where all employees go as a group. In this way, management thanks all of the employees for their good work as a group and does not single out individual workers. This arrangement provides several benefits:

  o Corporate trips build company morale.

  o Company vacations enhance employee loyalty.

  o Corporate junkets further strengthen the social bonds among workers.

  o Company getaways promote group harmony within the company.

The fact that companies function in a manner similar to that of a mini society is further seen in the words in the Japanese language for company and society. The word for company is *kaisha* (会社), and the word for society is *shakai* (社会). Both words are written with the same two characters, just in reverse order. In other words, company = society (会社 = 社会) and society = company (社会 = 会社).

The company functioning as a community or mini society is part of Japan's cultural heritage. It is a manifestation of the strong group orientation of the culture and the influence of Confucianism and Shinto. It reinforces, and is also reinforced by, the "inner

(内 *uchi*) versus outer (外 *soto*)" cultural dynamic that is discussed in the chapter on communication in Japan.

As can be seen through these examples, Japanese companies often take a paternalistic view toward their employees. The reason, in part, for that is management's desire to maintain a workforce that is content, loyal, stable, and well motivated. This allows staff to work without distractions and at higher levels of efficiency and productivity. This is another example of how cultural factors contribute directly to a company's performance in Japan.

The paternalistic approach of Japanese management is also seen in their sense of responsibility for the well-being of their employees. This is perhaps most evident in Japanese attitudes toward laying off workers. Morita Akio, the co-founder and President of the Sony Corporations stated:

> *I discovered very quickly that in Western countries, employers would get rid of some personnel when a recession seemed imminent. It was a shock to me, because in Japan we never do this, unless we are completely desperate. If the administration takes the risk and responsibility of hiring personnel, then it also assumes responsibility for giving them work. It's not the employee who is responsible for this agreement. Also, when there is a recession, why should the personnel suffer because of a decision made by the administration who gave them a job? That's my point of view. That's why, in periods of prosperity, we increase the number of our employees with great prudence. Once hired, we try to make them understand our idea of 'shared destiny' and our intention, if the business has to deal with a recession, to give up certain benefits so that they stay with us.*

> http://www.quoteswise.com/akio-morita-quotes-2.html

Returning to the subject of vacations, I have always been amazed at how Japanese workers in Japan rarely take individual vacations. Whenever I have discussed this with them, two reasons are consistently given:

- First, employees hesitate to take time off from work because their co-workers will have to cover their responsibilities while they are away. An employee taking a vacation would "bother" or "impose on" his or her fellow workers—*meiwaku o kakemasu* (迷惑をかけます).

- Second, workers fear that if management sees that a vacationing worker's responsibilities can be handled without them, the company may decide that the employee's position is not needed anymore.

XIII. SERVING SOCIETY AT LARGE

The pervasive paternalistic role that companies play has roots stemming from two ancient cultural traditions. The first is the essence of Japan's only native religion—Shinto. In this religion, as Ono Sokyo writes in *Shinto: The Kami Way*, salvation is not found in the next world, as is the case in Western religions, nor in any transcendental state. Instead, salvation is achieved in this life by looking out for each other and contributing to the harmonious development of society and the world.[1]

[1]*Ono Sokyo*, Shinto: The Kami Way
(Rutland, Vermont: Charles E. Tuttle Company, 1979), p. 107.

Confucianism is the second cultural tradition. The values of this Chinese philosophy are part of the bedrock of Japanese culture and society. Confucianism teaches that those in a position to lead have a social responsibility, and indeed moral obligation, to look after those under them. Accordingly, in their leadership roles, companies and their management have both a social responsibility and a moral obligation to look after their employees and society at large. This social responsibility and moral obligation of a company to benefit society at large is referred to in Japan as "corporate social responsibility" or "CSR" (コーポレートソーシャルリスポンシビリティー).

As a consequence, serving society at large and taking a family-like view of employees have long been fundamental parts of both the philosophy and the practice of management in Japan. To illustrate this point, I would like to share the words of the executive who is considered the most prominent CEO in present day Japan.

> Serving society at large and taking a family-like view of employees have long been fundamental parts of both the philosophy and the practice of management in Japan.

In 2011 Japan Airlines (JAL) went bankrupt. In its desire to save the nation's flagship carrier, the Japanese government asked one executive to turn the company around. His name is Inamori Kazuo. He is the president and CEO of the Kyocera Corporation, one of Japan's most successful Fortune 50 companies. Inamori succeeded in turning JAL around in three years.

Inamori saw the company as functioning like an extended family or mini society and that "family" had an obligation to benefit society at large. These two representative quotes underscore this vision:

> *(B)elieving in an environment in which all workers shared the same goals as management and regarded mutual cooperation as the ideal, I then looked to the traditional Japanese family for a model...*

If the company becomes a community held together by destiny, as one extended family, and its mutual understanding, encouragement, and help are freely given among managers and employees, just as any family, then it should be possible to run the company with management and labor as one body united for the same purposes.... I named this concept the extended family principle and made it part of the company's management foundation. — Kazuo Inamori, *Amoeba Management* (Boca Raton, Florida: CRC Press, 2013), pp. 18–19.

Inamori went on to explain:

The pursuit of profit is the driving force behind business as well as many other human endeavors, and there is thus nothing wrong with wanting to make money. We should not pursue profit, however, for the benefit of ourselves alone. We need to "greedily" desire what is best for others and strive to promote the common good. If we do so, we too will benefit and the scope of our profit will greatly expand in the process.

Running a company, for example, is in itself a service to others and to society. — Kazuo Inamori, *A Compass to Fulfillment: Passion and Spirituality in Life and Business* (New York: McGraw Hill, 2010), p. 82.

Matsushita Konosuke, the founder and CEO of the Panasonic Corporation (formerly known as the Matsushita Electric Co.), explained the social obligation of Japanese management and companies to employees and society at large:

If the result of hard work is not black ink, and if it does not contribute to the prosperity of the country and the society nor to the enhancement of the standards of living of our employees, Matsushita Electric has no reason to exist. If it has no reason for existence, we should dissolve Matsushita Electric. — PHP Institute, Inc., *Matsushita Konosuke (1894-1989): His Life & Legacy* (Tokyo: PHP Institute, Inc., 1994), pp. 34–35.

The following statement is a good demonstration of the social commitment and long-term horizon of management and business in Japan. In early 2015, I participated in a conversation via Skype in which Mr. Tanaka Yoichi, the president of the Tokyo-based company EDT Inc., articulated this philosophy in a clear fashion:

We deeply regret the level of sales this past year and today we renew our commitment to succeeding in 2015.

Sales in the short term have not recovered from the earthquake and tsunami of 2011. As you know, the difficult conditions of the economy in Japan remain a real obstacle even today. However, despite this we have not slackened off in our efforts to promote and sell the products. EDT remains as committed to this business in Japan today as we were when we first began.

The reason for our continued commitment is that we believe that the products and their underlying concept are indispensible for the health of the entire Japanese nation. All of the people of Japan stand to benefit from them and so I am fully committed to succeeding in this effort. For the sake of my fellow Japanese, I see it as my fate to make sure that this work succeeds. — Tanaka Yoichi, Skype conversation remarks, March 11, 2015.

As these remarks indicate, both his interest in and

commitment to the business are long term, so he will not be dissuaded by short-term setbacks. Note that the period of low sales had already lasted for four years by January 2015. And yet Mr. Tanaka characterized that period as being short term.

His statement indicates that in addition to promoting his company's sales and profits, EDT is committed to its social responsibility and moral obligation to bring the benefits of this American company's products and services to the entire nation of Japan so that all the people of Japan can benefit from them.

In one discussion I had with senior executives in Tokyo about Japan's family-like style of management and the societal role of the company, one company president stated he believed that the notion of being a good corporate citizen that we have in the U.S. is America's equivalent to Japan's philosophy of management and societal role for companies. However, while both may point in the same direction, they are nowhere near the same. In the States, being a good corporate citizen means that a company contributes to specific organizations or activities in society, e.g., supporting the arts, an education program, a sports team, a sports arena, etc. Making contributions to societal activities is not the same as endeavoring to benefit society at large while serving as a mini society for the company's workers.

XIV. WORK & SELF-GROWTH

It has often been noted how dedicated to work Japanese people have always been. They work earnestly and for long hours. Why is this so?

In the samurai tradition of *Bushido*, focusing and applying one's self singularly, earnestly, and wholeheartedly to the task at hand was a form of spiritual discipline and meditation. Given that, being diligent (勤勉 *kinben*) in one's work promotes one's growth as a person (仕事は人間成長 *shigoto wa ningen seichou*). As the company or other place of business is the venue where people work, the company has a role in facilitating the self-growth of its employees so they may become not only better members of the company but also full-fledged contributing members of society (社会人 *shakaijin*). This is another way in which companies in Japan are thought of as public vessels (公器 *kouki*) that contribute to society at large.

Matsushita Konosuke of the Panasonic Corporation (Matsushita Electric) aptly articulated this idea that a company has a social responsibility to facilitate the growth of employees when he wrote *Before Making Things, First Make People* ("物をつくる前にまず人をつくる"):

> The company has a role in facilitating the self-growth of its employees.

> *When asked what does Matsushita Electric make, reply that it is a place that makes people. At the same time it also makes electric products. Reply in that way...*
>
> *In my mind, "the enterprise of business is people." That is, my feeling is that if we don't first develop people, if we utilize people who have not grown as people, then that business is not one that can succeed. Accordingly, while the making of electric goods itself is an extremely important mission, to achieve that we first must develop people.* — **Matsushita Konosuke, "PHP Human Resource Development" (PHP 人材開発)**
>
> http://hrd.php.co.jp/shainkyouiku/cat21/post-73.php, my translation.

In the Shinto religion, as Ono Sokyo writes in *Shinto: The Kami Way*, life is seen as being a gift received from the gods. Man's daily existence is only possible due to his dependence on nature and society. As a result, man must embrace his obligations to society and reciprocate by contributing to the development of all things entrusted to him.[2]

[2]*Ono Sokyo*, Shinto: The Kami Way
(Rutland, Vermont: Charles E. Tuttle Company, 1979), p. 107.

Work—whether running a company as a member of management or working at a company as an employee—is one of the major ways people contribute and reciprocate.

As we can see, the Japanese work ethic and approach to business is based on deeply rooted cultural values that are quite different from those in many countries.

SUMMARY

Management in Japan is much more holistic and contains approaches and practices that are not found in America. A recap of some of the representative differences includes:

- Focus is on the group rather than the individual employee.

- Decision-making is group-based where all parties involved participate in the entire decision-making process.

- In Japanese hiring practices in most industries, companies hire significantly more generalists than specialists. In grooming the next generation of managers, generalists are preferred over specialists.

- Seniority is important to promotions and salary increases.

- Corporate management is exercised with a long-term horizon rather than a short-term approach in all facets of business.

- Japanese define short term, mid term, long term, and other frameworks of time differently than foreigners do.

- Japanese approach management and business in a highly detail-oriented manner.

- Change is managed differently in Japan.

- Business is relationship driven not only between companies but also within a company among its individual departments.

- The company takes a family-like approach regarding the welfare of employees.

- The company serves as a mini society for employees.

- Companies and management have an obligation to contribute to society at large.

- The Japanese work ethic and approach to business are based on deeply rooted cultural values wherein work is seen as being related to self-growth.

As discussed throughout this chapter, these different approaches and practices in Japanese management come from cultural values, norms, and preferences in Japan that are not present in America. More often than not, these culture-based differences in management and business practices are unknown to foreign executives and, as a result, present significant challenges to their business endeavors in the Japanese market. Foreign executives would benefit greatly from intercultural managment support to effectively deal with them.

伝達と共感

CHAPTER 3

The Challenges Of

Japanese Communication

"The single biggest problem in communication is the illusion that it has taken place." — **George Bernard Shaw**

When business executives sit down at a meeting table, they bring with them the communication dynamics and cultural norms of their own country and culture. These dynamics and norms include the cultural connotations, nuances, and expectations that the hearer attaches to what is said, heard, reflected upon, and experienced.

In America, we prefer communication to be direct and clear. We prefer either yes or no answers or I agree or I disagree statements. In our culture, directness and clarity are seen favorably as promoting understanding and reducing miscommunication. We feel directness and clarity add confidence that our communication will be effective and ensure that all parties are on the same page. In Japan, this is not the case at all. In fact, very different social values and cultural dynamics inform communication there. The result is that communicating with Japanese typically is highly problematic for foreigners and is a major obstacle to a foreign business attaining success in that market.

Japan's current Prime Minister, Abe Shinzo, acknowledged the difficulty that foreigners have communicating with Japanese when he wrote:

> *The Japanese have a reputation for being taciturn and hard to communicate with. Probably the most difficult part of Japanese communication for people from other countries is the way people here converse wordlessly.* — **The Government of Japan,** *We are Tomodachi (We are Friends)* **(Tokyo: Office of the Prime Minister, Spring/Summer 2014), Page 72.**

Communication is the lifeline of collaborative business ventures. The importance of communication is heightened when that collaborative venture is taking place between different countries and different cultures. Challenges in communicating with partners in Japan directly result in challenges in every facet of a foreign company's business in that market. Let's look at some of the major ways communication in Japan is different than communication in other countries, explore how these differences are problematic for foreigner businesses, and learn how American executives can most effectively deal with them.

I. DIFFERENT GOALS IN COMMUNICATION

The first challenge is that communication in Japan has a very different goal than in America. In the States, the purpose of communication is to express or share an idea or sentiment as clearly as one can. We are encouraged to do so as logically and convincingly as possible. In fact, in defining a good communicator we use such terms as easy to understand, clear, articulate, lucid, expressive, unambiguous, convincing, and compelling.

While the function of communication in Japan is likewise to convey a thought or sentiment, there is an underlying goal that does not exist in America that governs Japan's communication dynamics. That goal of communication in Japan is to promote smooth relationships and harmony; it does that by fostering a sense of mutual belonging and interdependence. As a result of having different goals and drivers, communication in Japan has very different dynamics and characteristics than we are accustomed to in the States.

> As a result of having different goals and drivers, communication in Japan has very different dynamics and characteristics.

In Japan, communication is intentionally vague. Japanese go to great lengths to avoid being too direct or clear when communicating. Statements that can be understood in more than one way are commonly used. Keeping communication vague means parties do not have to take sides by agreeing or disagreeing, thereby preserving group solidarity. As a result, "keeping things vague" (*aimai ni suru* 曖昧にする) is a common feature of Japanese communication used to promote harmony.

As a result of this common practice of keeping things vague, it is not unusual for business meetings to conclude with the parties wondering what just transpired and unsure as to where things stand. When I initially experienced this practice of intentional vagueness while living in Japan, I thought that my Japanese language skills still had a long way to go. However, I quickly realized I was not the only one who could not figure out the meaning of what was said. When I would ask Japanese colleagues, they replied that they also had no idea—the conversation was too vague to know what was meant. When that happens, Japanese understand that they will need a one-on-one follow-up meeting with the other party *outside of an official meeting* to find out where things stand.

It is much more important in Japan to promote the harmony of the group than to lay facts on the table, present a solution, or to express one's thoughts or feelings unambiguously. An excellent example of this is seen in how speakers who are considered good communicators in Japan read their audience for the purpose of promoting a sense of mutual agreement and group solidarity.

In the Japanese language, the structure of a sentence is first the subject, followed by the direct object, and finally the verb. Good communicators in Japan are those who are able to say the noun and the direct object and then, before concluding the sentence with the verb, are able to read the audience reaction. If the audience is displeased with the subject and direct object, the skilled speaker conjugates the verb in negative form to express his or her shared dislike. If the audience seems favorably disposed to the subject and direct object, then the speaker conjugates the verb in positive form expressing agreement with the audience.

For example, after saying "I" (the subject of the sentence) followed by "nuclear power" (the direct object in this example), the speaker will observe the reaction of the crowd. If the mood or faces of the audience indicate they are not favorably inclined after hearing

"I, nuclear power," the speaker is likely to complete the sentence by using the negative form of the verb so that he says "I disfavor nuclear power." On the other hand, if after saying "I" and "nuclear power," the speaker reads the audience reaction as favorable, he will say, "I favor nuclear power." In this way, the grammatical structure of Japanese allows speakers to read the audience and complete their sentences according to the reaction of those listening. The Japanese language thus provides flexibility to promote a sense of everyone being on the same page. The English language does not.

Since a primary objective of communication is promoting harmony and smooth relations, it is not appropriate to directly disagree, contradict, or challenge others in formal business meetings or discussions. This is especially true when parties do not yet have a strong relationship. It is likewise not polite to say "no."

Most foreigners are not only unaccustomed to this communication dynamic; for the most part, they do not even know it exists. As a result, while Japanese are seeking to promote a smooth relationship with foreigners through vague communication or an absence of a definitive yes or no reply, foreigners typically misunderstand and interpret it as a lack of interest or believe that the Japanese are being disingenuous in the business discussions.

II. A DIFFERENT & DIFFICULT LANGUAGE

Another reason communication with Japanese is problematic is that becoming fluent in the Japanese language is very difficult for Westerners. Linguists say Japanese is one of the most difficult languages for non-natives to learn. Part of the reason for that is that Japanese is so very different from most other languages. It shares similarities with the Korean language, but none with Chinese or Western languages.

Americans typically study French, Italian, Spanish, or other languages by finding similarities with English. That can be done given the similarities between those romance languages and English. However, Japanese is so different from Western languages that there are no points of comparison or similarities to draw on to help us learn it. Consequently, learning by association does not work with the Japanese language.

We immediately realize this when we encounter the writing system of the Japanese language. The roman letters used in English are also used in the European languages, so we use a shared writing system. This clearly is not the case with Japanese. This language has three writing systems, and each is unrelated to English.

> Linguists say Japanese is one of the most difficult languages.

One is the Chinese *kanji* (漢字) characters that Japan imported over a thousand years ago. *Kanji* were originally pictorial drawings of the word's meaning. A typical Japanese college graduate today knows approximately two thousand two hundred *kanji*.

The other two writing systems—called *hiragana* (ひらがな) and *katakana* (カタかナ)—are indigenous. They are phonetic letter systems for writing syllables and sounds just like the letters in the English alphabet and have no meaning in and of themselves.

There are forty-six *hiragana* symbols and forty-six *katakana*. These two writing systems do not pose significant difficulty for foreigners to learn. The Chinese *kanji* characters, however, are a different story.

Each *kanji* character has its own meaning that must be

memorized. What makes that especially challenging is that each character can have several meanings.

Another difficulty is the degree of complexity of the structure and the number of strokes required to write the *kanji* character. For instance, *kanji* characters can either be simple with only a few strokes or complex with numerous strokes. By way of example, the character 鍵 (*kagi*), meaning a key, has as many as seventeen strokes. Some characters have more than twenty strokes. If the number of strokes is not challenging enough, there is a prescribed order for writing each stroke and each one must be placed in the correct position. Since many characters look similar, deviations in writing the strokes can result in a different character being written which will create a different word and meaning.

The multiple meanings and numerous brush strokes of *kanji* are not the only difficult aspects of Japanese. Reading Japanese is another equally challenging task. First, there are several different ways to read each character, and they all must be memorized. For example, the *kanji* meaning "what" is 何. It has six different ways to read it—*ka, nan, nani, dore, izu(re),* and *dou(shite)*.

Second, most nouns are written by combining two or three *kanji* characters. As each character can have several possible ways to be read, the result of combining characters is that the number of possible ways to read any given noun can be overwhelming. They cannot be learned by association but must be committed to memory.

I remember how daunting a challenge it was when I studied the Japanese language as a graduate student at Columbia University. There are four levels of Japanese language instruction in that program, and the attrition rate is usually quite high. In the case of my class, level one Japanese language had sixty-four students.

Level two had thirty-two. Level three had twelve students, and level four had six students. Only six out of the original sixty-four students—or about ten percent—made it through all four levels. This ninety percent attrition rate was not just the result of students not registering for the next level at the start of a new academic year every September. Students would just simply stop coming to class throughout the academic year. The study was so demanding for me that I had to spend five hours a day, seven days a week just for Japanese language study to complete the program.

Due to the great degree of difficulty for foreigners to learn Japanese, there are few foreigners who can speak Japanese fluently enough to conduct business in that language. Consequently, American companies typically rely on the Japanese company to provide a translator. However, this reliance is a major strategic as well as tactical disadvantage for American companies as is discussed in chapter seven of this book.

III. HIGHLY INTUITIVE COMMUNICATION

Anthropologists refer to cultures where fewer words are needed to communicate as "high context cultures." Japan is certainly a high context culture.

Japanese communication is highly intuitive. For example, communication takes place quite often without the use of complete sentences. Phrases frequently are sufficient to convey one's meaning. For example, the phrase *"sore wa"* (それは) by itself literally means "that is." It is certainly not a complete sentence and is useless in conveying any meaning in English. In Japanese, however, it is more than enough to communicate its meaning: "That is not what I had in mind." "That's not it." "That's off the mark." "That's wrong."

This dynamic of communicating in incomplete sentences applies not only to stand-alone phrases but also applies to conversations as well. Can you imagine trying to carry on a conversation in our country using only incomplete sentences or phrases? It would not be possible.

Conversations in Japanese are further complicated for foreigners in yet another high context way. The subject of a sentence typically will be spoken once when the topic is first brought up. After that, it is not repeated. Incomplete sentences or phrases are used after that. This is not a problem when only one topic is being discussed; however, as a second, third, or even fourth topic is introduced into the conversation, each new subject will likewise be spoken only once. As the conversation jumps from one topic to another without the subject of the sentence being stated, it becomes a real challenge to follow what is going on. It is "expected" that each participant will be able to follow the conversation intuitively.

> There is a whole realm of non-verbal communication that is highly developed and commonly used in Japanese culture.

As a result of this highly intuitive nature of Japanese communication, there is a whole realm of non-verbal communication that is highly developed and commonly used in Japanese culture. The three most common types of intuitive communication are:

- **Hara-gei** (腹芸): "belly talk" or subtle, stomach-to-stomach communication

- **Ishin-denshin** (以心伝心): "mind to mind," non-verbal, tacit understanding

- **Ammoku no ryoukai** (暗黙の了解): understanding through silence, which has the very Zen-like literal meaning of "the understanding of silence"

The highly intuitive nature of Japanese communication is also well expressed in the term commonly used to describe the essence of customer service in Japan: *omote nashi* (おもてなし). While the literal dictionary meaning is simply "hospitality," its significance is so much broader and deeper. It means to have the mindset to understand all things from the perspective of the client, to intuitively know what is needed, and make sure it is taken care of without the customer ever becoming aware of it.

In explaining how this great degree of vague, cryptic, and intuitive communication is possible, Japanese commonly point to the fact that they have been such a homogeneous society with one common culture and language for so long that everyone can some-how or other intuitively follow what is being communicated (*nanto naku wakaru* 何となく分かる).

IV. MUTUAL CONNECTION & INTERDEPENDENCE

In addition to having one shared culture, however, Japan's unique communication dynamics are possible because of what Japanese commonly characterize as feeling that all Japanese are organically connected to each other and to the greater whole. This concept comes in part from Japan's native Shinto religion, which sees everyone as being connected and mutually dependent on each other, as well as from Taoism and Confucianism, which teach that each of us is one small part of the greater interconnected universe.

Being mutually connected and interdependent, then, is a fundamental feature of Japanese society and is exhibited in the strong group orientation of the Japanese. This trait influences the Japanese approach to communication and business as well as the dynamics that define them. Both this connectivity and interdependence are well expressed in the following common expressions:

- **Okagesama de** (お陰様で)**:** This phrase translates into English as an equivalent to "thanks to everyone's assistance or cooperation." This self-deprecating expression is typically used when one party is thanked for or is complimented by another party for a job well done. Rather than saying "You're welcome" or "Thank you," the party that completed the task responds with *okagesama de.* Since everyone is mutually connected and dependent, it is possible for things to be accomplished because of the presence and role of everyone that is part of the greater whole. In other words, it is possible for things to get done not because of any one individual's action but because everyone in the group does their part and contributes to the overall scheme of things.

  This view that the role played by every individual is necessary for things to function is the reason why Japanese value and take seriously every job from the chairman of the board all of the way down to the janitor. Everyone's role and contribution is important, necessary, and appreciated. This outlook, in turn, further reinforces the group-orientation idea that everyone is connected and interdependent.

  That everyone's role and contribution to the greater whole is to be valued is the reason why when asked what kind of work they do, Japanese always reply by stating only the name of the organization they work for, never the job function. For example, a Japanese would reply that he or she worked for Japan Airlines rather than identifying their specific position. In contrast, in the States we reply by stating our job function—"I am an accountant." Because our culture is oriented around the individual and not the group, we often do not even give the name of our employer. For the Japanese, the employer name is all they say. Since all job functions are important and the culture is oriented around the group, it is the group one belongs to that is paramount in Japan.

This notion of *okagesama de* is such a part of the Japanese mind-set and communication dynamic that often people have no idea who the "everyone" is when *okagesama de* is said to them. On countless occasions over the years, I have asked Japanese clients, associates, and friends whose help is it that is being acknowledged when *okagesama de* was said to them. The answer was always a variation of "I don't know. But it is our way of respecting and being appreciative for all that went into allowing this to happen."

- **Osewa ni natte orimasu** (お世話になっております): This means "I'm benefitting from your help" or "I'm succeeding thanks to your good graces." Japanese say this expression to each other even when in fact they have not been helped at all by anyone else. In using this phrase regularly, Japanese are confirming that everyone belongs to and is mutually dependent on the greater whole. So deeply embedded in Japan's culture and business practices is this idea that the phrase is commonly used as a greeting at the beginning of meetings, telephone conversations, e-mails, corporate newsletters, formal business correspondences, etc.

- **Yoroshiku onegai shimasu (**よろしくお願いします**):** This means "I'm counting on you." It also means "Thank you for your cooperation, understanding, or indulgence." The notion that Japanese are counting on others is again an affirmation of their mutual dependence and reliance on the group and greater whole.

When Japanese are not sure they can satisfactorily do or provide something, they ask for the other party's understanding or indulgence by saying *yoroshiku onegai shimasu*—or "Thank you for understanding that what I provide may not be good enough." This self-deprecating expression is a way for Japanese to indulge (*amaeru* 甘える) the group by saying "Thank you for understanding if things do not proceed as well as I intend or you may expect." In this way, the greater whole supports everyone and makes everything possible. Again, this is the influence of Shinto, Taoism, and Confucianism.

Japanese also commonly use *yoroshiku onegai shimasu* to express thanks and appreciation for each other's mutual cooperation and assistance. In that case, both parties say it, not just the receiving party.

The phrase is shortened to *yoroshiku* after which is added either the word *domo* (どうもwhich means "thanks") or *douzo* (どうぞ which means "please"). For example, if Mr. Tanaka is doing something for Mr. Suzuki, at the end of the conversation Mr. Suzuki will say *yoroshiku domo* which means "I'm counting on your assistance—thanks." Mr. Tanaka will reply to that by saying *yoroshiku dozo*, which means "happy to oblige you, please avail yourself of my help" or "I'm likewise counting on your assistance—go ahead."

Upon visiting Japan, one of the first things foreigners notice is how often Japanese nod their heads to each other while talking. What truly baffles foreigners, however, is that Japanese will nod their heads to the other party even when talking on the telephone. Why would anyone nod their head to someone when the nod cannot be seen by the other party? The reason is that whether they can see you or not, everyone is still connected and so it is natural to offer head bows in recognition of that mutual connection whether it can be seen or not. Therefore, while it may seem odd to Westerners, the nod makes sense in Japan's cultural context even if the other party cannot see it.

To counterbalance their sense that everyone is connected and mutually dependent and the import that comes with that, Japanese have a unique way of differentiating between those with whom they are obligated to follow all of Japan's demanding cultural norms and expectations and those to whom they are not obligated. The people or party that Japanese are obligated to are those who are on the "inside" of their group (*uchi* 内); those individuals or parties that Japanese are not obligated to are those on the "outside" (*soto* 外) of their group. Group means any entity an individual belongs to, whether their family, neighborhood, school, company, social club, team, country, etc.

What is noteworthy about this *uchi* versus *soto* differentiation is its impact on Japanese communication. Japanese do not have to relate and communicate in accordance with all the etiquette rules when dealing with those outside of their groups. For example, if the person is outside of their groups, they do not have to be concerned about who needs to bow more deeply. An equal bow suffices to outsiders. Bowing in Japanese culture is fully discussed later in this chapter.

The differentiation between insiders and outsiders also

impacts information sharing. In America, we value free access to information and tend to be very open in sharing it. We even codify it in our laws, such as the Freedom of Information Act. Japanese have a different attitude toward disclosing information.

In Japan, those on the inside are afforded meaningful access to relevant information pertaining to business activities. Those on the outside are not. Japanese will hold information very close to their vests and be very slow in divulging even information that is cursory in nature when they are in early dealings with foreigner executives because the foreigners are still on the outside at that point.

What does this mean in regard to Japanese communication dynamics and their impact on foreign businesses? Those on the inside are afforded meaningful access to relevant information pertaining to business activities. Those on the outside are not.

In a foreigner's early dealings with Japanese while they are still "outsiders," Japanese will be very slow in divulging information. As a trust relationship develops and a foreigner's status changes to that of an "insider," Japanese will be comfortable

> There is a direct correlation between the degree of information shared and the closeness of the mutual relationship.

sharing more meaningful information with them. So if Japanese are not as forthcoming as you would like with providing substantive information in your initial meetings, this is not necessarily a red flag. The amount of proprietary information they share with you will increase in proportion to the strength of the trust relationship you build with them. On the other hand, if they do not share more information over time, then it is clear they are not bringing you to the inside and, therefore, are not interested in engaging in business with you. In this way, there is a direct correlation between the degree of information shared and the closeness of the mutual relationship.

V. COMMUNICATING WITHOUT DIRECTLY DISAGREEING OR SAYING NO

In chapter one we learned that it is deemed impolite to directly disagree, contradict, or say no to others, especially in formal settings or when the parties do not have a relationship, and we have learned that this cultural preference can be attributed to the importance and priority of group harmony in their culture. Japanese go to great lengths to avoid disrupting that harmony, including avoiding disagreeing or saying no at inappropriate times.

We've also learned in chapters one and two that Japanese society and language do have culturally accepted ways of expressing disagreement and saying no in appropriate circumstances and at appropriate times. This is so foundational that I strongly encourage you to read these chapters if you have not done so already. Because of the great importance of this cultural taboo regarding inappropriate direct disagreement, I am going to repeat some information from those pages. If you have read those chapters, please consider these repeated passages a reminder!

> The Japanese have quite an array of words or phrases that culturally convey "no" to the knowing hearer.

We have three things in play when learning to disagree properly in Japan: the cultural preference for group harmony, the societal norms that govern politeness and showing respect, and the tendency, therefore, toward intentionally vague conversation unless the conversation is taking place in certain acceptable environments such as, for example, an "evaluation meeting" (*hanseikai* (反省会)). So let's look at ways Japanese communicate without creating undesired disharmony.

First, Japanese have quite an array of words or phrases that culturally convey "no" to the knowing hearer. I am including that list of words and phrases from chapter one here for quick reference. Review the list again and see that nearly all the accepted words to use when disagreeing have a literal meaning that has nothing to do with saying a direct "no." It bears reminding that in the Japanese language even "yes" can mean "no." Note my previous example where we saw that a very non-committal sounding word such as *"chotto"* (ちょっと), which literally means "a little," is culturally a term of clear disagreement. As a part of the phrase *"Sore wa chotto..."* (それはちょっと...), literally meaning "That is a little...," the cultural meaning again is crystal clear—a definite no!

1. *Iie* (いいえ): No.
2. *Hai* (はい): Yes.
3. *Chotto* (ちょっと): A little.
4. *Sore wa chotto.* (それはちょっと...): That is a little...
5. *Iya* (イヤ): Not really.
6. *Sore wa.* (それは): That is...
7. *Dou deshou* (どうでしょう): How about that?
8. *Saa* (さあ): Well...
9. *Jitsu wa* (実は): Actually...
10. *Honto wa* (本当は...): In truth...
11. *Wakarimashita* (分かりました): I understand.
12. *Wakarimasen* (分かりません): I do not know.
13. *Kentou shimasu* (検討します): It is worth our consideration.
14. *Zenshou shimasu* (善処します): I will do my utmost best for that.
15. *Suimasen* (すいません): I am sorry.

16. *Moshi wake nai desu*(申し訳ないです): I apologize.
17. *Moshika shitara* (もしかしたら): It could be such that...
18. *Muzukashii desu* (難しいです): That is difficult.
19. *Nanno koto* (何の事): What is that?
20. *Ittai nanno koto deshou* (一体何のことでしょう): What in the world?
21. Replying with silence.
22. Sucking in air through one's teeth.

To underscore the significance of understanding the power of an indirect no, in chapter one I related a true account about a visit between the Japanese prime minister and the U.S. president where both the president, speaking in English, and the prime minister, speaking in Japanese, each reiterated their take on the meeting they had just had. The president expressed his pleasure at the fruitful outcome of the meeting with the perspective that both parties were in agreement. The prime minister echoed him on the fruitfulness of the meeting, adding that he will *zensho shimasu* (善処します)—translated literally into English as "I will do my utmost best for that." The prime minister repeated this same phase when he returned home to Japan, expressing to his nation a clear disagreement with the requests made by the U.S. president.

In this case, the American government, including the president, now have certain expectations based on that meeting while the Japanese actually set very different expectations. While the literal meaning of *zensho shimasu* is "I will do my utmost best for that," the actual cultural meaning is a definite "thanks, but no thanks."

When Japan does not attempt to implement any of the meeting items in the future, America concludes Japan was disingenuous. Japan, however, has a clean conscious because, according to their cultural norms, they very politely replied at the meeting that they were not in agreement.

Foreigners almost always rely on Japanese to provide the translator when meeting. Because of Japan's code of respect, foreigners will only receive polite, literal translations. In order to understand the actual cultural meaning—what in fact is actually going on—foreigners must have a translator *on their team* who is in a position to provide accurate cultural interpretation. When they do not do this, the foreign company or executive is placed at a tactical and strategic disadvantage fraught with the possibilities of confusion, misunderstanding, and false expectations.

Now that awareness has been raised about the ways used by Japanese to disagree, the question becomes how can you, speaking in English, express your disagreement without offending your potential business partner? Once more I am going to refer to material already presented in this book because of the importance of the concepts. Based on my many years of experience I have found two methods that work very well to allow you to disagree politely with your Japanese partner.

The response "That might be difficult" translates well into Japanese—*Sore wa muzukashii kamo shiremasen* (それは難しいかもしれません). You are not directly saying no, but are indicating you are not in a position to agree. I like the Zen touch this response offers that leaves open the possibility of a different answer in the future.

An effective second way to handle disagreement is to reply with a counterproposal. Verbally recognize their approach as one option, and then ask if XYZ would be another option. This allows you to come across as being open-minded and considerate of your partner's interests. A benefit to this approach is being able to offer a more desirable option for you that still could serve the interests of both parties.

The wording used in this option is very important. When

Americans offer a counterproposal, we typically phrase it: "*I have an alternative option.*" By saying "*I have,*" the alternative becomes the idea of the person saying it—the American executive. Using the words "*would another option be*" instead of "*I have* an alternative" leaves the ownership of the idea up for grabs. Allowing the Japanese to take your suggestion as a variation of their own makes it easier for them to accept and lobby for that idea within their company, and it demonstrates you are a partner concerned about the interests of both companies.

VI. LITERAL MEANING VS. CULTURAL MEANING

When I was working in a Japanese company early on in my involvement with Japan before I became a speaker of Japanese, I had an interesting experience that highlights another very prominent feature of the Japanese language.

The president of the company I was working for at that time and I were waiting for the elevator. When the elevator door opened, an employee said to the president "*ohayou gozaimasu*" (おはようございます) as she got off the elevator. This means "good morning." The president replied, "*Doumo*" (どうも) which, according to the dictionary, means "thanks." I thought to myself that was rather an arrogant reply—the employee says "good morning" and the president says "thanks." As the company president and I were close

> The actual cultural meaning of words and phrases might well have nothing to do with their literal meaning.

friends, I felt comfortable asking him about that exchange. He laughed and said that while *doumo* certainly does mean "thanks," it also is culturally understood to mean "the same to you."

The problem is that "thanks" is given as the meaning of *doumo* in the dictionary, but "the same to you" is not. As this example illustrates, an additional challenge inherent in Japanese communication is that words and phrases often have meanings not listed in the dictionary in addition to their literal definitions. The actual cultural meaning of words and phrases might well have nothing to do with their literal meaning. Here are some common examples.

- **Doumo (どうも):** The literal meaning of *doumo* is "thanks," while also having a cultural meaning of "the same to you."

- **Sore wa (それは):** The literal meaning of this phrase is "that is." It is also used to express disagreement, disapproval, or dissatisfaction. For example: "That is not agreeable." "That is not accurate." "That is not what I had said." Or it may simply mean "no."

- **Chotto (ちょっと):** Despite its literal meaning of "a little," *chotto* also is used to express a negative response to what is being discussed.

- **Iie (いいえ):** This is the word for "no." In Japanese, however, no does not necessarily only mean no—it can be part of the polite process for saying "yes"!

In Japan, if someone is offering something significant, it is not polite to immediately accept the offer. The more significant the item is, the more immodest it would be to accept it right away. Instead, it is polite to go through the protocol of saying "no, thank you" three times and then after saying "no" to the third offer, to say "yes," thereby accepting what is offered in the end.

This interchange is similar to an American initially

replying "no, thank you" to something being offered and then replying "yes" by saying "well, since you twisted my arm."

As Japanese are very self-deprecating, it is considered presumptuous and immodest to reply "yes" to receiving something important before saying no three times.

An additional challenge for foreigners in communicating in Japan is that this discrepancy between the literal definition and the actual cultural meaning applies not only to words but also to actions and concepts. One example is when managers in Japanese companies are given corner desks by themselves in front of windows. In America, getting a window desk is seen as a positive development, a reward, or perhaps part of a promotion. As we have discussed, in Japan, the manager receiving a corner desk in front of a window is known as "a person by the window" (*mado giwa zoku* 窓ぎわ族) and his future lies outside the company.

Another differing cultural concept is that of an offer of an honorary position in a company or organization. In the States, we offer an honorary position to solidify the good working relationship between two parties or in recognition of assistance provided. In Japan, offering an honorary position is a polite way of asking someone to become one of the major financial investors in the entity!

Thus, not only the Japanese language but also business customs, concepts, and actions are full of instances where the cultural meaning (the actual meaning in daily life) is different from, even completely unrelated to, the literal meaning of what is said or done. In this way, there can be two levels of reality in Japanese communication. There is what appears to be the case literally as well as what actually is the reality of the communication or situation. So prevalent is this facet of Japanese culture and communication that the

Japanese have distinct words to clearly identify and express these two realities and meanings.

The first word is *tatemae* (建前). The meaning of these two *kanji* characters is "constructed façade" which means what is ostensibly the case or meaning. It represents what is apparently the situation, or seemingly the meaning, or supposedly the case.

The second word is *honne* (本音). These two *kanji* characters mean "the actual sound." *Honne* means the actual situation or meaning. It is what is actually going on, the reality, what rings true.

Both the Japanese language and culture go to great lengths to differentiate between what is apparently the case or meaning and what is actually the situation or meaning as a way to show proper respect and promote group harmony.

Tatemae is what is ostensibly the case. Honne is the actual situation.

It would not be respectful to directly and abruptly say to a manager who has dedicated many years working for the company that he is no longer effective and needs to find employment elsewhere. That would be the *honne*, the actual situation. Instead, to avoid upsetting the harmony within the company, senior management expresses the same point to him by taking the indirect *tatemae* action of giving him a window desk by itself. The earlier example of the miscommunication between the U.S. president and the Japanese prime minister is another example of *tatemae* and *honne*.

VII. SILENCE IN COMMUNICATION

Silence during communication is not viewed favorably

in the U.S. We are not comfortable with it. It feels awkward and we rush to fill it. When we experience silence in negotiations or conversations, we are concerned that it means the other party has lost interest or is possibly upset. In fact, when we get angry with someone and deliberately stop talking to them, we call it "giving them the silent treatment." In Japan's culture, however, silence is perceived quite differently; silence is used in communication to sharpen one's attention to the discussion at hand.

In Japan, silence is seen as a pause in the discussion to be used to sift through and digest what is being discussed. Or it could be a means to fully focus on what is being said. Japanese will even close their eyes during silence to fully focus on using silence as an opportunity to reflect on the points being made. In addition, silence is the only time that Japan's non-verbal communication methods discussed above—such as *ammoku no ryokai* (暗黙の了解) or "understanding through silence"—can take place. In this way, silence is a common part of communication in Japan. It is not viewed negatively or as something that must be filled.

Knowing that foreigners are not comfortable with silence, Japanese occasionally use it as a negotiating tool in business discussions to frustrate foreign parties and trip them up. This is discussed in greater detail in chapter one. What then is the best way for foreigners to deal with silence when communicating with Japanese? Do not rush to fill it or ask if anything is wrong. Instead, quietly sit and wait it out, perhaps reviewing the points you have just made or will address next. Let the Japanese break the silence and resume the dialogue.

VIII. RESPECT & COMMUNICATION DYNAMICS

Japanese society is well known for the priority it places on showing great respect to one another. There are numerous ways that respect is demonstrated. Two major ways are the bow and the use of polite language.

The bow is ubiquitous in Japan. It is an integral part of interaction in all areas and all levels of Japanese society. However, in Japan a bow is not just a bow. Like so many things there, the bow is its own ritualized art form. The bow is used to demonstrate different levels of respect in two fundamental ways.

The initial way is the level to which the parties bow to each other. There are three levels of bows. The first is the head nod in which the person slightly nods the head forward fifteen degrees. The upper torso remains straight and just the head moves forward slightly. This demonstrates the lowest degree of respect. This head bow is used by those of greater status to those of lesser status.

The second bow is the middle bow. This is when the upper body comes down thirty degrees. This represents the middle range of respect and is used between parties of comparable hierarchical status.

The third bow is the full bow in which the upper torso comes down a full forty-five degrees. This is used by those having lower status to those in higher positions and expresses the greatest degree of respect.

If a company president is meeting individuals of lower status, he would only use the head bow while the others of lower rank would engage in the full bow, lowering their upper bodies a full forty-five degrees.

The bow expresses different levels of respect not only by how deep it is but also by how long it is held. The deeper the bow, the longer the individual must hold it. So while the company president just nods his head down and up in one smooth motion, a middle bow between individuals of comparable status is held one or two seconds, and subordinates will hold their full bow in the forty-five degree position for a full three seconds.

The second manner in which different levels of respect are expressed in Japan is through various levels of politeness in the language used in communicating with others. Both written and spoken Japanese are structured such that several different levels of respect can be demonstrated through them. Specifically, this is done through verb conjugation and multiple versions of phrases, each with differing levels of politeness.

Verbs typically can be conjugated in multiple ways. Each different conjugation expresses a greater level of respect, going from a greater degree of closeness or familiarity in the relationship to a greater degree of respect. For example, here are twelve different ways in which the verb "to drink" can be conjugated when asking if someone wants something to drink.

1. *Nomu?* 飲む?
2. *Nomu-ka?* 飲むか?
3. *Nomanai?* 飲まない?
4. *Nomanai-ka?* 飲まないか?
5. *Momimasu?* 飲みます?
6. *Momimasu-ka?* 飲みますか?
7. *Nomimasen?* 飲みません?
8. *Nomimasen-ka?* 飲みませんか?
9. *Nomaremasu -ka?* 飲まれますか?
10. *Nomaremasen-ka?* 飲まれませんか?
11. *O-nomuni narimasu-ka?* お飲みになりますか?
12. *O-nomini narimasen-ka?* お飲みになりませんか?

All twelve of the above words are identical in meaning— "Would you like something to drink?" However, they vary in the degree of respect they express. The longer the phrase, the higher the number on the list above, the more respect the verb is showing.

As this example illustrates, the options for showing different levels of respect through verb conjugation are quite numerous. However, having so many options is cumbersome and therefore not always practical for trying to figure out which of these many forms of conjugation parties should use in addressing each other. As a result, Japanese typically use three levels of politeness in business in both spoken and written Japanese to express the proper level of respect to each other. Those three levels are:

- **Sonkei-go** 尊敬語: the *respectful form* which elevates the other party and is the most respectful

- **Teinei-go** 丁寧語: the *polite form* which is used between parties of comparable status (です, ます)

- **Kenjo-go** 謙譲語: the *humble form* which lowers oneself (いただく)

By way of example, here are the three different ways of saying "to drink" in these three levels of politeness:

- **onomininarimasu** お飲みになります: the respectful form

- **nomimasu** 飲みます: the polite form

- **itadakimasu** いただきます: the humble form

As we can see, the etiquette protocols and communication dynamics in Japanese society are very involved, and they can be complex and cumbersome. These protocols and dynamics add another layer of difficulty to the challenges foreigners face in learning Japanese. Foreign executives would benefit greatly by receiving proper intercultural training on Japanese etiquette and communication dynamics before venturing to Japan to engage in business.

IX. SIGNIFICANCE OF THE BUSINESS CARD

Japanese are very deliberate when exchanging business cards. They present and receive business cards with two hands and take a moment to study the business card while the person is standing in front of them. It is only after that moment of silently examining the card that they continue their interaction with that person.

Westerners have suggested the reason for this examination is so the individuals can identify which *kanji* characters are used in writing the other party's name. While that is partially true, there are other reasons that are much more fundamental and significant.

> The reason business cards carry such great significance is that they are a primary means for determining what level of respect parties need to demonstrate to each other.

First, the exchange of business cards signifies that a connection (*kone* コネ) has been established. With that, it is now both possible and proper to begin communication with each other. Without having a connection, it is not socially accepted to initiate contact with another party. Because of this communication dynamic, cold calling does not work in Japan. One either needs to be introduced to the other party or to have the occasion to exchange business cards and establish a connection and thereby be able to commence communication with them.

Besides making it possible to contact another party, exchanging business cards socially obligates the other party to respond. In short, exchanging business cards is a prerequisite for initiating communication and a new business relationship.

Given the power—and inherent obligation—of the business card exchange, it is quite common for company chairmen, presidents, and other VIPs in Japan to deliberately not carry their business cards with them. By not carrying their business cards with them, they can avoid the business card exchange. They can thereby remain free from the obligation to respond when they have no interest in communicating with that party because no connection was established.

Simply receiving a card does not constitute a business card exchange. Each party must give his or her card and receive the other party's card in order for an exchange to occur. Only then are both parties in a position to communicate. As those high level executives do not want to be without their business cards in the event they meet someone with whom they would like to connect, they have their assistants carry their business cards. They are readily available for exchange—but only at the discretion of these high-ranking executives. When they are interested in exchanging business cards, they will instruct their subordinate to present their card to the other party.

The second reason business cards carry such great significance in Japan is that they are a primary means for determining what level of respect parties need to demonstrate to each other. As we have seen, Japanese society is strictly hierarchical and both business and social etiquette dictate that the parties show proper levels of respect to each other according to their respective status. The business card is the only way Japanese can know what their standing is relative to the person they are meeting. That is why Japanese study the card the instant they receive it—to determine their relative status to each other.

The person in the lower hierarchical position needs to relate to individuals with a higher standing with a greater degree of respect. Conversely, the person with the higher standing need not express as great a degree of politeness to individuals with lower standing. As discussed above, those different degrees of politeness are expressed through the bow and the level of politeness of language used.

Given the significant and important role that business cards have, they are treated with great respect in Japan. They are always presented and received with both hands—never just one hand. Never, ever slide a card across the table to the other party. And also, unlike in America, it is not appropriate to write on a business card.

Japanese always keep business cards in a high-quality business card carrying case—usually made out of leather. After business cards are exchanged in a meeting and the parties sit down at the table, they do not stack those cards or immediately place them in their business card case. Instead, once seated, Japanese will line up the business cards they received in front of them on the table corresponding to where those individuals are seated across the table.

In a final step of demonstrating respect, Japanese will elevate the business card they received from the senior most person in the other party by placing it on top of their business card case on the table. As the senior most executive is usually sitting in the middle across the table, his elevated card will be in the center of the row of business cards for those sitting on the other side of the table. In this way, they show greater respect for the senior most executive sitting across the table.

In Japan, business cards are viewed as a symbol of one's company, just as a flag is a symbol of one's country. This symbolism is another reason business cards are treated with great respect and why writing on a Japanese business card is inappropriate.

When engaging in business with Japanese, Americans should always prepare bilingual English-Japanese business cards to allow the Japanese not only to keep track of your name and that of your company but also, as described above, to better understand what your standing is in your company. Japanese are more comfortable interacting with foreigners who are on a similar level in their respective company, so receiving a bilingual business card will assist them in figuring out that status.

Along with preparing bilingual business cards, it is always beneficial to send to the Japanese who will be in the meeting the profiles of all those on your team who will be joining the discussion. It is wise to include a professional headshot for each profile as well.

X. JAPANESE COMMUNICATION PROTOCOL

We have already noted it is not polite to directly disagree, contradict, or say no to others in formal meetings. As is true with so much in Japanese culture, there is a proper time and place to negotiate and engage in substantive communication.

Official meetings, such as negotiations or formal business discussions, can often be more ceremonial than substantive in Japan. They are often the opportunity to confirm formally what has been informally discussed and decided outside of the official meetings. A common practice is for key participants from both parties to meet in smaller, unofficial meetings to discuss the substantive points. These discussions will be open and candid. These meetings are one of the appropriate times and places to openly express contrary opinions and work to resolve points of disagreement.

This dynamic is more common in the initial stages of the relationship between the parties. As a trust relationship is established, communication in official meetings may become more open and candid.

Another common way to express contrary opinions in Japan is through third parties such as consultants, intermediaries who may have introduced the two parties, mutual business partners, banks, or attorneys. Because these intermediaries are third parties and not the principals, they are not bound by the same rules of etiquette the principal parties are and, therefore, can candidly relay and work to resolve conflicting opinions, sparing the main parties from having to do so.

In the same way, third parties are used for conflict resolution when the principals are not able to work out matters between themselves on their own. While the Western style of rule of law is firmly established in Japan, Japanese society is not as litigious a society as America is. Although Japan has about forty percent of the U.S.'s population, it has only three percent of the number of attorneys America has. Unlike in the West, lawsuits between companies are uncommon.

> Just as there is an *appropriate time* to discuss substantive business matters in Japan, there are *appropriate places* to do so as well.

When conflicts do arise in Japan, it is expected that the principal parties will meet face-to-face and work out their differences in good faith. If they are not able to do this, they will utilize the assistance of a third party or parties. In the end, if the principals still are not able to resolve their conflict, it reflects negatively on *both* parties—both the aggrieved party as well as the party responsible for causing the problem. The result is that both parties loose face in the eyes of society, which is never desirable in the Japanese business community or in society at large.

Just as there is an *appropriate time* to discuss substantive business matters in Japan, there are *appropriate places* to do so as well. Customary venues for discussing business matters include the following:

- Formal business meetings held in official business venues such as either company's office or factory, the offices of an intermediary if involved, a meeting room in a hotel or conference center, etc.

- During meals—preferably if the Japanese initiate

- Over evening drinks

- On the golf course

Representative examples of places where substantive business topics are not discussed include:

- In the lobby of a hotel or company offices

- In hallways

- In elevators

- On the street

- In taxis or other cars

- In rest rooms

- While walking

Other communication dynamics and protocol items to avoid when communicating with Japanese include the following:

- **Humor:** What is humorous in one culture might not be so in another. While it is common in America to start a presentation or meeting with a joke to break the ice and help everyone relax and feel comfortable, this custom does not exist in Japan. In Japan, humor has no place in formal business meetings and discussions. In addition, it is very difficult for humor to be understood and translated appropriately from one culture to another.

- **Slang:** This is difficult to be understood and translated correctly.

- **Double negatives:** They are confusing and difficult to translate. For instance, "We wouldn't disagree with your strategy." or "I can't not agree with your proposal." If the translator is skilled enough to be able to figure out the meaning of such double negative sentences, the amount of time they need to figure it out is time they are not following the subsequent conversation. The result is that you will lose translation of that part of what is being said. Either way, the use of double negatives impedes complete and accurate interpretation of business discussions.

- **Idioms:** For the most part idioms are misunderstood and thus translated incorrectly. As a result, they can cause significant confusion in business discussions with Japanese. As you can imagine, the following idiom examples translated literally into Japanese would be confusing:

  o "We had to cancel our outdoor marketing event because it was raining cats and dogs."

○ "My company's CEO was so upset with my counterproposal that I was thrown under a bus."

○ "There is more than one way to skin that cat."

To share a specific example, I have witnessed the "I was thrown under a bus" idiom being used on multiple occasions. On one occasion, it was translated literally by the Japanese company's translator, and all of the Japanese were quite shocked to hear that the American executive was thrown under a bus.

During a subsequent coffee break two senior Japanese executives pulled me aside to ask me about the international sales director having been "thrown under a bus." One asked if the American CEO was that much of a madman and if he was that crazy. He said he was not sure his company would want to do business with that company. The second executive said, "On the other hand, if their sales director survived being run over by a bus, perhaps we *should* work with their company. Who knows what other miracles he might be able to perform."

- **Sarcasm:** This is highly difficult for interpreters to understand. The result is that it is usually mistranslated.

- **Long and compound sentences:** The longer the sentence, the more difficult it is for the translator to keep up and appropriately translate it. There is a direct inverse correlation between length of the sentence and the accuracy of translation: the longer the sentence, the more unlikely it is to be translated both fully and accurately.

I mention both fully and accurately. Longer, complex

sentences often result in the translator translating correctly part of the sentence, but not translating the complete English thought in an effort to keep up with the ongoing conversation. This results in incomplete communication. If you cannot be confident the whole of the English was translated, you cannot be sure the Japanese have received your entire message. Likewise, if the Japanese say they agree with your position, you cannot be certain they are referring to or agreeing with all of your position points.

- **Speaking in long intervals:** Just as using long sentences increases the likelihood of weak and inaccurate translation, speaking in long stretches likewise is a constant obstacle to complete and accurate interpretations. For example, speaking for three minutes and then pausing for translation is a much higher hurdle for the translator than stopping after twenty or thirty seconds to allow for translation. When making very important points it is better to break up a key sentence into parts to allow for full and accurate translation, part by part, than to risk an inferior translation. Speaking in smaller snippets will increase the effectiveness of your communication.

- **Body language and hand gestures:** In Western countries, body language and hand gestures can play a significant part in communication. A frown, the shaking of one's head, or rolling one's eyes powerfully express that one is not interested or not in agreement. Hand gestures can be used to give added emphasis to a statement— such as pointing your index finger as you state your point. A thumbs up or OK hand gesture can replace saying an entire sentence. These forms of communication are common in America. In Japan, however, body language and hand gestures are not used when communicating.

- **Physical contact:** Japanese traditionally do not use physical contact when communicating. While younger or more internationally experienced Japanese will shake hands when meeting foreigners, unlike Westerners, Japanese do not hug or kiss when greeting each other. Japanese are usually greatly embarrassed by these gestures. Instead they are accustomed to bowing to the other party when saying hello and goodbye.

  When Americans feel a connection with the other party, we may reach out and touch their forearm or hand while making a point or slap the other party on the back to express camaraderie or pleasure with a favorable discussion. This is not done in Japan and should be avoided.

- **Eye Contact:** It is important to note that Japanese do not engage in eye contact to the degree that Westerners do. While in our culture it is rude *not* to maintain good eye contact when speaking with someone, the opposite is true in Japan. It is impolite to maintain continuous, direct eye contact. Instead, Japanese will typically glance at your eyes for two or three seconds and then rotate their glance to look at a few other places on your person, before returning for a quick glance at your eyes again. For instance, after a quick glance at your eyes, their eyes will fix on one of your shoulders for a bit, then your necktie, then the other shoulder. They will then return for a quick two or three second glance at your eyes and repeat the process again. Younger or more internationally experienced Japanese may make more direct eye contact in their conversations with foreigners.

We have seen in this chapter that the way Japanese approach communication is remarkably different from the approach commonly found in America. Here's a representative summary of these differences:

- Having different goals for communication

- Using highly intuitive means of communication

- Using communication to reinforce a sense of mutual connection and interdependence

- Following complex cultural rules for saying no or disagreeing

- Using the cultural meaning of words, concepts, and actions which often have nothing to do with the literal meaning of those words, concepts, or actions

> Communicating in Japan can be like working through a maze even for native Japanese themselves.

- Socially condoning the use of both *tatemae* (what is ostensibly the case) and *honne* (what is actually the case) in communication to promote harmony

- Using different communication dynamics for those parties that are on the inside (*uchi*) and those who are on the outside (*soto*)

- Using silence both as thinking time to further focus on the discussion and as a tactical tool in negotiating with foreigners

- Having different sensibilities regarding physical contact and eye contact

- Having appropriate times and venues for substantive business discussions

As a result of the significant differences from Western communication, communicating in Japan can be like working through a maze. This is true not only for foreigners, but even for native Japanese themselves.

Westerners going to Japan often are concerned about being polite enough and not insulting their Japanese hosts, especially potential business partners. While this is certainly important, this chapter illustrates that the real challenges arising from Japan's different communication dynamics are much more fundamental and far reaching. Not knowing these different communication dynamics and how to effectively deal with them will directly reduce the level of success foreign companies attain in Japan—from simply limiting a company's success to outright derailing their business. We will look at options foreign executives can utilize to successfully navigate these challenges in section two of this book.

販売

CHAPTER 4

Sales

The Japanese Way

In the areas of sales and marketing, foreign companies face numerous challenges in the Japanese market that derive from culture-based differences in consumer preferences and business practices. Included in these are differences in the areas of consumer sensibilities, quality standards, marketing, distribution, advertising, and customer service. Geographical characteristics also present obstacles in the distribution and sale of products in Japan. This chapter discusses these challenges.

I. PRODUCT QUALITY

Japan is well known for having some of the highest product quality standards in the world. In America, product defect rates vary greatly from industry to industry with defect rates greater than fifteen percent in certain industries. This is commonplace and accepted by both manufacturers and consumers.

In contrast, companies in Japan have no tolerance for defective products going to market. This "zero tolerance" policy has become closely studied and emulated all over the world since the 1980s. The market in Japan—that is, both the manufacturer and the consumer—does not accept products that have any kind of defect or imperfection. There is an actual "zero tolerance" with regard to less than perfect product quality. Matsushita Konosuke, the founder of the Panasonic Corporation, went so far as to penalize suppliers who sent Panasonic defective parts by unilaterally discounting Panasonic's per unit purchase price for the parts Panasonic did accept.[3]

[3]*Matsushita Konosuke*, Not for Bread Alone: A Business Ethos, A Management Ethic *(Tokyo: PHP Institute, Inc., 1984), p. 59.*

As Inamori Kazuo, the founder of the Kyocera Corporation and one of Japan's foremost business leaders in the twenty-first century, explained:

> *Demands for superior product quality today are such that defective goods are altogether unacceptable. In Sales, Production, Research and Development, and all other processes, perfection is demanded.* — **Inamori Kazuo, *Amoeba Management* (Boca Raton, Florida: CRC Press, 2013), p. 74.**

While respected by manufacturers all over the world, this zero tolerance policy can present a daunting level of quality control that foreign manufacturers have to meet if they want to succeed in the Japanese market. Failure to meet that product quality standard has done in many foreign companies' efforts to engage in business in Japan.

Meeting this quality standard can require varying investment levels of time, resources, capital, and manpower. When U.S. products are already at or close to those standards, only minor product adjustments may be needed. In those cases, typically little or no additional product investment is needed to sell those products in Japan. In cases where the product quality needs major improvement, the investment can be significant. So significant, in fact, that meeting those quality standards can render that product unprofitable and, therefore, not worth pursuing in Japan. The costs in time and resources to meet expected product quality requirements have kept many foreign products out of the Japanese market.

Meeting Japan's product quality standards requires foreign company management to examine numerous aspects of their overall business operations. For example, the company needs to examine not only how much it would need to invest to improve its ingredient or component quality but also look at its manufacturing processes, packaging, product handling, shipping methods, storage options, and other factors that determine the quality of the products that end up in the hands of the ultimate consumer in Japan.

In the experience of many American companies, making the adjustments needed to meet the more stringent quality levels of the Japanese market turns out to bring windfall benefit in other markets. Making the alterations required for the Japan market results in increased sales revenue not only from Japan but also from the company's established markets around the world. Typically the improvements that American management makes to engage in business in Japan are subsequently applied to the company's operations worldwide. The result can be improved manufacturing processes and products with a higher level of quality company-wide, both of which enhance the company's competitive standing in markets not only in Japan but also around the globe.

One of the verses in the song "New York, New York" boldly states, "If you can make it there (New York City), you can make it anywhere." The same is true with regard to Japan and product quality—if a manufacturer's product quality can make it in Japan, chances are good the product can succeed in any market worldwide. It is often said that Japan can be the gateway to the rest of Asia and the reason assumed for this is its geographic location. However, Japan's superior quality standards are the more fundamental reason why Japan is viewed by its neighbors as the gateway to Pacific markets. If an American product succeeds in Japan, then it has already passed the quality requirements of other Asian markets.

In entering the Japanese market, American companies are invariably surprised to discover that product quality and zero tolerance apply not only to the product itself—that is, the quality with which a product is manufactured—but also far beyond that. Product quality and zero tolerance are also applied to the process by which the product is brought to market and eventually reaches the customer—namely the quality of the product after it has passed through the distribution system and ultimately is in the hands of the customer. The following are representative experiences my clients have had with Japanese quality standards applying to both the product itself and how it is brought to market.

In the States, it is not unusual for the boxes that products are shipped in to arrive with some damage. Nothing is really thought about damage to the shipping carton as long as the product itself inside is in good condition. After all, the purpose of the packaging is to protect the product inside. For example, a mashed in corner of the shipping box is not a big deal. Likewise, cuts, holes, or dents in boxes are not normally an issue in the American market. In many instances, not only is damage to the shipping box accepted, so is damage to the individual retail box or packaging for the product inside the shipping box.

In Japan, the opposite is true. Product is routinely rejected as defective with the slightest damage or imperfection in any of the three types of packaging:

- Damage to the shipping carton

- Damage to the retail box

- Imperfections in the product package or wrapper

The appearance of the product and its packaging must be entirely without defect.

Western manufacturers are often surprised when their Japanese distributor informs them that a whole shipment of product needs to be returned and replaced—at the manufacturer's expense—because of the slightest imperfection. In the case of nutritional supplements, for example, occasionally the number of capsules in a single bottle is incorrect. In America, if a bottle either is short or has a few extra capsules, it is not a great concern. In Japan, that miscount would be unacceptable. Zero tolerance applies to product count as well as product quality and product packaging.

Likewise, boxes of energy or snack bars occasionally will be shipped to market containing an incorrect number of bars. In the States, this usually does not raise much concern. Not so in Japan. In the experience of a client who is one of the leading American health bar manufacturers, each box of bars was sold packed with fourteen bars in it. Once boxes with an incorrect number of bars started to be returned to the distributor in Japan by wholesalers and retailers throughout the country, the distributor was forced to initiate quality control checks of all subsequent shipments. This entailed checking every single box in every shipment of bars from America. Each box was opened, every bar was counted, and the box was then resealed. Hundreds of thousands of bars were regularly checked with each order.

Of course, the process of removing the exterior wrapping around the box, manually counting the bars in every box, then replacing the wrap was uneconomical, so the distributor decided to weigh every box. If a box weighed less than the weight of a box with fourteen bars, then that box was pulled aside, opened, and given an additional bar or bars. Likewise, if a box weighed more than a box of fourteen bars, that box was opened so any extra bars could be removed.

In America, consumers would be happy to receive a box with fifteen bars instead of fourteen—it would be considered a "bonus bar"! Not so in Japan, however, where there is no such thing as an acceptable imperfection or deviation from the proper form. Instead, Japanese question the quality control capability of the manufacturer. So even the boxes that contained fifteen bars were deemed defective and were returned by wholesalers and retail customers. The distributor had to pull those boxes from the market place and manually correct the problem. Zero tolerance rules.

A challenge U.S. manufacturers of topical skin care products face in Japan is the rejection of their product by their Japanese distributor when ingredients clump together or sediment is found in them. Again, if a product has any imperfection, then the distributor will pull it from the market and return it to the manufacturer.

In America, not much attention is paid if the quality of the printing on a product label is not perfect. For example, if the name of the company, brand, product, ingredients, usage instruction, etc. is faded, smeared, or otherwise not clear in places, it is not a major issue. In Japan, that imperfection would result in the product being returned to the manufacturer by the wholesalers and/or retailers handling it.

Likewise, the appearance of the product label itself must be correct. The company logo must be consistent on all products and product literature. The type font for the name of the company, brand, and product must be identical. So too must the shades of color used on product labels, boxes, product literature, and so on. Again, the appearance must be completely without defect.

> To insist on products being entirely defect free in all aspects is part of the Japanese cultural sensibility referred to as *kirei-zuki* (綺麗好き).

To insist on products being entirely defect free in all aspects is part of the Japanese cultural sensibility referred to as *kirei-zuki* (綺麗好き). *Kirei-zuki* means products are in perfect condition in every way, from appearance to operation. Zero tolerance in quality control applies not only to the products themselves but also to every facet of the product from packaging to appearance to operation.

This cultural value of *kirei-zuki* is applied not only to product quality but also to most other facets of conducting business in Japan. *Kirei-zuki* means planning, negotiating, managing, manufacturing, marketing, distributing, selling, taking care of customers—everything—being done in correct form without blemish or defect. It means engaging in the various facets of business by doing it "exactly right" as discussed in the next section of this chapter.

In addition to *kirei-zuki*, the cultural sensibility of being *komakai* (細かい) means being detail oriented with the expectation of every detail being perfect.

II. "ABOUT RIGHT" VS. "EXACTLY RIGHT"

Komakai is the culture of being exact in every detail—in other words, being "exactly right." In Japan, this is applied to a degree rarely done in the U.S. In contrast, Americans are often comfortable with things being "good enough." As one Japanese executive client of mine expressed it, Americans are comfortable with things being "about right." Therefore, boxes of snack bars that are supposed to contain fourteen bars can be shipped with thirteen or fifteen—because the quantity is about right.

This Japanese mindset of being exact in every detail permeates all aspects of Japanese society, including the business world. American executives must ensure that their business operations, products, and all their dealings meet Japan's *komakai* requirements if they are to have a chance at succeeding in that market. As Inamori Kazuo explained:

> *Kyocera does not except the notion that "very close is good enough" in management goals for order bookings, sales, production, hourly efficiency, or other areas. The statement "We didn't achieve 100%, but we did reach 99%, so let's go with that" is not acceptable. For production and sales targets, full accomplishment is required.* — **Inamori Kazuo,** *Amoeba Management* **(Boca Raton, Florida: CRC Press, 2013), p. 74.**

Interestingly, there are areas where Americans need things to be done in as exacting a manner as found in the Japanese mindset.

This is perhaps best seen in the U.S. approach to negotiating and contract writing where every term and obligation is clearly stated and carefully defined. The goal is to be as exact as possible with the expectation that the more clearly things are defined in the negotiation and business agreement, the less likely there will be misunderstanding in the future. Japanese, in contrast, are very comfortable with contract terms not being as detailed or definitive. In fact, Japanese are comfortable with not even using business agreements at all because business is based on mutual trust relationships.

> This Japanese mindset of being exact in every detail permeates all aspects of Japanese society, including the business world.

III. REGULATORY APPROVAL

Obtaining government approval to import and sell products in Japan is another area that is often a high hurdle for foreign companies wanting to engage in business in that market.

For example, Food and Drug Administration (FDA) approval for an American product is not enough to secure Japanese government approval for sale of a foreign product in Japan. Products requiring government approval in Japan must be approved by the Japanese government. Having FDA approval in the States is very helpful for establishing credibility for foreign products, but it is not enough.

In the event clinical data is required for product approval, the Japanese Ministry of Health, Labor, and Welfare (*Koseiroudousho* 厚生労働省) requires clinical data that is obtained in Japan. Again, clinical data from the U.S. is helpful and serves as supporting documentation, but alone it is not enough. Regulatory approval in Japan can be costly and require considerable time. A medical device, for instance, can take up to three years and cost several million dollars to go through the regulatory approval process with no guarantee that the product will be approved.

Another hurdle that regulatory approval can present in Japan is that making the changes required to meet the regulations can transform the product so fundamentally that it is no longer effective in serving the purpose for which it was originally designed. For example, in the case of obtaining approval for a topical skin care product, if the problematic ingredients are not active or other major ingredients, the change is not usually too difficult to accommodate. However, if active or other major ingredients need to be changed, then replacing them can result in the product losing its original efficacy or becoming a totally different product.

IV. JAPANESE CONSUMER PREFERENCES

There probably is nothing more subjective from one country's culture to another's than consumer preferences. The impact of these consumer preferences cannot be emphasized enough. These preferences are the bottom line factors in a consumer's decision to buy or not to buy your product. As a result, these cultural preferences directly impact the bottom line sales for foreign companies in the Japanese market. Let's look at some representative consumer preferences that foreign companies must deal with in Japan.

- **Taste:** In the case of food products, taste is highly subjective and what is considered a desirable taste in the States may not necessarily be agreeable in Japan. Perhaps the most problematic taste characteristic of American foods is that many of them are too sweet.

- **Portion and serving sizes:** U.S. portion sizes for food products are almost always too large for the Japanese market and frequently need to be made smaller. Japanese typically have smaller body frames and eat less than Westerners do. Food products domestically made and sold in Japan invariably come in smaller portions than portions in the States. For example, power bars in America are approximately two ounces, while in Japan, they are half that weight.

  Portion sizes are a consideration not only for food products but also for products such as supplements, medicine tablets (such as prescriptions or aspirin), and candy.

  The size of a dose of a drug in Japan is usually smaller than the dose size in America for the same product. For example, the American aspirin Bufferin is popularly used as a painkiller in Japan. Each Bufferin tablet in Japan contains 330 mg of aspirin. In the States, each tablet contains 325 mg. The maximum daily dose in Japan is four tablets per day—or 1,320 mg in one day. In America, it is 4,000 mg per day—three times greater than Japan's dose. In Japan, Bufferin cannot be used every day; its use is limited to ten days per month. In the U.S., Bufferin is commonly used on a daily basis.

- **Product size:** Japanese usually prefer products that are smaller in scale than those found in the West.

  Japan is smaller in size than the state of California and ninety percent of the country is uninhabitable due to its mountainous terrain. As a result, the majority of the nation's population is squeezed into cities strung along the edges of Japan's four major islands. Simply put, Japan is space constrained. Houses, offices, hospitals, roads, and cars, to name a few, are all smaller in scale than in most other countries. Consequently, products necessarily are smaller. Here are some specific examples.

o *Cars*: Most American automobiles are too big for Japan's narrow roads. Only smaller foreign models sell in meaningful numbers. The only big cars that sell in Japan are luxury cars that are bought as status symbols.

o *Refrigerators*: U.S.-made refrigerators are too big for Japanese kitchens, and, therefore, they are of no interest to Japanese.

o *Furniture*: Western furniture—desks, seats, sofas— are too large for Japan's smaller rooms and too large for the body size of the typical Japanese person. Subway riders in New York City had the opportunity to experience the mirror image of this problem back in the late 1970's.

Graffiti on the NYC subway cars had become so bad that the City government opened a subway car replacement project to international bidding. The Japanese company Kawasaki Steel Corporation won the international bid to supply graffiti-proof subway cars to NYC. Given the high quality of Japanese products, New Yorkers were very pleased when this was announced. However, joy was short-lived.

Once the subway cars arrived, all subway riders immediately realized that the seat size was designed for people with smaller size buttocks. NYC passenger complaints continued for as long as those cars were used.

o   *Medical devices*: Foreign made lasers and anti-aging devices such as liposuction units and microdermabrasion devices can be too large for Japanese hospitals and clinics.

In one client project I managed in Japan, the manu-facturer, let's call them the Adams Corporation, was the leading dermatological laser producer in the States. Their best selling product was a specialty laser that combined four different types of lasers into one unit. This combination laser was extremely popular among physicians in America because it was a true money saver. It eliminated the need for doctors to buy each of those four lasers separately, and it offered the convenient use of multiple lasers during a single procedure.

When we launched the company's combination laser in Japan, however, this product did not sell well. Japanese doctors commented that it was too big and bulky for their streamlined procedure rooms.

As it turned out, the company also had a countertop laser that was designed for doctors to become familiar with how to use lasers. Viewing this countertop laser as a teaching aid, the manufacturer never promoted it in the States. However, after realizing the combination unit would not sell in Japan due to its size, the company launched the compact laser there, and this product went on to sell very well given its appropriate size. In the end, the product expected to sell well (the combination laser) did not, but the one that was a sleeper product in the States became the company's best selling unit in Japan.

- o *Capsules*: Western capsules are generally too large for Japanese consumers. The capsule size makes them difficult to swallow. Products that come in capsule form need to be rescaled to a smaller, more appropriate size for the Japanese market.

- **Fragrance free**: Westerners generally enjoy fragrance in their products and, when deciding which product to purchase, often decide based on which fragrance they like the best. In contrast, Japanese consumers prefer products that are fragrance neutral. This applies to skin care products and personal care products such as soaps, shampoos, and conditioners as well as other products.

When I investigated this fragrance-free preference in Japan, I learned two things:

- o The first is that Japanese traditionally have not used fragranced products of any kind, unlike Westerners who have long used perfumes and fragranced powders.

- o The second is that in the Japanese view, it would be imposing on those around them if they were to use fragrances. After all, it would be presumptuous to think that those around you would also enjoy your fragrance. This is yet another example of the group-oriented nature of Japanese culture.

- **Product purpose or function:** Different consumer preferences in Japan regarding a product's purpose or benefit also impact which products sell in that market and which do not. By way of example, let's look at the skincare industry.

The top three skin care concerns in the U.S. are (1) fine lines and wrinkles, (2) acne, and (3) sun damage. Accordingly, products treating those conditions are the top three selling skincare products in America. In Japan, the top three skin care concerns and best-selling products are for (1) whitening, (2) acne, and (3) pigmentation.

For centuries in Japan, as well as in China and Korea, beautiful skin has been thought to be white, porcelain-like skin. That is why beautiful women portrayed in traditional paintings in the Far East all have pure white toned skin, just as Japanese dolls of women do. The sun parasol was invented in China to protect the skin of Chinese women from the sun, keeping the skin as fair as possible. The sun parasol commonly has been used throughout the Far East for centuries and has been mentioned and painted in traditional Far Eastern literature and art for hundreds of years.

Until recently, whitening products did not exist in the States because there traditionally has never been any demand for them. Until very recently, in contrast, sun tanning and sun tan products are what consumers wanted in America. As a result, when Western skincare manufacturers entered the Japanese market, their product line did not include whitening products. They were unable to sell in the greatest product category in the market—whitening products. Only after developing their own whitening products to accommodate the cultural preferences of Japanese consumers did foreign product makers become players in the largest segment of the skincare market there.

Japanese consumers' preference for white skin is another example of how Japan's cultural preferences can require foreign manufacturers to not only alter their current products but even to develop entirely new products to satisfy customer demand and obtain greater sales levels in the Japanese market.

- **Product Features:** Providing the product features that Japanese consumers prefer can also require foreign manufacturers to alter their products. For years American automobile manufacturers could not sell their cars in Japan in meaningful quantities. Anyone who has seen the roads in Japan can immediately understand that large U.S. cars are not practical for Japan's very narrow and winding streets. Being a natural resource-less country, Japan imports ninety-eight percent of its oil. As a result, the price of gas in Japan is typically double that in the U.S. Consequently, the Japanese market needs cars with higher fuel efficiency than American cars have traditionally offered.

Also, keeping the steering wheel on the left side of the American car even though the steering wheel is located on the right hand side in Japanese vehicles did not help American cars sell in Japan. In contrast, by the 1980s, Japanese automobile manufacturers accounted for as much as thirty-eight percent of the total U.S. automobile market. That would never have happened if Japanese manufacturers had kept the steering wheels on the right hand side. After all, the only ones who drive right-handed vehicles in America are postal employees as they deliver mail, and those vehicles constitute less than one percent of the total U.S. auto market.

As could be expected, many of Japan's consumer preferences are different from those in the West, and foreign companies need to be willing and able to accommodate those preferences if they are to succeed in the Japanese market in a meaningful way. Likewise, Japan's cultural preferences are based on sensibilities from Japan's traditional culture and provide another illustration of how culture-based differences, rather than being "fluff" and an insignificant aspect of global business, directly impact a foreign company's level of success and bottom line sales in the Japanese market.

V. SHELF LIFE

Shelf life is another factor that often hinders American products from selling well in Japan. The Japanese market has different shelf life requirements than the U.S. market.

The Japanese market generally requires a longer shelf life for products than the U.S. market. This affects products in diverse categories, ranging from perishable products such as food and beverages to pharmaceutical drugs to sterilized components of medical devices to topical skin care products, as examples. Part of the problem lies in the shipping time for products sent from the States to Japan.

Generally speaking, 60 percent of the world's manufactured exports are shipped by sea, while 40 percent are transported by air. Sea freight can take six to eight weeks to arrive in Japan from the

States. Another one to two weeks can be required to clear Japanese Customs inspection and get product delivered to the distributor's warehouse in Japan. So far, up to two-and-a-half months have elapsed since the products left America.

The product might stay in the distributor's warehouse for between one and two months before being shipped to fulfill orders. It is now four-and-a-half months since the production date of the product. Depending on what part of the country the product is being shipped to, it can take another one to two weeks for the products to be shipped from the distributor's national or regional warehouse to local wholesalers, then to local distributors, and subsequently to the local retailer. The product is now up to five months old, and it still is not in the hands of the end-user.

If that product has a shelf life of eight months, for example, then it has three months left before expiring. In America, a product with three months left in its shelf life would still be sellable. But that is not the case in Japan where the norm is that a product upon arriving in the final retail outlet must have at least half of its shelf life left to be sellable. Japanese customers will not purchase a product that is further along its way to shelf life expiration. Given that, distributors will not accept delivery of product that is close to or already more than half way to its expiration. Such products are simply considered no longer sellable.

As a result of this shelf life requirement, it is not uncommon for wholesalers, sub-distributors, and retailers with product that reaches the halfway point of its shelf life while still in their possession to return it to the manufacturer or distributor either to be replaced with newer product or refunded.

The following is a typical timetable for products shipped from America by sea until they reach retailers throughout Japan.

Table 4: Time Required for American Products to Reach Retailers in Japan

Action	Number of Weeks	Cumulative Time
Product arrives in Japan by sea freight from America	6 - 8 weeks	2 months
Product clears Japanese Customs and arrives at Japanese distributor's warehouse	1 - 2 weeks	2½ months
Product is inspected, inventoried, and kept in warehouse until shipped to fulfill customer orders	1 - 2 months	4½ months
Product shipped from main warehouse to local warehouses to sub-distributors to retailers	1 - 2 weeks	5 months

Source: Robert Charles Azar

As can be seen from the timetable above, products with expiration dates need to have a shelf life of at least one year if they are going to be shipped by sea to Japan. This can be a hurdle for manufacturers in many product categories. If the manufacturer is not able to produce the product with the necessary shelf life, then there are two possible options:

- Ship the product by air instead of sea. This is a viable option only if the higher shipping cost to Japan does not make the product too expensive to compete.

- Produce the product locally in Japan, thereby removing the international transportation time and reducing the domestic shipping time. This, like the previous option, is only possible if it is cost effective to manufacture the products in Japan.

The following is an example from a client of how shelf life directly impacts, or can even prevent, foreign products from selling in Japan.

Doctors in Japan often will not stock or sell medical products or goods that have a remaining shelf life shorter than one year. This is far more stringent than requiring at least six months left on a twelve-month shelf life. Products must arrive at the hospital or clinic with at least twelve months of shelf life remaining. Here is a letter to me from the president of a sales partner in Japan whose company is a leading supplier of medical goods in that country:

Dear Azar-san,

In the Japanese business custom, doctors don't buy the medical products or medicine if shelf life is shorter than 1 year.

If they (the manufacturer) can ship the latest batch of the product to Japan with more than 1 year shelf life, that would be okay.

If they can supply the product with 1.5 years or 2 years shelf life, then we will be able to buy more units with each order, stock them, and sell them with at least 1 year remaining.

Best Regards,

T.Y.

As the president of this medical distribution company indicates, Japanese distributors would prefer the products they distribute be manufactured with a shelf life of one-and-a-half to two years. This would give them the opportunity to sell products with at least one year still remaining on the shelf life by the time the product reaches the end-user.

Not being able to meet expected shelf life requirements,

then, will limit or outright prevent the sale of foreign products in the Japanese market.

VI. CLIMATE

Japan's climate has a major impact on the salability of products in a way that companies in the States do not experience. Japan consistently experiences high humidity many months during the year, and it is commonplace for products to be stored in offices and warehouses that do not have air conditioning. This can present a major challenge for products in numerous categories. This is especially true because American products are not designed to take into account Japan's unusual humidity conditions.

The following is a client example with the challenges Japan's climate can present to foreign companies. The company is a leading manufacturer of nutritional meal replacement bars in the U.S.

> Distributors prefer certain products they distribute be manufactured with a shelf life of one-and-a-half to two years.

Market research and numerous focus groups in Japan concluded that the company's chocolate flavored bar was by far the one with the greatest appeal to Japanese tastes. It clearly should be the main bar the company sells in Japan. Upon shipping the bars to Japan in bulk, the humidity problem immediately made itself known to my client and their sales partner in Japan at the time. Bars were melting in large numbers. In some instances, ingredients even leaked out of the bars' individually sealed foil wrappers.

The manufacturer was greatly surprised by this development

because they had never experienced this before anywhere in the world—including in other markets with very high humidity in southern Europe, Mexico, and South America. Furthermore, the bar was manufactured with ingredients that were specifically designed to be "melt proof." The problem, of course, was that all the melt proof ingredient development and testing was based on humidity conditions typical in the United States. The Japanese market presented an entirely different and more difficult climatic challenge. This meant succeeding in Japan would require a higher level of product stability than the U.S. market.

Meanwhile, for their part, the Japanese distributor was shocked. Given the quality standards in Japan, this problem would never have happened with a Japanese product. They were disappointed to have been shipped what turned out to be defective product. The marketing plan called for pharmacies to be the main sales channel for the bars, and the distributor had lined up the number one wholesale company in the pharmacy channel. We were poised to launch nationwide distribution in Japan. However, when the wholesaler discovered that the bars melted, they immediately returned the entire shipment to the distributor who not only had to refund the wholesaler for the bars but also experienced losing face.

The leading manufacturer of microdermabrasion devices offers another example of how Japan's climate can wreak havoc on the sale of American products and require product alteration for sales in Japan. Based in the States, the product line of this client had become the frontrunner in the microdermabrasion industry worldwide. They were very excited to enter the Japanese market given that Japanese spend two times more than Americans per capita for skin care products and treatments. Japan was the largest skin care market in the world at that time and thus represented a huge opportunity.

The American company's microdermabrasion device worked by shooting crystals at high pressure onto the face to treat such things as sunspots and fine lines. For the machine to work properly and effectively, the crystals must be able to flow smoothly through the device, be shot out onto the patient's face, and then be vacuumed back into the machine through its hand piece. Immediately upon commencing sales in Japan, however, a major problem appeared— the machine's crystals clumped together and would not flow freely through the device. Instead the crystals clogged the machines, which thereby made them inoperable. This malfunction happened not only in the warehouse of the Japanese distributor but also in the clinics and spas that had purchased the devices. The cause of this unfortunate and totally unforeseen development? Japan's high humidity.

The problem is that it is common for warehouses not to be air-conditioned. In addition, while stores, offices, and clinics may use air conditioning during business hours, many reduce or totally shut off air conditioning after hours due to the high cost of electricity and a sense that it is wasteful to use air conditioning when no one is there.

VII. CUSTOMER SERVICE

As we have seen above, Japanese have a very different approach to quality standards for products. The market in Japan expects and demands some of the highest standards in the world. This applies not only to products and their condition as they move through the distribution system as discussed earlier in this chapter but to customer service as well.

This difference in customer service standards between America and Japan is clearly illustrated in the catch phrase each country uses regarding how the customer is viewed and valued. In America, the saying is that "the customer is king." The comparable saying in Japan is "the customer is god" (*ogyakusama wa kamisama desu*—お客様は神様です).

> In America, the saying is that "the customer is king." The comparable saying in Japan is "the customer is god."

These two sayings epitomize the different levels of importance of and commitment to customer satisfaction in the two countries. The Japanese saying demonstrates the length to which Japanese companies will go to satisfy the customer. Japanese apply their above-discussed quality standards and zero tolerance for product imperfection to customer service as well. Further, Japanese engage in customer service with the same level of attention to detail (*komakai* 細かい) and commitment to continual improvement (*kaizen* 改善) that they apply to manufacturing standards. According to Japanese sensibilities, it would be an insult to the customer if product and customer service were not both "exactly right."

The heightened importance of customer service in the conducting of business in Japan was well described in this article quoting the founder and CEO of the Panasonic Corporation, Matsushita Konosuke:

> In addition to his extraordinary passion for manufacturing, Matsushita Konosuke kept track of the products his company made after they were sold. "The goods we make here everyday," he would tell his employees, "are like children we raise with tender care. Selling them is like seeing those children grow up and go out into the world. It is only natural, then, that we should be concerned

about how they're getting on in their lives, and to go and see for ourselves." He believed that maintaining this concern for what you produce is the first step to building an extra ordinary supplier–client relationship into a stronger link based on mutual trust. — **PHP Institute, Inc.,** *Matsushita Konosuke (1894-1989): His Life & Legacy,* (**Tokyo: PHP Institute, Inc., 1994), p. 52.**

Matsushita went even further to take the position that customer service is even more important than a company's product itself. Matsushita explained:

After-sales service is the key to keeping your customers. No matter how good the product you put on the market, if you do not provide equally good after-sales service, the customer will not come back. He will shower you with complaints and then go elsewhere. In many respects service is more important than the product itself. — **PHP Institute, Inc.,** *Matsushita Konosuke (1894-1989): His Life & Legacy,* (**Tokyo: PHP Institute, Inc., 1994), p. 70.**

Japanese have a saying that aptly expresses the essence of customer service in their country: *omotenashi* (おもてなし). The literal dictionary meaning is "hospitality." However, its cultural nuance, as well as its significance and social practice, is so much deeper and far-reaching. *Omotenashi* means to have the mindset to look at all things from the perspective of the client—to prepare all things from the perspective of the client—from manufacturing to presentation to customer service, and even to anticipate

> Omotenashi means to anticipate and take care of every potential need of your customers before they articulate them.

and take care of every potential need of your customers before they articulate them.

Japan's cultural differences in the various areas of sales covered in this chapter are usually not on the radar of most foreign companies seeking to engage in business in the Japanese market. Consequently, these market differences present a genuine challenge for foreign companies and often result in diminished business performance in Japan.

VIII. PRODUCT SALES & DISTRIBUTION

In the U.S., nationwide marketing, distribution, and sales are usually readily available and commonplace. Manufacturers expect a company to be able to get their products on retail shelves and in showrooms from coast to coast, utilizing distribution companies, sales companies, or a combination of both to get access to nationwide capability.

In Japan, nationwide marketing, distribution, and sales are, of course, present but not always achieved in the direct, straightforward manner, or to the same extent they are in America. Instead, marketing, distribution, and sales can be highly fragmented into regional and local distribution networks. This may require putting in place a network of different regional or local companies to execute nationwide sales. As a result, product marketing, distribution, and sales can be more cumbersome, costly, and time consuming in Japan than in the States. There are several reasons for this.

A. TRADITIONAL SALES NETWORKS

Japan is comprised of forty-seven prefectures (provinces). Historically these prefectures—or domains as they were referred to in pre-modern days—were independent of and isolated from each other, often warring against each other at different times throughout Japan's history. This isolation of domains from each other was often reinforced by Japan's highly mountainous topography, which inhibited travel between many of them. So isolated was each domain historically that until Japan started the process of becoming a modern nation in 1868, the domains were considered independent countries. This is seen even today in the phrase Japanese use to ask what part of Japan someone is from. That phrase is O-*kuni wa doko desuka* (お国はどこですか) or "Where is your *country?*"

As a result of this historical isolation of prefectures, both product distribution and sales networks developed throughout Japan's history on a local, prefecture level, much of which remains entrenched today. It is hard for newcomers to participate in these local distribution networks, a situation Japanese refer to as O-*kuni ishiki* (お国意識) or "country mentality," reflecting that these prefectures were historically separate entities.

B. BUSINESS IS RELATIONSHIP DRIVEN

As discussed earlier in this book, developing and maintaining a business relationship is a critical part of business in Japan. This cultural dynamic has made it very difficult for small- and medium-sized companies to expand into other parts of the country to start business there because they do not have the requisite relationships in those areas.

C. CONCENTRATION OF POPULATION

With ninety percent of the country's land being uninhabitable, Japan's population is highly concentrated in several cities. For example, the country's five largest metropolitan areas account for just under sixty percent of the country's total population. The Tokyo and Osaka urban areas alone hold forty-six percent of Japan's people—nearly half the population of the entire country. High population concentrations encourage selective focus on areas for sales and distribution.

The following table illustrates the population of Japan's top five geographic markets.

Table 5: Population of Japan's Top Five Geographic Markets

Geographic Markets	Population (2014)	% of Japan's Total Population	% of Total Population Cumulative
Tokyo	39 million	31%	–
Osaka	19 million	15%	46%
Nagoya	9 million	7%	53%
Shizuoka	2.7 million	2%	55%
Fukuoka	2.5 million	2%	57%

Source: Robert Charles Azar

As a result of these factors, distribution in Japan today remains more fragmented and localized than in the States. In certain industries where small, local sales companies have long histories and close relationships with retail outlets and customers, companies often cannot engage in business in other prefectures on their own as they lack the requisite relationships to do so. To deal with this, companies must partner with those entrenched companies in other prefectures and have them distribute and sell products.

The medical device industry is a good example of this situation in Japan. For hospitals and medical clinics, the decision-maker regarding the purchase of products is an individual physician. A local company's relationship with that doctor is the key to selling products to that medical establishment. If salesmen from another company outside that area call and try to schedule an appointment, the doctor will not agree to a meeting because a relationship between them does not exist.

This is why cold calling does not work in Japan. If, for example, a company in Tokyo wants to sell its medical devices in the southwestern prefecture of Fukuoka, the company needs to work through a local sales company based there that does have relationships with the physicians in that prefecture. These relationships take years to develop and are fiercely guarded by the local sales companies. As a result, distribution and sales of products are often more cumbersome and time consuming than in the U.S. In addition, because additional layers are added to the distribution process and each layer adds a mark up, the end price to consumers is higher than it would be with more direct nationwide distribution and sales.

D. PRACTICAL BUSINESS APPLICATION

What are the practical, business implications of Japan's distribution situation for American companies seeking to sell products in that market? When conducting due diligence checks on potential sales partners in Japan, American companies must directly discuss this topic and find out exactly how extensive the companies' distribution and sales capabilities are. Specifically:

- Does the company possess its own national distribution and sales capability through its own branch offices, subsidiary companies, or otherwise related firms?

- If not, does it already have in place a widespread distribution and sales capability through working relationships with appropriate distribution and sales companies in the major parts of the country? Is that coverage both sufficient and appropriate for your business objectives?

- If not, does the company possess some other way to sell

your products beyond the area where it is located? How well does that meet your needs?

- In the case of small- and medium-sized potential Japanese partners, it is imperative that foreign executives confirm the sales and distribution option to be utilized in selling their products before signing a business agreement. If the Japanese company cannot provide adequate market coverage on their own, then foreign executives can request the potential Japanese partner company take them to other parts of Japan to visit the sales and distribution companies that would be involved.

In one project in the medical channel that I worked on, my U.S. client had discussed the Japanese company's experience selling in that sales channel and was told that the company had more than a twenty-five year history selling in the specific segment of my client's product in the medical channel. After signing a sales agreement and commencing business in Japan, it became clear that the Japanese sales company had very few relationships with or experience in selling products to doctors. Why? Because it had only sold products as a wholesaler to other vendors and never directly to end-user customers such as hospitals and clinics.

Another fundamental difference in product marketing, distribution, and sales in Japan is consignment (*saihan seido*再販制度). Consignment is used in the selling of products to wholesalers, distribution firms, and retail companies in Japan to a significantly greater degree than in the States. Consignment allows those companies buying products on a consignment basis to return any unsold product to the manufacturer at any time without explanation. The cost of returning the product is borne by the manufacturer. Consequently, selling products on a consignment basis leaves the manufacturer at risk for having to refund all returned product.

When doing due diligence reviews on a potential sales partner in Japan, it is critical to consider the exact nature and extent of the sales outreach of the Japanese company; the strength of their relationships with your potential customers; and the extent they utilize consignment. The more the Japanese company's sales approach and network of relationships are in line with your business objectives and needs, the more likely your company is to achieve success.

Conversely, the more fragmented the sales and distribution network a Japanese company brings to the table, the weaker their network of relationships. The more a company uses consignment, the less desirable they are as a partner: product sales and distribution costs will be greater and the retail price for your product to its end users will be higher. Also the sales company will be less able to manage the marketing, sales, distribution, and customer service related to your products. Furthermore, not having a sales capability beyond the city where the company is located would limit your company's sales even before you commence your business in the Japanese market.

Distribution costs and delivery time in Japan are high to begin with. There are several reasons for this:

- The cost of fuel for trucks and cars is high.

- All roads in Japan, from local streets to major highways, are narrow with few lanes. The major arteries with four or more lanes in each direction found in the U.S. simply do not exist in Japan. Two lane roads in each direction are typical for major highways in Japan. Given the very narrow and curvy roads in Japan, trucks are smaller than in America, so more trucks are required to distribute the same amount of merchandize in Japan than in the States.

- Since small parking lots make it impractical to operate large fleets of trucks, each truck must make a greater number of runs to deliver merchandise. This not only raises the cost of distribution but also the length of time required to deliver the same amount of merchandise that could be delivered in America.

All of these factors combine to make the cost, manpower, and time required for product distribution and sales in Japan higher than in America. These factors can limit the geographic penetration into the Japanese market as well. Whenever possible, American companies want to avoid selecting a Japanese sales company that utilizes a fragmented sales and distribution network and instead work with a company that has access to a nationwide network either through its own already existing network or through another Japanese sales company with whom it has a strong working relationship.

日本における
資本主義

CHAPTER 5

Japan's Brand Of Capitalism

*"Japanese Samurai spirit together with commercial
talent!"* — **Shikon shosai** (士魂商才)

As we have seen throughout this book, the Japanese approach
to and practice of management and business is often quite different than that of the West. We have noted that these differences
are rooted in the country's cultural values and social traditions.

However, equally significantly, these differences stem from how capitalism as an ideology was deliberately altered by the Japanese when it was adopted in Japan, creating the second reason for Japan's differing management and business practices. This chapter explores how Japan deliberately created and implemented its own brand of capitalism based on its traditional culture.

I. EARLY JAPANESE CAPITALISM: 1868–1945

When Japanese discuss the origins of capitalism in their country, the name of one individual is unanimously put forth as

PHOTO COURTESY OF SHIBUSAWA MEMORIAL MUSEUM COLLECTION, TOKYO, JAPAN.

its founder, pioneer, and greatest practitioner. No one did more to establish capitalism and develop the specific management and business practices of modern Japan than Shibusawa Eiichi (渋沢栄一1840-1931).

As Japan opened to the West in 1868 and began the process of modernization, Shibusawa led the effort to bring capitalism to his country, an endeavor that became his mission for the rest of his life. Through his dedica-

Shibusawa Eiichi (渋沢栄一), the father of Japanese capitalism

tion to capitalism, he may very well be considered one of the most prolific practitioners of capitalism any country in the world has ever seen. The following are a few of his monumental accomplishments:

- **Formed the Tokyo Stock Exchange:** This was Japan's first exchange and is the major stock exchange today.

- **Created the Tokyo Chamber of Commerce and Industry:** Japan's first chamber is its primary chamber today.

- **Established over five hundred companies:** Yes, 500! These were not small or inconsequential firms, but rather the main corporations that still dominate their respective industries even today, serving as the pillars of Japan's modern economy and the models for conducting business in Japan. The companies founded by Shibusawa include:

  o *Daiichi Kokuritsu Bank*: Japan's first modern bank. It is the predecessor of the Daiichi Kangyo Bank that today is known as the Mizuho Bank and remains a leading money center bank in Japan. Shibusawa headed this bank for more than forty years.
  o *Japan Industrial Bank*: The Nippon Kogyo Bank, through which the government provided funding for the development of Japan's modern economy, is part of today's Mizuho Bank.
  o *Japan Railroad*: The country's first and primary railroad is known today as Japan Railroad Group.
  o *Tokyo Electric Power Company*: This was Japan's initial electric utility and is now the largest electric utility in Japan.
  o *Chugai Business Journal*: Today known as Nikkei Shimbun Inc., it is Japan's largest business publisher and news organization and is the publisher of the Nikkei newspaper—Japan's leading business newspaper today.
  o *The Imperial Hotel*: This is Japan's premier hotel to this day.
  o *Tokyo Marine Insurance*: This leading insurance company is now known as Tokio Marine and Nichido Fire Insurance.
  o *Tokyo Gas Company*: The country's first gas utility is now the country's largest.

- o *Uraga Docks*: The company is known today as Sumitomo Heavy Industries.
- o *Steam Engine Manufacturing Co.*: This company is now known as Kawasaki Heavy Industries.
- o *Osaka Cotton Spinning Company*: The first in its industry, this company is now the largest in its industry.
- o *Oji Paper*
- o *Japan Chemical Fertilizer*: This company became Nissan Chemical Industries.
- o *Tokyo Brick Manufacturing Company*: This company operates today as Japan Brick Manufacturing.
- o *Tokyo Ishikawajima Shipyard*: This company is known as IHI Corporation today.
- o *Toyo Steamship*: This company became Nippon Yusen Co. (NYK Line).
- o *Asano Cement*: This company is still in operation today as Nihon Cement Co.
- o *Dai-Nippon Brewery*: This company now operates as Asahi Breweries and Sapporo Breweries.
- o *Japan Leather*: This company became Nippi Inc.
- o *Imperial Theater*: This company is now Toho Company.

- **Co-founder and first president of the Japan Association for the League of Nations**

- **Organized and participated in many of Japan's commercial delegations and study trips to America and Europe**, including:

  - o The Paris International Exposition of 1867
  - o A two-month commercial study group that toured America in 1909
  - o Numerous visits to America as the founder of the Japanese-American Relations Committee

As the most prominent, and in many instances the first, companies in their industries, Shibusawa's corporations became the very models of how business is conducted in Japan. Moreover, Shibusawa's lectures and writings provided the cultural framework for capitalism as it was imported and implemented in Japan. As a result, his influence was as far reaching as it was fundamental to the establishment of Japan's way of practicing management and business in its modern economy.

Shibusawa believed that if capitalism was to succeed in his country, it needed its own variety or brand of capitalism, one that would be suited to the cultural values and social practices of his homeland. Specifically, he believed that Western capitalism must be combined with Japan's traditional values and social practices in order for it to work in Japan. He pointed to two major cultural traditions in particular— samurai values and Confucianism.

> Western capitalism must be combined with Japan's traditional values and social practices.

Shibusawa was born into a poor samurai family in the prefecture of current day Saitama, Japan. Because his family was part of the samurai class, he was profoundly influenced by the values and outlooks of *Bushido*, the centuries old code of the samurai. *Bushido*, however, did more than inform the values of the samurai class. It set the moral standard for the rest of the country as well. Nitobe Inazo (新渡戸稲造1862–1933), a prominent figure in Japan's drive to modernize, expressed the far-reaching social influence of *Bushido* in the following manner:

> *What Japan was she owed to the samurai. They were not only the flower of the nation, but its root as well.... Though they kept themselves socially aloof from the*

populace, they set a moral standard for them and guided them by their example. — Nitobe Inazo, *Bushido: The Soul of Japan* (New York: Kodansha USA, Inc., 2012), p. 34.

In addition to Bushido, Shibusawa greatly valued the traditional Confucian precepts that form a large part the bedrock of Japan's culture and society. Shibusawa lived his life guided by those cultural traditions.

While he was a traditionalist in his cultural and social values, his progressive views about wanting his country to succeed in the modern world led him to see that traditional and new could and must be *deliberately* combined to allow capitalism to help build Japan into a strong, modern country.

The following quotes illustrate Shibusawa's perspective on how Western capitalism needed to be altered when imported into Japan:

I have firmly adhered to the conviction that morality and economy can be perfectly harmonized.... The promotion of industry and commerce...must be controlled by sound and solid moral reason; and that there is but one standard for moral reason, which is the teachings of Confucius.

I have a fond dream that my view on the harmony between morality and economy based upon the principle of the teachings of Confucius may spread among men. — Obata Kyugoro, *An Interpretation of the Life of Viscount Shibusawa* (Tokyo: Tokyo Printing Company, 1937), pp. 269–270.

Civilization must depend upon the advancement of economic power. Economic progress cannot be achieved simply aiming for personal gain and the prosperity of commerce and industry per se, unless it is based on the strong foundation of morality. There is no other way but to fall back on the practice of the principal of the union of economics and morality, if we desire human progress. — Jeremy Matsumura, "Shibusawa Eiichi: Japan's Great Industrialist Guided by Confucian Morals." *The East Vol. 39, No. 3 September-October 2003*, p. 9.

Books about morality and those about business talent seem to have nothing in common with each other. However, business talent is based on morality. "Business talent" that is lacking in morality, fake, superficial and without substance is not true business talent.... If we think that business talent and morality cannot be separated, then it is through the book of morality called "Rongo" (the teachings of Confucius) that you can develop business talent. — Shibusawa Eiichi, *Rongo To Soroban: Gendai Goyaku* 『現代語訳論語と算盤』 *Analects and Abacus: Modern Translation* (Tokyo: Chikumashobo, 2010), pages 16–17, my translation.

Commerce is not commerce without morality. Morality is not morality without commerce. — Taguchi Yoshifumi, *The Managerial Ideas from the East* (Honolulu: Babel Press U.S.A., 2012), p. 4.

Shibusawa also taught that companies have an obligation to contribute to and benefit society at large—not just pursue their own profit. Shibusawa wrote:

A person once asked me: "What is the true meaning of business? That is, is the true meaning of business to focus on profit for all of society only and not on one's own personal profit? Or is the true meaning of business to focus on one's own personal profit only and only consider the benefit to society as a secondary consideration? Or is the true meaning of business to pursue both personal and societal interests simultaneously and, as long as one does not violate society's morals, seek personal profit?"

Confucius said that: "The benevolent man (仁者 jinsha), in wanting to stand on his own, first helps others to stand on their own. In the same way, he who wants to achieve his own goal, first helps others achieve their goal." Based on these words of Confucius, I believe that Confucius also lived placing greater priority on the perspective of society's benefit.

The person engaged in business must also hold this basic thought: Fundamentally, starting a business is for one's own self. However, it would be a major mistake to think of business as being only for your own benefit.

In my view, engaging in true business is not for self-profit or self-interest, rather public profit and public benefit. So the profit that I made from business is in the end public profit. Creating profit for society at large also creates profit for oneself. This is the true form of business. Therefore, it is completely mistaken to differentiate between public and private profit. Business that attempts to differentiate between the two is not a legitimate business. — Shibusawa Eiichi, *Kokufu-ron: Jitsugyou to Koueki* 『国富論：実業と公益』 *Theory of National Wealth: Business and Social Benefit* (Tokyo: Kokusho Kankokai, Inc., 2010), pp 41–42, my translation.

In addition to establishing capitalism in Japan, Shibusawa

saw himself as having another mission, a higher and more noble one: constant moral improvement—that is, continuously striving to make things better. Shibusawa stressed business ethics, such as honesty, education, virtue, and the cooperative spirit, all based on Confucian and samurai (*Bushido*) values.[4]

[4]Jeremy Matsumura, "Shibusawa Eiichi: Japan's Great Industrialist Guided by Confucian Morals." *The East Vol. 39, No. 3 September-October 2003*, p. 9.

This notion of constant moral improvement from *Bushido* is one of the cultural sources of Japan's practice of continual improvement later applied to manufacturing and other areas of business in Japan's modern period. It has become famous throughout the world as *kaizen* (改善): continual improvement.

Shibusawa strongly advocated that his country needed to harmonize the traditional cultural values and social practices of Japan with Western capitalism. Was his belief correct or mistaken? Hindsight has shown that Shibusawa was wise indeed.

For his monumental role in establishing the country's modern economy and its management and business practices, Shibusawa is rightly known as "the father of capitalism in Japan" even today.

II. TITANS OF POST-WORLD WAR II JAPANESE CAPITALISM: 1945–2000

The hybrid form of capitalism that Shibusawa and his peers set in motion and modeled in Japan when the country embarked on its course of modernization was a great success. However, Shibusawa died in 1931 and for the next fourteen years Japan was engaged in armed conflict throughout Asia while under the control of its military which had co-opted traditional Japanese values to serve their militaristic aims.

When World War II ended in 1945, many of Japan's cultural values and national traditions were called into question and looked upon with disapproval. What impact did that have on capitalism in Japan? Did the capitalism that Shibusawa established in Japan with its reliance on traditional cultural values survive this period of national soul searching and rejection of the past? Did Japan's brand of capitalism survive into the post-war period after Shibusawa's death? Let's look at the lives of the three titans of Japan's post-war business world to find the answers.

Out of the ashes of defeat in WWII, Japan's business leaders built an economy that became the marvel of the world. In just over twenty-five years, it surpassed all of the European nations and by the 1970s became the world's second largest economy behind only the United States. At its height, Japan produced as much as fifteen percent of the world's gross domestic product (GDP). It held this position from the 1970s until it was surpassed by China in 2012, making Japan the world's third greatest economy. Its corporations became some of the most successful and dominating global business entities the world has ever known—including such powerhouses as Toyota, Sony, Canon, and Panasonic. And many of Japan's management and business practices—such as "just in time" production and inventory control and *kaizen's* continual improvement—have been held up as models for corporations everywhere to emulate.

Let's briefly look at some of the major industrialists who led Japan to the heights of its economic success in the post-war period and see if the business and management practices they utilized in achieving Japan's historic success were those of Shibusawa.

A. MATSUSHITA KONOSUKE — 松下幸之助

Matsushita Konosuke (1894–1989) was the founder and first President and CEO of the Matsushita Corporation. The company is better known in the West as the Panasonic Corporation, the name it adopted as its business expanded internationally. Matsushita created what became one of the most successful multinational electronics firms in the world. Did Matsushita carry on Shibusawa's brand of capitalism or did he veer from it with different management precepts and business practices?

1. Social Role of the Company

Like Shibusawa before him, Matsushita viewed companies as having a strong social responsibility. He felt management and the company's business are meant to give high priority to that responsibility. His position that social responsibility is at least as important as a company's goal of making profit is clear in this quote from him:

> *For me as an entrepreneur, the primary duty, or mission, of management lies in satisfying the human instinct for improving the quality of life (of the country).... In this social role is found the answer to the question that all managers must constantly ask themselves: 'Why is this company necessary?' And the answer—that the enterprise exists to benefit people and improve society—should be the same for all businesses....*

> *Some people believe that the whole purpose of an enterprise is to make profit, but while profit is an essential part of business, it is not the only part. Profit is only important as a means of achieving the ultimate goal— that of improving the people's standard of living.*

> *Seen in this light, an enterprise is very much a part of the social fabric, and management should thus be considered a public, not a private, concern. We are all accustomed*

to the term 'private enterprise,' but since business activities are so closely connected with society, an enterprise must operate with a public perspective. A purely personal, selfish motivation cannot be central even for the self-employed entrepreneur, for management decisions must take into account how society will be affected when they are implemented. — PHP Institute, Inc., *Konosuke Matsushita: His Life and Management Philosophy* (Tokyo: PHP Institute, Inc., 2002), pp. 20-22.

Matsushita described the role of his company's contribution to the enhancement of society's well-being this way:

The mission of a manufacturer is to overcome poverty, to relieve society as a whole from the misery of poverty and bring it wealth. Business and production are not meant simply to enrich the shop or the factories of the enterprise concerns, but all of society. And society needs the dynamism and vitality of business and industry to generate its wealth. Only under such conditions will businesses and factories truly prosper.... The real mission of Matsushita Electric is to produce an inexhaustible supply of goods, thus creating peace and prosperity throughout the land. — Matsushita Konosuke, *Not for Bread Alone: A Business Ethos, A Management Ethic* (Tokyo: PHP Institute, Inc., 1984), p. 22.

Given that companies are public entities in every sense of the word, they are responsible for contributing not only to the general welfare of society but also to the growth and development of their own employees. This is discussed in section XIV of chapter two. Matsushita articulated this when he wrote:

When you think about it, a private enterprise is really a

public institution, insofar as it is expected to contribute some benefit to society as a whole. Given the public nature of its raison d'être, a private firm, large or small, must help its members grow as people and become responsible citizens. — Matsushita Konosuke, *Not for Bread Alone: A Business Ethos, A Management Ethic* (Tokyo: PHP Institute, Inc., 1984), p. 30.

This great emphasis on the social role and responsibility of the company was not pursued at the expense of making profit. That is, a company's focus on contributing to society was not meant to reduce the importance of generating profit. Matsushita fully realized the need for businesses to make meaningful profits. He emphasized that companies and their management should pursue these two overriding goals in tandem, and they must focus equally on both. In fact, Matsushita went so far as to say that making a profit and returning benefit to shareholders was actually not only part of a company's corporate responsibility but also a part of its social responsibility. Accordingly, the inability to produce a profit was a company's failure in its responsibility to society as well as to its shareholders.

> Companies are public entities responsible for contributing to society [and] to the growth of their own employees.

In this way, profits are essential to a company's fulfillment of its mission to make a positive contribution to society. When there is no profit, then a corporation can be said to be failing in its social responsibility.... A concrete example of this social responsibility is found in a company's obligation toward its shareholders. — PHP Institute, Inc., *Konosuke Matsushita: His Life and Management Philosophy* (Tokyo: PHP Institute, Inc., 2002), pp. 32–33.

Matsushita believed so strongly in these two priorities for every company that he went so far as to say that if a company cannot achieve both of them, it had no reason to exist.

> *If the results of hard work is not black ink, and if it does not contribute to the prosperity of the country and the society nor to the enhancement of the standards of living of our employees, Matsushita Electric has no reason to exist. If it has no reason for existence, we should dissolve Matsushita Electric.* — **PHP** Institute, Inc., *Matsushita Konosuke (1894–1989): His Life & Legacy* (Tokyo: PHP Institute, Inc., 1994), pp. 34–35.

Matsushita's outlook on the social role of the company was not limited to contributing to just Japan. In his view, it was the responsibility of all Japanese business leaders to strive to contribute to the welfare of people throughout the world. As Matsushita explained:

> *Recognizing our responsibilities as industrialists, we will devote ourselves to the progress and development of society and the well-being of people through our business activities, thereby enhancing the quality of life throughout the world.* — **PHP** Institute, Inc., *Matsushita Konosuke (1894–1989): His Life & Legacy* (Tokyo: PHP Institute, Inc., 1994), p. 20.

2. Bushido & Japan's Business Culture

Shibusawa said that business and ethics cannot be separated in Japan. Matsushita echoed this, teaching that business must contribute to the ethical well-being of the people:

> *We do not live by bread alone, however; possessing*

*material comforts in no way guarantees happiness. Only
spiritual wealth can bring true happiness. If that is true,
should business be concerned only with the material aspect
of life and leave the care of the human spirit to religion
or ethics? I don't think so. Businessmen, too, should be
able to share creating a society that is spiritually rich
and materially affluent.* — Matsushita Konosuke, *Not
for Bread Alone: A Business Ethos, A Management Ethic* (Tokyo:
PHP Institute, Inc., 1984), pp. 87–88.

The importance to people and society of living by convictions or a code of ethics is a theme long rooted in Japan's samurai
tradition of *Bushido*—"the way of the samurai." It was central not
only to the samurai themselves but also became an integral part of
Japan's traditional business and social culture in general. As Matsushita said:

Hagakure, *the eighteenth-century work that was a kind
of bible of the samurai code of honor, declared that when
forced to choose between life and death in a situation,
the samurai should choose death. This may seem a little
extreme in our day and age, yet a similar ethic was the
source of the merchant's backbone.*

*Times are different. People think differently than in the
past. But the value of living by a code—of sticking by
your convictions—has not changed. Indeed, I'm often
struck that nothing is more precious in succeeding in
business than faithfulness to one's principles, one's code
of conduct.* — Matsushita Konosuke, *The Path* (New York:
McGraw Hill, 1968), p. 175.

Bushido's influence on Japan's management style and way of
conducting business is also seen in the way Matsushita compares

business and management to an encounter between two samurai and their swords:

> *Business is not a matter of the luck-of-the-draw; it is a sword fight. In a real sword fight, one slip up and you've lost your head. It's the same in business... Business does not go badly because of timing, luck or any other external factor. You must always see problems as arising from some fault within your own style of management.* — PHP Institute, Inc., *Matsushita Konosuke (1894–1989): His Life & Legacy* (Tokyo: PHP Institute, Inc., 1994), pp. 51–52.

> Constant reflection and constant improvement in *Bushido* is the basis for Japan's world famous business practice of *kaizen*.

Viewing problems as being caused not by factors external to one's company but rather as stemming from internal issues within one's own management is another theme from *Bushido*. In the code of the samurai, victory or defeat was determined within one's self, even before drawing one's sword in battle. It was determined by how diligently one had worked at honing their martial skills, day in and day out, as well as by one's mental focus at the moment of the encounter. That demanded of the samurai constant reflection, spiritual self-discipline, and constant improvement (*kaizen*) of one's swordsmanship and mental focus. Matsushita believed that the path to success for business executives is exactly the same path

> *by giving your best to each and every task you take on, and by reflecting on your performance with an honest and unprejudiced eye. If you do this constantly, day after day, eventually you will be able to do your job*

unerringly. — PHP Institute, Inc., *Matsushita Konosuke (1894–1989): His Life & Legacy* (Tokyo: PHP Institute, Inc., 1994), p. 61.

As we can see, this deliberate focus on constant reflection and constant improvement in *Bushido* is the basis for Japan's world famous business practice of *kaizen* (constant improvement). It is also causally related to two other traditional cultural values of Japan. The first is the earnestness that characterizes how Japanese approach all tasks. The second is the willingness of Japanese to work so diligently in the highly focused manner that they do. These *Bushido* roots of earnestness and diligence are discussed further in chapter two.

Meanwhile, *Bushido's* emphasis on constant reflection for the sake of improving is the cultural foundation for the evaluation meeting (*hansei–kai*) so prevalent in Japanese companies in which company members reflect on how things are currently done and seek ways to improve them. The importance of constant reflection and the evaluation meeting is discussed in section X of chapter two.

In traditional Japanese culture, the quest for constant improvement is itself a constant. In its business application, the pursuit of constant improvement is never ending and is what drives the success of an enterprise. Matsushita said:

> *The process of making improvements is eternal. How it is done, or to what extent, determines whether a company will continue to develop or cease to grow. The fact that we can always do better is what makes business so exciting and fulfilling, for it means that management attitudes are directly responsible for progress.* — Matsushita Konosuke, *Not for Bread Alone: A Business Ethos, A Management Ethic* (Tokyo: PHP Institute, Inc., 1984), p. 56.

In looking at the cultural roots of *kaizen* in Japan, we see that in addition to *Bushido*, it is also based on the Buddhist teaching that we are reborn into each life to attain continual improvement in our spiritual development, ultimately to the point where we no longer need to be reincarnated because we have attained the highest level of growth or enlightenment (nirvana). In Matsushita's view, the constant improvement idea of *kaizen* applies not only to aspects of business and man's spiritual growth but is also an approach that should be used in life in general and even applied to one's country as well:

> *Progress—inherent in the nature of the universe and of humanity—is the necessary consequence of the natural law of birth, growth, development, and transformation in the physical world and in society.* — **PHP Institute, Inc.,** *Konosuke Matsushita: His Life and Management Philosophy* **(Tokyo: PHP Institute, Inc., 2002), pp. 17–18.**

> *Ours is a good country; there are not many other countries like it in the world. So we want to make it an ever-better country and live in harmony with others, in lives that are affluent in tangible and intangible ways. When you are blessed, if you do not know that you are blessed, it is as if you had nothing at all. Let us reflect again upon the good of our country and give ourselves a new chance to take pride in it.* — **Matsushita Konosuke,** *The Path* **(New York: McGraw Hill, 1968), p. 188.**

B. HONDA SOICHIRO — 本田宗一郎

Honda Soichiro (1906–1991) was the founder and first President and CEO of the Honda Motor Co., Ltd., Japan's world famous automobile, motorcycle, and race car manufacturer. As was true with Shibusawa Eiichi and Matsushita Konosuke, Honda followed the hybrid capitalism that Shibusawa implemented in Japan that relied heavily on the country's traditional cultural values and social practices.

1. Social Role of the Company

Echoing the notion that a company does not exist only for its own profit but also to contribute to its country, Honda stated:

> *Japan was still a poor country, so for me to be happy, I had to make Japan happy, too.* — The NHK Group, *Good Mileage: The High-Performance Business Philosophy of Shoichiro Honda* (Tokyo: NHK Publishing, 1996), p. 23.

2. Bushido & Japan's Business Culture

The samurai of Japan's past valued honor more than anything. Honda saw enhancing the honor of Japan and its industry as the greatest purpose of his company. Honda wrote:

> *The greatest purpose of Honda Motor is to raise the honor of Japanese manufacturing.* — The NHK Group, *Good Mileage: The High-Performance Business Philosophy of Shoichiro Honda* (Tokyo: NHK Publishing, 1996), p. 22.

For Honda, the values of *Bushido* were not only to inform corporate management but even to inform how Honda Motor designed cars. A master samurai could detect the presence of his enemy just by sensing him. In the same way, Honda sought to design and produce a "sensing automobile."

> *Honda once told workers at the lab to "make a 'sensing automobile.'" At first no one had a clue as to what he meant. When Honda explained, he said that he wanted a car that*

let the drivers "sense" the feel of the car running, turning, and stopping—just like a motorcycle felt to the rider.

The image of a car that operated in tune with the 'senses' sounds a bit like a 'master samurai' (a master samurai could detect the presence of his enemy just by using his senses). — The NHK Group, *Good Mileage: The High-Performance Business Philosophy of Shoichiro Honda* (Tokyo: NHK Publishing, 1996), p. 179.

Japan's traditional value of *kaizen* with its approach of constantly striving to improve and be the best—to seek perfection in whatever one engages in—was a principle that Honda practiced very strictly in managing his company and demanded from all of his employees. Indeed, Honda's policy was that every single product and every single component must be perfect. Honda stated:

Since human lives are in the hands of our vehicles, we must be careful about every single nut, every single bolt. We must ensure perfect, trustworthy products, or our products will be worthless. — The NHK Group, *Good Mileage: The High-Performance Business Philosophy of Shoichiro Honda* (Tokyo: NHK Publishing, 1996), p. 38.

Sugiura Hideo, a chief engineer at Honda Motor Co., described how Honda had zero tolerance for any product defects:

On many occasions Honda struck me. One time, he hit me in front of 20 or 30 of my subordinates. Earlier that day, I was working in my office when an employee ran in with a panic expression, saying that the president was asking for me. I ran out and asked Honda what was wrong. Without saying a word, he suddenly hit me.

It turned out that the cause of his anger was a bolt that was supposed to stick out by a maximum of 2 mm was protruding by 5 mm. Honda screamed, 'Who was in charge of such a ridiculous design? It was you!'

What was truly wonderful about Honda was that he was not calculating (motivated only by saving); rather, he was sincere in his search for expedience and perfection. — The NHK Group, *Good Mileage: The High-Performance Business Philosophy of Shoichiro Honda* (Tokyo: NHK Publishing, 1996), pp. 38–39, 41.

Here we see how constant improvement (*kaizen*) and zero defect tolerance—Honda's search for "perfection"—are clearly based on traditional Japanese cultural values, and how Honda practiced Japan's brand of capitalism that incorporated Japan's traditional cultural values and social practices.

C. MORITA AKIO & IBUKA MASARU — 盛田昭夫と井深大

Morita Akio (1921–1999) and Ibuka Masaru (1908–1997) were the co-founders of the Sony Corporation, Japan's world famous electronics manufacturer. Ibuka was the first CEO, while Morita was its first president. As was true with Shibusawa Eiichi, Matsushita Konosuke, and Honda Soichiro, these two titans of post-World War II Japanese business also managed and conducted business with Japan's hybrid form capitalism that incorporated the country's traditional cultural values and social practices.

1. Social Role of the Company

Ibuka Masaru clearly believed that the company, in addition to achieving success for its own benefit, must contribute to the well-being of society and the country at large. In 1946 Ibuka wrote his vision for the Sony Corporation outlining its purpose in a document entitled "Founding Prospectus." In it he noted that:

> *All future products or inventions must make a positive contribution to society.... (Furthermore, the Sony Corporation must) take an active role in helping and leading the development of technical industrialization for the reformation and cultural advancement of Japan....* — The NHK Group, *Good Mileage: The High-Performance Business Philosophy of Shoichiro Honda* (Tokyo: NHK Publishing, 1996), p. 17.

Ibuka likewise believed in the Japanese view that a company is a family, and should be run as such. As Ibuka succinctly put it:

> *People should think of companies as merely a 'family register.'* — The NHK Group, *Good Mileage: The High-Performance Business Philosophy of Shoichiro Honda* (Tokyo: NHK Publishing, 1996), p. 168.

Morita Akio also viewed the company as a family:

> *There is no secret ingredient or hidden formula responsible for the success of the best Japanese companies. No theory or plan or government policy will make a business a success; that can only be done by people. The most important mission for a Japanese manager is to develop a healthy relationship with his employees, to create a family like feeling within the corporation, a feeling that employees and managers share the same fate. Those companies that are most successful in Japan are those that have managed to create a shared sense of fate among all employees, what Americans call labor and management, and the shareholders.*

I have not found this simple management system applied anywhere else in the world, and yet we have demonstrated convincingly, I believe, that it works. — Morita Akio, *Made In Japan* (New York: E.P. Dutton, 1986), p. 130.

The following are several examples of how Morita stressed the need to have employees work as family:

(W)e think it is unwise and unnecessary to define individual responsibility too clearly, because everyone is taught to act like a family member ready to do what is necessary. — Morita Akio, *Made In Japan* (New York: E.P. Dutton, 1986), p. 149.

What we in industry learned in dealing with people is that people do not work just for money and that if you are trying to motivate, money is not the most effective tool. To motivate people, you must bring them into the family and treat them like respected members of it. — Morita Akio, *Made In Japan* (New York: E.P. Dutton, 1986), p. 138.

At Sony we learned that the problem with an employee who is accustomed to work only for the sake of money is that he often forgets that he is expected to work for the group entity, and this self-centered attitude of working for himself and his family to the exclusion of the goals of his coworkers and the company is not healthy. It is management's responsibility to keep challenging each employee to do important work that he will find satisfying and to work within the family. To do this, we often reorganize the work at Sony to suit the talents and abilities of the workers. — Morita Akio, *Made In Japan* (New York: E.P. Dutton, 1986), p. 189.

Morita strove to include Japan's "company as family" approach to management and business operations not only in Japan but also in other companies as Sony expanded abroad. Noted Morita:

> *We have a policy that wherever we are in the world we deal with our employees as members of the Sony family, as valued colleagues, and that is why even before we opened our U.K. factory, we brought management people, including engineers, to Tokyo and let them work with us and trained them and treated them just like members of our family, all of whom wear the same jackets and eat in our one-class cafeteria. This way they got to understand that people should not be treated differently; we didn't give a private office to any executive, even to the head of the factory.* — **Morita Akio**, *Made In Japan* (New York: E.P. Dutton, 1986), p. 143.

The approach of Japan's management to treat employees as family is not done only due to the influence of Shinto and Confucianism as discussed in this book's chapter on management. Japan's "company as family" approach is also followed out of the realization that a company's future is ultimately decided by its employees. No matter how capable management might be, the degree to which a company succeeds over time is ultimately determined by how well the company—more specifically, the employees—perform. Morita explained:

> *But in the long run—and I emphasize this—no matter how good or successful you are or how clever or crafty, your business and its future are in the hands of the people you hire. To put it a bit more dramatically, the fate of your business is actually in the hands of the youngest recruit on the staff.* — **Morita Akio**, *Made In Japan* (New York: E.P. Dutton, 1986), p. 131.

These statements show that management in Japan acknowledges the importance of employees to the company's long-term performance and survivability and assigns great value to them. This is also one of the reasons that employees are treated as family in Japan's style of management and why employees traditionally have long-term employment and are not laid off during recessions.

2. Bushido & Japan's Business Culture

In addition, this value placed on the importance of every employee's role is a big part of why the salary difference between management and employees in Japan is nowhere as great as it is in America. In the States, top executives on average earn seventy times as much as rank and file employees, while top executives in Japan typically earn no more than sixteen times the earnings of their company's employees. As Morita explained:

> *(T)he company must not throw money away on huge bonuses for executives or other frivolities but must share its fate with the workers.* — **Morita Akio,** *Made In Japan* **(New York: E.P. Dutton, 1986), p. 187.**

Morita believed in the stability and other benefits of Japan's long-term and group-oriented approach to business:

> *Since Japanese management of the company is long-range and collective, the departure of any one top official is not likely to change the long-range goals of the company or the way it deals with its employees and suppliers.* — **Morita Akio,** *Made In Japan* **(New York: E.P. Dutton, 1986), p. 179.**

> *You must also consider the return that comes in five or ten years... not just the immediate return.* — **Morita Akio,** *Made In Japan* **(New York: E.P. Dutton, 1986), p. 155.**

Morita understood that the *Bushido* notion that all work is honorable is an outlook that helps differentiate capitalism in Japan from that in the West. He wrote:

> *Japanese attitudes toward work seem to be critically different from American attitudes. Japanese people tend to be much better adjusted to the notion of work, any kind of work, as honorable.* — **Morita Akio**, *Made In Japan* (New York: E.P. Dutton, 1986), p. 184.

Akio Morita was the last of these titans of Japan's post-World War II business era, passing away in 1999. Consequently, none of these giants of Japan's post-war economic development lived past the twentieth century. Did Japan's hybrid form of capitalism survive into the twenty-first century? Next, let's look at representative leaders of Japan's business world in the twenty-first century for the answer.

III. JAPANESE CAPITALISM IN THE 21ST CENTURY

A. INAMORI KAZUO — 稲盛和夫

Within Japan, Inamori Kazuo (1932–) is considered to be the country's most prominent business leader of the twenty-first century. His numerous and significant achievements include founding and leading the Kyocera Corporation, a world leader in industrial ceramics and the KDDI Corporation, Japan's second largest telecommunications giant.

When Japan Air Lines (JAL), the country's first and largest airline company, was in bankruptcy and on the brink of going out of business, Inamori was the only executive the Japanese government called in to rescue JAL and return it to profitability. He took over JAL in 2011 and within three years had successfully turned it around.

Inamori's prominence and impact on business management is so great not only in Japan but also internationally that the world-famous magazine *The Economist* called Inamori "one of the five management gurus in the world."[5]

[5]*Inamori Kazuo,* A Compass to Fulfillment: Passion and Spirituality in Life and Business *(New York: McGraw Hill, 2010), front cover of book.*

What views of management and business have guided Inamori's distinguished career? Does he subscribe to the hybrid capitalism that Shibusawa implemented in Japan? Or does he view—and, more importantly, practice—capitalism differently now as Japan has faced the challenges of the twenty-first century, including Japan's "lost two decades" (失われた20年 *ushinawareta nijuu nen*) in which its economy has stagnated from 1992 to today?

Like the leader's of Japan's business world before him, Inamori believes management and business must be guided by Japanese culture as will be seen from excerpts from Inamori's writings.

1. Traditional Cultural Values & Business

Regarding the values that management and business practices should be based on, Inamori stated:

> *Around the time I started the company (Kyocera Corporation), like it or not, I was called upon to make all kinds of decisions as a manager. This being a start-up venture, one wrong decision could push the company off the rails. Day after day, I continued to rack my brains over some kind of criteria to adopt for making decisions.*

At the end of all the worry, I realized that what was good for day-to-day life should also be the basis for management decisions—in other words, "Do what is right as a human being." If we operate in violation of generally accepted ethics and morals, then we cannot expect to do well in the long term. Therefore, I felt the basis for decisions should be the concepts drummed into us when we were children: what is right and what is wrong for human beings. — **Inamori Kazuo** *Amoeba Management* **(Boca Raton, Florida: CRC Press, 2013), p. 10.**

Basing business decisions on "doing what is right as a human being," "generally accepted ethics and morals," and "the concepts drummed into us when we were children," of course, refer to basing decisions on Japan's traditional cultural values and social practices.

Inamori also believes that leadership in the business world as well as every sphere of human endeavor should be based on virtue more than ability or achievements. This is another traditional Japanese cultural value found in the tradition of *Bushido*. It also is an important part of Confucianism, which taught that a ruler must lead a country virtuously—failure to do so would result in the people having the divine right to revolt and replace that ruler. As Inamori stated:

It is an executive overflowing with resourcefulness that can create a new market. However, a leader without superior character cannot manage a company. — **"Meigen Ijin: Inamori Kazuo** (*Quotes of Famous People: Inamori Kazuo*)**" http://meigen-ijin.com/inamorikazuo, p. 4.**

In emphasizing the importance of leading by virtue, Inamori goes back to the words of Saigo Takamori (西郷隆盛 1828–1877),

the great 19th century samurai leader who championed Japan's drive to modernize and became one of the country's leading statesmen, and quotes him as saying:

> *To men of high virtue, give high office; to men of many* *achievements, give cash.* — **Inamori Kazuo,** *A Compass to* **Fulfillment: Passion and Spirituality in Life and Business** (New York: McGraw Hill, 2010), p. 56.

As is common in Japan's style of management, Inamori saw the company as being an extended family:

> *Believing in an environment in which all workers* *shared the same goals as management and regarded* *mutual cooperation as the ideal, I then looked to the tra-* *ditional Japanese family for a model. The word family* *is used here for the traditional family group in which* *grandparents, parents, and children all do their utmost* *for the good of the family. Parents are considerate of their* *children; children are considerate of their parents. The* *family is a community held together by destiny, with* *everyone obtaining a sense of enjoyment as the family* *grows and develops. Such a family relationship is one* *of mutual love, with members ready and willing to* *do anything for each other. This is what I mean by the* *extended-family principle.*

> *If the company becomes a community held together by* *destiny, as one extended family, and it's mutual under-* *standing, encouragement, and help are freely given* *among managers and employees, just as any fam-* *ily, then it should be possible to run the company with* *management and labor as one body united for the same* *purposes. Even in the face of severe market competition,*

operations should naturally proceed well, as united efforts are directed toward the development of the company. I named this concept the extended family principle and made it part of the company's [Kyocera's] management foundation. — Inamori Kazuo, *Amoeba Management* (Boca Raton, Florida: CRC Press, 2013), pp. 18–19.

2. Social Role of the Company

As was true of the leaders of Japanese business that preceded him, Inamori likewise believes that a company does not exist solely for the benefit of its shareholders and management. Instead, a business has a greater social role and function—namely, to promote the welfare of society at large as Inamori says:

The pursuit of profit is the driving force behind business as well as many other human endeavors, and there is thus nothing wrong with wanting to make money. We should not pursue profit, however, for the benefit of ourselves alone. We need to "greedily" desire what is best for others and strive to promote the common good. If we do so, we too will benefit and the scope of our profit will greatly expand in the process.

Running a company, for example, is in itself a service to others and to society. — Inamori Kazuo, *A Compass to Fulfillment: Passion and Spirituality in Life and Business* (New York: McGraw Hill, 2010), p. 82.

Making the same point about his personal experience in establishing and running the Kyocera Corporation, Inamori writes:

The purpose of the company is to safeguard the employees and their families, and to aim for their happiness.

My destiny is to take the lead and aim for the happiness of our employees. From that, I established the Kyocera management rationale as follows: "To provide opportunities for the material and intellectual growth of all our employees, and, through our joint efforts, contribute to the advancement of society and humankind." — Inamori Kazuo, *Amoeba Management* (Boca Raton, Florida: CRC Press, 2013), pp. 5–6.

In incorporating traditional Japanese cultural values in capitalism, Inamori goes all the way back to the teachings of the Japanese philosopher Ishida Baigan (石田梅岩1685–1744), who stressed the importance of following an ethical code of supporting the common greater good through one's own commercial activity:

"A true merchant thinks from the other's standpoint, not just his own." Ishida believed that the pursuit of profiting the customer as well as the merchant constituted the very core of business, which led to his claim that a spirit of "profiting self, profiting others" should drive all business activity. — Inamori Kazuo, *A Compass to Fulfillment: Passion and Spirituality in Life and Business* (New York: McGraw Hill, 2010), p. 82.

B. TSUKAKOSHI HIROSHI — 塚越寛

The guiding influence of traditional Japanese cultural values and social practices in Japan's capitalism is well seen in the management and business practices of another noteworthy corporate thought leader in 21st century Japan—Tsukakoshi Hiroshi.

Born in 1937, Tsukakoshi is the Chairman of Ina Foods Industry Co., Ltd., located in the rural prefecture of Nagano in central Japan. The company is a leader in manufacturing powdered agar, a traditional gelatin product made from seaweed.

While only a medium-sized company with annual sales of $148 million in 2015, Ina Foods has distinguished itself under the leadership of Mr. Tsukakoshi as a pioneering company in the areas of management, supply systems, and sales and marketing. In 1996, Tsukakoshi was awarded the highly prestigious Government of Japan's Medal of Honor with Yellow Ribbon, the Outstanding Businessperson Award in 2002, and the Good Company Award Grand Prize from the Small Business Research Institute for his management philosophy and for achieving forty-eight consecutive years of increased sales and profits at Ina Foods.

Given its noteworthy business results, executives from Japan's major corporations—companies like Toyota Motor Company—that have been global leaders dominating their industries all over the world regularly visit Ina Foods to meet with Tsukakoshi and learn about his highly successful management strategies.

And what is the management philosophy of this thought leader in 21st century Japan? Does he believe that traditional cultural values and social practices should play a role in how business is conducted in Japan? Or has Japan's economic stagnation in the 21st century and the resulting questioning of Japan's way of conducting business prompted him to seek alternative management approaches? For Tsukakoshi, traditional cultural values and social practices remain an integral part of engaging in business and succeeding in the Japanese market. Let's take a look at his views of the principles of management and business in Japan.

1. Traditional Cultural Values & Business

More than just emphasizing the need for and importance of

harmony and cooperation as his predecessors have, Tsukakoshi tells how they directly impact a company's performance. He believes that attaining harmony within a company is the very essence of management in Japan.

I think of management as a game, one whose goal is to figure out how to raise everyone's sense of solidarity. To use a sports analogy, it is like soccer in the sense that it requires teamwork. The work of a company manager is to concentrate everyone's power—that of directors, employees, part-time workers, and even trading partners—and get it moving in same direction. If people are dissonant, their power is diminished, but when everyone acts in perfect harmony, the company is able to exert its greatest possible power.... .

> Attaining harmony within a company is the very essence of management in Japan.

This is why I value the spirit of harmony: because it is essential for concentrating people's power. — Tsuka-koshi Hiroshi, *Tree-Ring Management: Take the Long View and Grow Your Business Slowly* (Tokyo: Japan Publishing Industry Foundation for Culture, 2015), pp. 131–132.

Tsukakoshi says harmony is so important to a business' performance that it is the primary consideration in human resource management. Specifically, he believes that harmony is more important than talent or education in deciding who should be hired:

My highest priority when hiring employees is their ability to cooperate. No matter how talented or well educated a potential employee might be, I will not hire someone who lacks the ability to cooperate.

Having the ability to cooperate means thinking about others and being open to mutual support. Those who are cooperative can therefore be expected to be highly attentive in their everyday lives. — Tsukakoshi Hiroshi, **Tree-Ring Management: Take the Long View and Grow Your Business Slowly** (Tokyo: **Japan Publishing Industry Foundation for Culture, 2015), p. 147.**

Without a relationship it is not possible to engage in business with another party.

As noted throughout this book, Japanese place central importance to relationships in conducting business. Chapter one explains how establishing a mutual relationship of trust is a primary facet of Japan's approach to conducting business, and that without a relationship it is not possible to engage in business with another party. Tsukakoshi champions this traditional notion. He speaks to this traditional cultural value and approach to business when he writes:

It is important to develop a relationship of trust before beginning to trade with one another. We carefully consider whether the company is one with which we can develop a long-term relationship....

Indeed, you cannot really call it business unless you are able to develop a relationship in which both sides prosper through long-term fidelity. — Tsukakoshi Hiroshi, *Tree-Ring Management: Take the Long View and Grow Your Business Slowly* (Tokyo: **Japan Publishing Industry Foundation for Culture, 2015), pp. 71–72.**

Tsukakoshi likewise points out that, based on a mutual trust relationship, Japanese companies do not emphasize contracts and are committed to advancing the business interests of both companies:

> *But once a relationship of trust has been built, it becomes a bond stronger than any contract, because both parties have come to an agreement and feel confident in the shared desire to develop further together.* — Tsukakoshi Hiroshi, *Tree-Ring Management: Take the Long View and Grow Your Business Slowly* (Tokyo: Japan Publishing Industry Foundation for Culture, 2015), p. 76.

Tsukakoshi explains that in Japanese culture "relationship" means not only having mutual trust and a shared desire to develop further together but also includes taking into account the interests of the other party and accommodating what you reasonably can to ensure that they also grow through the relationship. He writes:

> *We pursued our business in a way that took the other party's position into account and tried to ensure that the other party grew....*
>
> *Before we knew it, thinking earnestly about the other parties and working together with them over a long period led to the development of relationships of deep trust. Today, even without a contract, they will make whatever we need and provide it just the way we want it.* — Tsukakoshi Hiroshi, *Tree-Ring Management: Take the Long View and Grow Your Business Slowly* (Tokyo: Japan Publishing Industry Foundation for Culture, 2015), p. 102.

In addition to the centrality of relationships in doing business in Japan, Tsukakoshi stresses the importance of the traditional Japanese cultural value of taking the long-term perspective in business. He quotes a prominent Japanese philosopher from two centuries ago to make his point:

> *Ninomiya Sontoku, the 19ᵗʰ century Japanese philosopher, wrote: "Those who take the long view will prosper. Those who are short-sighted will become poor." I came across these words perhaps 30 years ago, around the time I began to think that a company's greatest virtue is its endurance. It suddenly struck me then that in order to build a good company that would endure, I needed to take the long view.*
>
> *Ever since then, my management strategy has been to take the long view.* — **Tsukakoshi Hiroshi**, *Tree-Ring Management: Take the Long View and Grow Your Business Slowly* (Tokyo: **Japan Publishing Industry Foundation for Culture, 2015), p. 25.**

In taking the long-term view of business, Tsukakoshi emphasizes that the goal of management is to steadily grow the company from year to year. It does not matter how large or small the company's growth is, just that it grows.

> *I called this management style "tree-ring management": growing a little bit each year, slowly and reliably, in the same way that a tree adds rings. I believe that this is the ideal form of management. The rings vary in width with each year's weather, sometimes growing a great deal and sometimes only a little, but the tree always grows bigger than it was the year before. Even if a given ring happens to be narrow, the important thing is that the tree continues to grow.* — **Tsukakoshi Hiroshi**, *Tree-Ring Management: Take the Long View and Grow Your Business Slowly* (Tokyo: **Japan Publishing Industry Foundation for Culture, 2015), p. 29.**

Tsukakoshi believed that blaming factors outside of one's company for poor business results is never correct:

> *Tree rings exhibit a mechanism for endurance. Trees do not stop growing even during years with bad weather. Their rings are narrower, but they continue to grow at a pace that is right for them. They do not say, "Well, the weather is bad this year, so I'm not going to grow." It is the same with our company. I want us to continue to grow steadily at our own pace, even if it is a slow one, without blaming others or our environment. This is the essence of tree-ring management.* — Tsukakoshi Hiroshi, *Tree-Ring Management: Take the Long View and Grow Your Business Slowly* (Tokyo: Japan Publishing Industry Foundation for Culture, 2015), p. 165.

The theme in Tsukakoshi's management philosophy of not blaming external factors for poor company results is consistent with the traditions of *Bushido* and echoes Matshushita Konosuke's words that problems in business need to be resolved from within by management rather than through the result of external influences.

Another traditional Japanese cultural value that Tsukakoshi emphasizes is *kaizen*—continual improvement or innovation. Far beyond discussing the need to constantly improve a company's products, he stresses the importance to management of applying *kaizen* to every facet of the company:

> *In order for a company to endure, it must continually innovate. We try to ensure that waves of innovation are constantly sweeping across every division, through the introduction of new management techniques, new products, new technologies, and new services.* — Tsukakoshi Hiroshi, *Tree-Ring Management: Take the Long View and*

Grow Your Business Slowly (Tokyo: Japan Publishing Industry Foundation for Culture, 2015), pp. 160-161.

2. Social Role of the Company

Tsukakoshi firmly believes in the traditional notion that a business has an important social role to play and must contribute to society; that a company should be managed as a family; and that employees should not be laid off. He summarizes his philosophy writing:

> When it comes to management, "the way things really ought to be" means building the kind of company that contributes to society by making its employees happy. Sales and profits are nothing more than a means of achieving this end.
>
> This might be easier to understand if you think of a company as a family. When a family runs short of food, it does not expel one of its members so those who remain can eat what is left. A company is the same. Just as you wish for the happiness of your family, it is important to wish for the happiness of your employees; doing so generates a succession of virtuous cycles in company management. This is the secret to Ina Food Industry's continually rising revenues and profits over the course of a half a century. — Tsukakoshi Hiroshi, *Tree-Ring Management: Take the Long View and Grow Your Business Slowly* (Tokyo: Japan Publishing Industry Foundation for Culture, 2015), pp. 6–7.

To him, management's role in an employee's life includes making the employees happy and being educators to help the employees grow as people to become productive and contributing members of society.

Tsukakoshi contrasts this traditional Japanese business practice of valuing employee well-being with the American focus on giving priority to increasing profits and shareholder return:

Doctrines emphasizing sales above all, the expansion of profits, or market capitalization seem all too often to come at the expense of employee happiness.

It is impossible to manage a company whose sales do not grow, and in the absence of profits, the company's very survival may be in doubt. Yet, once you make increased sales and profit your sole objective, employee happiness becomes secondary. In short, you start and think about how profits could be effectively raised by reducing labor costs and welfare expenditures, or by cutting back on activities that give back to the community and support culture and the arts.

This seems completely backward to me. Management is all about finding a balance between the company's numbers and the happiness of its employees. This balance is what management should pursue above all else. Corporate management these days seems to have placed too much emphasis on company numbers, throwing things out of balance. — Tsukakoshi Hiroshi, *Tree-Ring Management: Take the Long View and Grow Your Business Slowly* (Tokyo: Japan Publishing Industry Foundation for Culture, 2015), pp. 22–23.

In emphasizing the fundamental aspect of Japan's business culture that a company is like a family, Tsukakoshi teaches:

A company is a community that shares a common purpose. I would even go so far as to say it is a family. Indeed, employees at my company often refer to themselves as the Ina Foods family. — Tsukakoshi Hiroshi, *Tree-Ring Management: Take the Long View and Grow Your Business Slowly* (Tokyo: Japan Publishing Industry Foundation for Culture, 2015), p. 65.

We want those who join our company to understand that the employees of Ina Foods are family. Because we are a family, there is no labor union. There is no need for one. — Tsukakoshi Hiroshi, *Tree-Ring Management: Take the Long View and Grow Your Business Slowly* (Tokyo: Japan Publishing Industry Foundation for Culture, 2015), p. 148.

C. OKUDA HIROSHI — 奥田碩

Okuda Hiroshi (1932–) was the president of Toyota Motor Company from 1995 through 2006 as well as its chairman from 1999 to 2006. He also served as the chairman of the Keidanren from 1998 through 2006. The Keidanren (系団連), or Japan Business Federation, is one of the most prominent business organizations of major corporations in Japan. An important thought leader in Japan's business world, Okuda was selected to be a member of the Prime Minister's Economic Strategy Council of Japan in 1998.

In 2005 when Okuda was chairman of the Keidanren and at the helm of Toyota, he was asked what he thought about laying off employees. In his reply now widely famous throughout all of Japan, Okuda replied: "Fellow Executives, if you lay off employees, then also slit your own stomachs (経営者よ. 従業員の首を切るなら, 腹を切れ)." The idea of cutting one's own stomach is a reference to the old samurai tradition of ritual disembowelment known as *seppuku* or *hara-kiri* (切腹). This ritual of suicide was engaged in by samurai to take responsibility for a major action that violated society's rules and, thereby, caused one to lose their honor.

By answering that corporate executives must commit *seppuku* if they lay off employees, Okuda stated in the strongest of terms that layoffs violate society's rule and that he opposes them.

The use of *seppuku* in Okuda's reply indicates the great degree of influence on his management philosophy of the traditional values of the samurai code (*Bushido*). Specifically, what social rule would corporate layoffs violate from the perspective of *Bushido* that would necessitate ceremonial suicide? In the ways of the samurai code, samurai pledged absolute loyalty, including their very lives, to the lords they served. In return for his loyalty, the lords provided room and board and a modest stipend to their samurai. In the context of modern Japan's business practices, this *Bushido* value is present in the idea that company executives are obligated to repay employee loyalty to the company by providing for their well-being through stable employment and salary. In this way, corporate layoffs violate the values of *Bushido* in the context of Japan's culture.

In addition, by answering that laying off employees is an action that is contrary to social rules and is dishonorable to the degree necessitating executives to engage in ritual suicide to take responsibility for it, Okuda is confirming four other cultural values that preclude corporate layoffs in Japan:

- Maintaining the employment of workers is part of how every business fulfills its social obligation to promote social stability and the welfare of the nation.

- A company is considered a mini society in which workers are managed in a family-like manner.

- According to the teachings of Confucianism, leaders have a moral obligation to look after the well-being of those in their charge.

- The Shinto religion teaches that salvation is attained in this life by caring for each other and maintaining harmonious relationships.

In this way, all five of these long-standing cultural values make it difficult for Japanese companies to lay off workers in the framework of Japan's mainstream style of management.

SUMMARY

From its inception in the 19th century, Japan's style of capitalism grew with deliberate and intentional direction, weaving traditional Japanese cultural values and social traditions into Western capitalism in fundamental and far-reaching ways. This effort was so deliberate that the Japanese created a phrase at the time to express it—*wakon yousai* (和魂洋才), meaning "Japanese spirit, Western know-how."

From the wise and far-seeing Shibusawa and his peers to post-WWII titans Matsushita Konosuke, Morita Akio, and Honda Soichiro on to powerful 21st century leaders such as Inamori Kazuo, Tsukakoshi Hiroshi, and Okuda Hiroshi, this hybrid form of capitalism has been practiced for 150 years, creating iconic companies and landmark products, upholding this same philosophical framework for Japan's modern economy.

As a result, from its inception, Japan's brand of capitalism has been different from that of the West. Therein lie the roots of Japan's distinct style of business and management that is practiced to this day. It is the culture-based differences in management and business in Japan that resulted from Japan's implementation of its distinct brand of capitalism that present some of the greatest challenges to foreign companies seeking to engage in business in that market. They comprise the submerged part of the iceberg described in this book's preface.

The result of this intentional hybridization is that when we compare the capitalism that is practiced in Japan with that functioning in America and Europe, the differentiating factor is traditional Japanese cultural values and social practices. Just how different is the practice of management and business in Japan and in the West? Honda Soichiro, founder of the Honda Motor Company, put it in perspective by writing:

> *Japanese and American management styles are 95 percent the same—and different in all important aspects.*
>
> *QuotesWise: Soichiro Honda.*
> http://www.quoteswise.com/soichiro-honda-quotes-3.html, p. 3.

As we have seen in this chapter, Japan's brand of capitalism has remained consistent from the time it was first implemented through the present day. However, in 1992 Japan's economic bubble burst and its economy has for the most part remained stagnant through the present day. There are several factors that contributed to this protracted economic malaise:

- A declining population means there are fewer workers available than before.

- Off-shoring significant amounts of manufacturing to Asian neighbors has resulted in a smaller manufacturing base available in Japan to contribute to its domestic economic growth.

- There are significantly greater levels of competition from China, South Korea, Taiwan, and Southeast Asian countries.

- A near doubling of the value of the Japanese yen in relation to the U.S. dollar from 1992 to today has made Japanese exports more expensive to buy.

Given these challenging economic circumstances in Japan, there are business leaders who are questioning if Japan's traditional way of conducting business can continue to serve the country well. Indeed, they are wondering if a new approach to business is needed to reinvigorate the country and its economy.

At the same time, since becoming prime minister of Japan in 2012, Abe Shinzo has been pushing Japanese companies to adopt an American way of doing business and style of corporate governance—that is a short-term orientation and a focus on returning profit to company shareholders rather than looking out for employees.

Some Japanese companies have tried an American approach but the results have not been favorable. So while Japan's traditional management practices remain intact for the most part at this point in time, there is a real sense that Japan's economy is at a turning point and a new business approach may be needed. So far, however, no alternatives have emerged as viable or desirable.

PART TWO

MACRO-LEVEL MEASURES FOR SUCCEEDING IN JAPAN

Real On-The-Ground

Management Strategies

挑戦と失敗

CHAPTER 6

Challenges & Foibles In Japan

Client Case Study Vignettes & Lessons Learned

This chapter is a collection of case study vignettes that depict challenges, successes, and foibles experienced by client companies in Japan. These accounts provide representative examples of some of the actual challenges and pitfalls that American companies encounter in the Japanese market as well as lessons to be learned from them.

I. GGD, INC.

A. GGD, Inc.'s Experience

GGD, Inc. is an American company that pioneered and commercialized magnetized fluids. By successfully magnetizing fluids, the location and movement of those fluids can be precisely controlled with magnets. The GGD product came to be used in ninety percent of the world's audio speakers, half of the world's computer hard disc drives, and in numerous products in other categories. With tremendous sales success and market share domination throughout North America, Europe, Asia, and South America, they were the acknowledged global leader of that niche technology and product category.

The company already had a history of doing business in Japan for several years when they requested my assistance to help manage and improve their performance in that market. While their efforts in countries around the world tended to be very rewarding, their business results in Japan were not. This was doubly surprising because so many of the audio speakers, computer hard drives, and semiconductors being produced in the world were being made in Japan at that time. The Japanese market should have been one of their top markets. However, it was not.

To deal with this situation, they hired a new director of international sales who reported that he not only had years of business experience in Japan but also was fluent in the Japanese language. They were quite optimistic that under his leadership their sales performance would improve significantly in the Japanese market.

John Allen, the new international sales director, had already been employed with GGD for six months when I began working with the company. I was living in Japan and met him for the first time in Yokohama during his next visit to the country. We were meeting with executives of a Fortune 50 Japanese corporation that was interested in using GGD components in its world-class products.

When meeting with Japanese executives together with American clients, I always translate the discussions—both English to Japanese and Japanese to English—in addition to facilitating the discussions and providing strategic advice. However, as everyone at GGD and I understood that John was fluent in Japanese, I did no translations as that meeting began. Right away I felt someone kicking my foot under the table. When I realized it was John and looked at him, he had this panicked S.O.S. look on his face. He signaled that he could not follow the discussion. I immediately began to translate both directions for the rest of the meeting.

When the meeting concluded, John and I huddled to discuss it. I asked why he needed me to translate the meeting. He replied that his Japanese was not good enough for discussing business matters. Keeping in mind that he had claimed to be fluent in Japanese, I asked him to clarify the level at which he was comfortable speaking the language. He replied: "To order sushi and beer in a restaurant." Knowing a few words and social greetings was the extent of his Japanese language ability. Needless to say, I was stunned. And so were GGD's executives back in the U.S. headquarters when they heard this.

The next day, John and I were to meet at the Tokyo headquarters of GGD's Japan subsidiary. It was my first visit to GGD Japan, and I was looking forward to it. John explained to me how proud he was of his track record of visiting the Tokyo office two weeks out of every month over the past six months of his employment at GGD. He informed me that he was confident that he had good working relationships with all of GGD's employees in Tokyo and that he was doing a good job managing the Japan subsidiary. However, surprises awaited.

The surprises started immediately upon arriving at the office. The first thing I noticed was the telephone greeting for incoming calls. When several of the staff answered the telephone in Japanese, they did not say something along the lines of "GGD. How may I help you?" Instead, they answered with a different company name. This was puzzling. John and I attended several meetings that day with most of the business conducted in Japanese. I was flabbergasted when many of the discussions were about matters unrelated to GGD's business.

I decided not to approach John about this for two reasons. I had just learned the evening before that his Japanese language skills were minimal, so it was possible that he was not aware of this strange business situation. And if he *did* know what was going on, then most likely he was a part of whatever was happening. I decided to investigate quietly on my own. I went to the office almost everyday, conversed with employees, attended meetings, listened to conversations among the staff, took a quick look at incoming faxes, and checked shipping invoices and other business documents.

It was not long before I realized that my fear was correct. In addition to engaging in GGD, Inc.'s work, the Tokyo subsidiary was also running a business completely unrelated to GGD.

This shadow business used all of GGD's resources—the office space, staff, telephones, and office equipment such as computers and copy and fax machines. Even worse, as I was able to review more and more information regarding the company's income and spending, my suspicion was confirmed that GGD funds were being used to support this side business.

When GGD retained me as a consultant, I was given the title Assistant to the Chairman and was to report directly to him at the U.S. headquarters. I made my initial report about this unusual situation in Tokyo through a lengthy international telephone call. The U.S. chairman was incredulous. He requested that I try to determine the extent of this illegal business activity and bring back proof to him.

I thought long and hard about what proof I could show GGD headquarters. If I brought any products or other objects back to America, the Tokyo staff would notice they were missing and realize that I was on to what they were doing. All of the documents in the Tokyo office were in Japanese and would be of little use to GGD headquarters in evaluating what was going on at their Tokyo subsidiary. I had to find a source of proof that would not raise any suspicions with the staff yet would demonstrate that unsanctioned business activities were being engaged in by the Tokyo office.

I remembered when I first visited GGD headquarters in the States, the Director of Human Resources showed me photos of all the employees in their Tokyo office. It was GGD's policy, she informed me, that all staff from around the world must come to the U.S. headquarters for a company orientation and training upon commencing employment at GGD's overseas locations. She was proud of her practice of keeping photos and information on all GGD staff employed at all of GGD's offices around the world.

As it happened to be the latter part of December when all of this was happening, I asked the Tokyo staff to take Christmas photos with me and gave all of them copies of the photos, which they enjoyed. I then brought additional copies of the photos back to U.S. headquarters. The Chairman, HR Director, other key executives, and I met privately in their boardroom. I first requested the HR Director place the photos of the Tokyo staff she had on file in a row on the table. I then placed the pictures of the Tokyo staff that I had just taken in a row underneath those employee photos so we could compare who was in both sets.

It quickly became clear that there were several "extra people" at GGD's Japan subsidiary. Those were the Tokyo staff members in the photos who had never come to headquarters for the mandatory new employee training and who were totally unknown to headquarters staff. They were working full time for the Tokyo subsidiary's shadow business.

Not knowing where the international sales director stood in all of this, I had requested this meeting take place when he was out of town. GGD U.S. executives accepted the fact that they had a renegade business being simultaneously run out of their Tokyo subsidiary. They now needed to ascertain whether John was involved as well. They immediately called him back to the U.S. headquarters to discuss the situation. He acted surprised and claimed that he knew nothing of this unauthorized, shadow business. Giving John the benefit of the doubt for the moment, the Chairman then ordered him to do three things:

- Tell Tokyo that he needed to focus on challenges the GGD subsidiaries in Europe were facing and that I would act as the U.S. Chairman's exclusive representative with GGD Japan going forward

- Keep in confidence that the U.S. headquarters knew about the unauthorized business activities in Japan

- Completely cease working and communicating with Japan thereafter

It was now clear why GGD Japan was not performing at the levels everyone expected in what should have been one of the company's biggest markets. The Chairman requested that I promptly return to Japan and thoroughly investigate this situation. With this further investigation, it became clear that the president of the Japan subsidiary and a majority of its employees were involved in this shadow business operation. Some of those involved were official employees of GGD and others were hired by the shadow business. After a period of time to investigate and corroborate the full extent of their activities in Japan, GGD's U.S. Chairman had all those involved, including the Tokyo subsidiary's president, fired and requested that I assume day-to-day control of the company, hire the staff necessary to replace those just let go, and get the Japan subsidiary back on track.

The impact of this shadow business was not only seen in the company's sales performance but also in its dealings with other companies that GGD conducted business with in Japan while this shadow business existed. The following incident is one example of this, and it took place while I was investigating the shadow business.

It was around 3:30 a.m. when my Tokyo apartment phone rang and woke me up. It was GGD's Chairman calling from America with what he described as "an emergency situation that required immediate resolution." As I scrambled to find my eyeglasses and turn on a light, he went on to describe what I could only think was a bizarre dream I must be having. Either that or this was some kind of prank.

The Chairman kept repeating to me that "we have a crazed samurai camped out in our Tokyo office." He went on to instruct me "to go and find out what in the world was going on there." Of course, I could not imagine what he was talking about. The only actual information he had on the situation was that this "samurai" was engaged in a sit-in inside GGD's Tokyo office and was claiming that GGD Japan owed his company several hundred thousand dollars and was refusing to pay him. Given that this situation was so bizarre and that the Chairman was not getting clear answers from Mr. Takahashi, GGD Japan's President, about what was going on, he charged me to go there immediately and get to the bottom of this situation.

The subways in Tokyo pause service every night, generally from between midnight or 1:00 a.m. and 5:00 a.m. I waited for the first train at sunrise and set out for GGD's Tokyo office. Upon arriving, Mr. Takahashi, who had no choice but to spend the night at the office as a result of this "crazed samurai" camping out there all night, gave me basically the same information that the Chairman had. He claimed he did not understand the reason for this sit-in and would not give me any further information about the circumstances.

When I inquired as to why the protester was referred to as a "crazed samurai," Mr. Takahashi explained to me that the protester was the proud descendant of a very prestigious samurai family in Japan's Nagano prefecture. His company had been established by his samurai great grandfather and been handed down through the generations. Furthermore, this "samurai" president maintained a first-rate collection of samurai swords that had been family heirlooms for centuries. This collection was housed in his company's headquarters in Nagano. He was well known for being highly skilled in *kendou* (剣道)—traditional Japanese swordsmanship or "the Way of the sword." He also was known for taking one of those swords with him to business meetings "for added effect in negotiating," as Mr. Takahashi explained to me.

The "crazed samurai" whose name was Mr. Ito had camped out in the conference room at GGD Tokyo's office. I could see through the glass wall that he had politely removed his shoes and was sitting on the floor with his legs crossed in front of him and his upper torso completely straight as a samurai in the Zen meditation position. Sure enough, one of his family's vaunted samurai swords was strategically placed on the floor in front of him.

As I reached for the doorknob to enter the conference room to talk with Mr. Ito, Mr. Takahashi abruptly declared that he had changed his mind and was not going in that room. I was on my own. I quickly came to appreciate the meaning of what I had heard about Mr. Ito's taking a sword to meetings "for added effect in negotiating." I had always believed in that old adage that the pen is mightier than the sword, but as I entered the room and saw the intensity in Mr. Ito's eyes and that samurai sword in front of him, I was not sure how much mightier my Mont Blanc pen would be in this particular instance.

For his part, Mr. Ito was surprised to see a foreigner coming in to meet with him. He immediately growled at me in Japanese: "What do *you* want? Anyway, I am tired of people telling me excuses as to why GGD is not paying what it duly owes my company. That's all I've heard for the past eighteen hours—nothing but excuses…"

I replied to him in Japanese, "I'm not here to tell you anything, sir… I'm here simply to listen to you." I paused, assumed a Zen sitting position, and just sat quietly on the floor opposite him. He apparently wasn't expecting anything like this and was clearly puzzled. He again asked: "So who are you? What do you want?"

I answered that I was the personal assistant to GGD, Inc.'s Chairman in the corporate headquarters in America. I said, "The Chairman sent me here to meet directly with *you* and resolve *your* grievance. How can he and I help you, sir?"

He said, "So you're here on behalf of the Chairman? To help resolve the problem I have with his company?"

I confirmed, "Yes, sir, that is correct." He then went into a period of silence in the manner Japanese engage in silence to consider a situation (as explained in this book's chapter on negotiating). After a good two or more minutes of no words or eye contact from him, he took a deep breath and then exhaled. Instantly I could feel the energy in the room change. His entire countenance relaxed, and he reengaged. He began to tell me all of the details of the situation.

Despite all of the theatrics, I quickly came to realize through listening to him that this "crazed samurai" was as sensible as he was sincere. He was there to protest GGD Japan's failure to pay his company for the contract manufacturing work he had done at GGD's explicit request. While the agreed upon terms of payment called for GGD Japan to pay his company within thirty days of receiving the products, more than six months had passed and he had not received any payment whatsoever for the many orders his company had already completed and delivered to GGD in good faith during that period.

In addition, GGD had been ignoring all of his communications about the payments owed for more than five months. I inquired if he had any documentation to back up his position. He immediately handed me a neatly organized binder of documents. These documents ranged from the sales orders specifying thirty day payment due dates signed by GGD Japan's president to the shipping documents signed by GGD Japan confirming receipt of delivery of the products to their invoices to GGD for each order. As I reviewed the documents, I could see that his grievance with GGD Japan was valid.

GGD's payments to Mr. Ito's company were now five months late. Mr. Ito had reached the end of his patience. While inquiring about his business, I learned that his company was a very small OEM manufacturer with annual sales of about twenty-eight million dollars and that he had taken out a bank loan to purchase the equipment and supplies needed to make the products GGD was ordering and cover the expenses related to this production work. Without GGD's payment for these orders, he was not able to make loan payments to his company's bank.

He explained that his bank was now demanding the monthly payments as specified in the loan, but that his company was not able to make them due to GGD's lack of payment. The bank was getting ready to call the loan. If that transpired, Mr. Ito's company would no longer be able to continue operating. As a result, he was taking this drastic action of staging a sit-in at GGD's office to secure their payment. He had begun his camp out in GGD's office at noon the day before and declared that he would not leave until the payments owed his company by GGD were duly paid in full.

After I listened and took detailed notes for about fifty minutes, he stopped talking and asked me what I thought. I said I needed to take a moment and confer with GGD Japan's president and that I would return in a few minutes. When I showed copies of all the relevant supporting documents to Mr. Takahashi and asked if Mr. Ito's story was accurate, he admitted that it was. Previously he had not wanted to inform GGD's Chairman of this because then it would have become clear that the reason why GGD Japan did not have the funds to pay what it owed Mr. Ito's company was that Mr. Takahashi had siphoned off GGD Japan's funds to run his shadow business.

I returned to Mr. Ito and replied that I would immediately report and recommend to the Chairman that GGD promptly pay Mr. Ito's company the entire amount due. GGD headquarters made full payment first thing the next day by international bank wire transfer and the situation was resolved.

B. Lessons from GGD, Inc.'s Experience

1. Effective Oversight

For American companies engaged in business in the Japanese market, effective management and oversight capability are imperative. This is important not only to prevent unwanted developments such as Mr. Takahashi's shadow business but also to ensure the company is meeting these fundamental goals:

- Consistently proceeding in sync with the company's market strategy

- Operating in the most effective way possible to achieve corporate goals

- Advancing the corporate image and brand identity to the greatest degree possible and in the most desirable fashion

Without effective management and oversight capability there is no way to know what is actually going on and, therefore, to successfully deal with the many challenges foreign businesses encounter in Japan. As seen in GGD's experience, American companies are confronted with three types of challenges:

- Challenges that are typical and, therefore, expected when conducting business in any highly competitive overseas market such as Japan's—the generic challenges mentioned in the preface of this book

- Potential problems that foreign executives are aware of but do not typically expect to be a factor

- Difficulties not imagined by foreign executives, including those that are unique to Japan due to its business culture

It cannot be emphasized enough how critical both effective management and oversight are to your business in Japan. In my thirty-five years of experience working with U.S. businesses that had a presence in Asian markets via a subsidiary, a joint venture, or simply through a sales agreement, the quality of oversight and management was the second most important factor impacting the level and longevity of success in the Japanese market. The most important factor was being able to effectively manage Japan's culture-based differences in business practices.

In the case of larger corporations, oversight is commonly conducted not only through multiple layers of executives and managers in the international sales department but also through several departments, such as the organization's auditing department. For example, larger corporations may well have directors of sales for individual countries of the world or even for the regions where the company has a market. This allows each country or region to receive a greater degree of oversight and management.

However, with small and medium sized companies, it is typically a very different story. Often there is only one manager overseeing the entire international sales department. The result is that one individual is responsible for all of the international markets and there are no other executives or managers providing additional oversight or management power. Frequently smaller businesses do not have an auditing department to help with oversight. As a result of these and other factors, small and medium sized companies generally have weaker oversight and management of overseas business operations than do larger corporations. Typically the oversight function is insufficient or even non-existent in smaller companies.

> Effective management and oversight capability are imperative.

To be most effective, management and oversight must be conducted in the international markets themselves. No matter how effective the oversight and management function might be when conducted from the U.S. headquarters, optimal success can only be attained with in-country, hands-on oversight and management. That is where the rubber meets the road. Trying to manage and properly oversee an international business from America by remote control has severe limitations and often leaves American executives and their companies' business in a weaker position.

To achieve optimal oversight and management of a business in the Japanese market, those operations need to be conducted by someone who has the following three qualifications:

- Familiarity with Japan's business culture, rules, and regulations

- Meaningful and successful experience in conducting business in Japan

- Sufficient proficiency in the Japanese language to be able to engage in business in the language (Ideally, this includes not only speaking Japanese but also reading and writing Japanese.)

2. Verifying Proficiency in Japanese Language & Culture

As GGD, Inc. experienced with its international sales director, even when a potential employee claims to be fluent in the Japanese language, it is imperative that the company confirms the level of fluency to determine if the prospective executive can in fact conduct business in Japanese.

It is not uncommon in America for individuals to state they are "fluent" or can "speak" a foreign language if they are able to exchange social pleasantries or carry on elementary social conversation. Unlike in Europe where it is common for people to grow up speaking three or four languages, most Americans do not speak foreign languages. When an individual becomes socially conversant in a foreign language, they are often considered to be able to speak it. In the case of GGD, Inc., their director of international sales claimed to be fluent in Japanese but could not do much more than, as he put it, order beer and sushi in Japanese.

In addition, given the high degree of difficulty in mastering the Japanese language, it is common in the States for claims about being fluent in Japanese to mean only the ability to speak the language to some degree. It is rare to find Americans who can not only speak Japanese fluently but also read and write it to the extent necessary to conduct business in that language. Obviously, the greater the degree an executive can function in terms of all three areas of language ability, the more effective and impactful they will be in overseeing, managing, and growing a company's success in the Japanese market.

While verifying the Japanese language ability of a prospective executive is critically important, American companies typically do not have a fluent Japanese language speaker already in their employ who can assist with this verification. As a result, the prospective executive's claim about language fluency is often not verified. This can have a disastrous effect. A company is gravely selling itself short by omitting this verification as we have seen with GGD. So how, then, can a company verify language ability? The following are a few options I developed for dealing with this:

- Find a native Japanese student studying at a nearby university who speaks English and pay him for an hour of his or her time to converse with the prospective executive in Japanese. Give him a written script or list of points in English that he is to discuss with the American executive. In addition to conversing in Japanese, have the American executive translate into English the points as they are discussed in Japanese. The student can then confirm to you the accuracy of the American's Japanese. To check the prospective executive's Japanese reading skills, the student can bring to this interview a Japanese language document or article for the executive to read and then briefly discuss.

- Request assistance through a local university from a Japanese language instructor or teaching assistant who is bilingual in Japanese and English in return for a small fee. The instructor or TA could follow the same protocol described in option one.

- Hire a professional translation company that handles Japanese. They can conduct a discussion in Japanese with your prospective executive and evaluate his or her level of proficiency. This can even be done via Skype for the cost of an hour of translating.

II. PNQ, INC.

A. PNQ, INC.'S EXPERIENCE

PNQ, Inc. is the leading manufacturer of topical skin care products sold in the medical channel in the United States. Designed and developed in California, the company has dominated this product category for the past thirty plus years, often enjoying sales levels twice that of their main competitor. Their brand is likewise recognized as a leader in its product category throughout the world. They retained me as their consultant to assist with developing and managing their business in Japan, Korea, China, and Taiwan.

The physician who designed the product line is a very high

profile individual. He is considered the pioneer of modern day skin care—the concept, the products, and the protocols. He is charismatic and has been a frequently invited speaker at major dermatology and plastic surgery conferences around the world for decades.

Given the prestige and popularity of PNQ's products and their inventor, both had been in very high demand in markets all around the globe. Heightened popularity and demand such as PNQ was experiencing usually become the drivers for exceptional sales and market domination, and are, therefore, every manufacturer's dream come true. This was the case for PNQ in every other country where they were in the market. However, this situation created a nightmare in the Japanese market.

PNQ's first involvement in Japan occurred when it was approached by a mid-tier Japanese pharmaceutical company about setting up a joint venture in Japan to import and sell PNQ's world famous products there. As a pharmaceutical company, the Suzuki Corporation had all the requisite licenses and qualifications to import and sell PNQ's products, which needed to be sold by physicians in hospitals and clinics by prescription rather than in regular retail sales channels because the product contained ingredients categorized as drugs.

Having a fifty-year history, Suzuki presented to PNQ's management that it was well experienced in selling topical skin care products in Japan's medical channel. Suzuki proposed that the two corporations establish a joint venture in Japan. After each company invested $47 million in this joint venture, Suzuki then looked into getting regulatory approval from the Japanese government to import and sell PNQ product. It quickly became clear that a main PNQ ingredient was not approved for importation and sale in Japan.

If the ingredient had been a secondary ingredient, such

as a preservative, it would not have been a great concern. PNQ could easily have replaced it with a substitute ingredient that was approved. As it turned out, however, the problematic ingredient was the main active ingredient in PNQ's product line and it could not be easily replaced. Replacing it would have resulted in a different product, one that was untested, had no clinical track record, and no recognition. Needless to say, learning that the product line's main active ingredient was not approved in Japan was an utter disaster for both PNQ and the Suzuki Corporation and their combined $94 million investment.

If news of this disastrous outcome had leaked to the press or otherwise had become public knowledge, Suzuki would have suffered a tremendous embarrassment or "loss of face" (*kao o tsubusu* 顔をつぶす). It moved quickly to do something to avoid that situation while also recovering its $47 million investment.

By that point, Suzuki had received from PNQ all of the details of the formulations for PNQ's products. Within a few weeks of discovering that the main ingredient was not approved in Japan, Suzuki executives shocked PNQ by telling them that Suzuki had already developed a non-prescription, over-the-counter version of PNQ's product line, and it was ready to produce the line in Japan. As it contained no drug ingredients, it was easily approved as a cosmetic product for sale in Japan and could be sold in retail sales channels. Suzuki informed PNQ that in return for the rights to produce and sell this new retail channel PNQ brand product in Japan, Suzuki would pay PNQ a small percentage of the product sales as a royalty.

PNQ had neither been aware of nor ever given Suzuki any permission to develop an alternative, non-medical product line based on PNQ's products. Nor did PNQ grant Suzuki the right to use the PNQ brand in Japan for any other product line other than PNQ's original medical channel products. In short, Suzuki developed, produced, and was ready to launch product sales for this alternative, over-the-counter product line entirely on its own without PNQ's prior knowledge or authorization.

Normally it takes months, if not years, to develop a whole new skin care product line. Given the fact that the Suzuki Corporation had their alternative product line ready within just a few weeks of learning that PNQ's product would not receive government approval, it was obvious that Suzuki had not started to develop their product line *after* it became clear that PNQ's product was without government approval—rather they had been developing it in secret all along while working to set up the joint venture.

As if this situation was not problematic enough, there were several other detrimental circumstances that had developed around PNQ's products and brand name in Japan.

Given the high regard and great demand for PNQ's product throughout Asia, both patients and physicians in Japan were eager to obtain and use the products years before PNQ decided to enter the Japanese market. Aware of this untapped business opportunity, companies in Asia began to sell PNQ products in Japan. The problem was that those sales were not made by PNQ or authorized by PNQ. Millions of dollars of PNQ product was being sold in Japan, just not by PNQ. There were two major sources of unauthorized PNQ products entering Japan.

The first was a large-scale dermatology clinic in Florida that was purchasing great quantities of the product from PNQ in America. The clinic was not authorized to sell products in Japan. In fact, its agreement with PNQ clearly stated that it would only purchase product for treating patients in its clinic—sales outside of the United States were strictly prohibited. In addition, as several of the products are categorized as drugs in America, it was illegal for the clinic to export them as they were not licensed to do so.

The second source of unauthorized PNQ product sales to Japan was PNQ's exclusive distributor in another Asian country— the TI Company. According to the terms of its sales agreement with PNQ, the TI Company did not have the right to sell PNQ products outside of its own country. So sales from that Asian country to Japan were unauthorized and taking place without PNQ's knowledge.

The TI Company was selling millions of dollars worth of product to Japan through black market activity. Making matters worse, the PNQ products that the TI Company was exporting to Japan were actually knockoffs. They did not contain the superior ingredients that the bona fide products did—the ingredients that enabled the product line's exceptional clinical results. Instead they were made with inexpensive filler ingredients. However, because the labeling and packaging were identical to the product made by PNQ, these knock off products were indistinguishable from PNQ's authentic products. The result: Both physicians and con-sumers in Japan became highly disappointed with the lack of results when using PNQ product, not realizing that they were using imi-tation products. Needless to say, this dealt a severe blow to PNQ's brand name in Japan *even before PNQ had entered that market.*

PNQ's challenges did not end there. Japanese traveling abroad to countries where PNQ product was legally sold were hand carrying back to Japan suitcases full of PNQ product not only for personal use but also to sell to others. These products were being sold by individuals who had no training in the products' cor-rect usage protocols. The result was numerous cases of users who experienced disappointing results, skin irritation, and even damage to their skin from improper product usage.

In addition, numerous physicians in Japan fraudulently

claimed to have been personally trained by the American physician who formulated the PNQ product line and founded the PNQ company. Those doctors claimed they were qualified to train other physicians as well as consumers on how to use the product correctly. Given the very high profile nature of PNQ's brand, these doctors could charge attendees thousands of dollars for each training. There turned out to be dozens of physicians throughout Japan conducting these bogus training programs every month.

With all of this activity, PNQ product was a big business in Japan even before PNQ entered the market. The problem for PNQ, of course, was that it was all unauthorized, illegal activity that was hurting PNQ's brand name and corporate reputation.

To recap, PNQ's product and brand name faced several major travails in Japan well before the company started business in that market. Those included the following eight circumstances:

- The Suzuki Corporation, a pharmaceutical company with whom PNQ created a $94 million joint venture, was unable to obtain Japanese government approval to import and sell PNQ products in Japan. In response and without PNQ's prior authorization, Suzuki developed an over-the-counter equivalent of PNQ's medical skin care product line to sell in traditional retail channels with PNQ to receive a royalty payment. Suzuki presented this to PNQ as a *fait accompli.*

- PNQ products were being illegally shipped to Japan from the U.S. without PNQ's knowledge or permission.

- Huge quantities of counterfeit PNQ product were being sold into Japan from PNQ's exclusive distributor in another Asian country.

- Great numbers of Japanese tourists hand-carried suitcases full of PNQ product back to Japan on a regular basis to sell to other users.

- Dozens of physicians in Japan were claiming they had been personally trained in PNQ product usage by PNQ's founder. They were travelling all over Japan offering seminars on PNQ product usage protocols when in fact they had received no such training at all. As a result, an incredible amount of inaccurate and contradictory information about product usage was being disseminated to both physicians and users throughout the country.

- There were numerous cases of poor or even harmful results from using PNQ products because the product was either an imitation or the user was never taught how to use these prescription medical skin care products correctly or safely.

- Japanese Custom's agents were intercepting huge volumes of PNQ product at airports and ports all over Japan, none of which had received approval from the Japanese government to be imported or sold in Japan.

- News of these developments became such a concern to government authorities in Japan that the Ministry of Health, Labor and Welfare (Japan's Food and Drug Administration) was getting ready to place PNQ product on its black list of products that were officially banned from importation and sale in Japan. If that happened, PNQ would lose the opportunity to sell its products in the world's largest skin care market.

Put all together, these different developments resulted

in incredible confusion in Japan regarding PNQ's product. In particular:

- Were the PNQ products being bought and used by doctors and customers in Japan authentic PNQ products?

- Who was the authorized sales agent for PNQ in Japan?

- Was the physician training occurring throughout the country for PNQ product usage bona fide training?

- Were correct PNQ product usage protocols being used?

- What clinical results could a consumer expect?

- Would PNQ products be banned from importation and sale in Japan by the Ministry of Health, Labor and Welfare because of these concerns?

In short, PNQ faced quite a challenging situation in the Japanese market.

It was at that juncture that PNQ retained me as their consultant. I was charged with resolving these issues and spearheading PNQ's official launch in the Japanese medical market. I gave highest priority to putting in place the most appropriate exclusive distributor in Japan for PNQ while simultaneously putting an end to the unauthorized and illegal activities related to PNQ's product in Japan discussed above.

For major business projects, it can typically take twelve to eighteen months for an American company to identify, approach, negotiate with, and build enough of a relationship with a Japanese firm to execute an exclusive sales agreement. Within the first three months of the project, I identified an effective partner for PNQ in Japan; secured their interest in partnering with PNQ to import and sell the product in Japan's medical channel; and successfully negotiated and concluded an exclusive sales agreement between PNQ and that distributor. This distributor, Hayashi, Inc., was a highly regarded company in Japan.

Next, I wanted to find the most effective and timely solution for eliminating the confusion in Japan regarding PNQ's product among physicians, patients, the public, customers, customs officials, and the Ministry of Health, Labor and Welfare. To that end, I formulated and spearheaded the implementation of the following measures.

First, I devised a strategy for Hayashi, Inc. to engage in a comprehensive print ad campaign in major industry journals as well as appropriate social newspapers and magazines (as this was before the advent of social media) announcing the following:

- Hayashi, Inc. has been selected by PNQ to be their official and exclusive distributor in Japan's medical market.

- Hayashi, Inc. is the only company in Japan that is authorized to import and sell PNQ's medical product there. Accordingly, all PNQ products must be purchased from Hayashi. Only PNQ product sold by Hayashi, Inc. in Japan is bona fide PNQ product.

- Hayashi, Inc. is the only entity in Japan authorized by PNQ to provide training to physicians on product usage as well as information on correct usage for customers.

I simultaneously had Hayashi meet with senior members of

Japan's Customs Authority as well as the Ministry of Health, Labor and Welfare to discuss the following issues:

- Hayashi, Inc., as PNQ's exclusive distributor, would take responsibility for putting an end to the confusion, incidents of product users suffering harmful side effects from inappropriate product usage, and unauthorized and illegal activities regarding PNQ's product in Japan.

- Hayashi, Inc. would provide proper product usage training to physicians and usage protocols for customers for PNQ product.

- Hayashi, Inc. would assure that PNQ product arriving in Japan was safe and authentic PNQ product shipped from PNQ in America.

- Hayashi, Inc. asked government authorities to provide Hayashi with complete information on all other shippers of PNQ products going through Customs throughout Japan to aid efforts to identify the sources of and to eradicate unauthorized PNQ product shipments to Japan.

With the above measures in place, from that point on, genuine PNQ product would be safe to import and use in Japan. Based on that, we argued that there was no longer any need for the Ministry of Health, Labor and Welfare to consider banning PNQ products from Japan. Satisfied with the comprehensive and swift actions we were taking, the Ministry, fortunately, agreed to not to ban PNQ product.

To ensure that PNQ product could only be purchased and used by physicians who had been duly trained by Hayashi, Inc., I set up a training system that required any physician interested in handling PNQ products to complete one of Hayashi's official PNQ product training workshops. Upon finishing these day-long seminars, physicians would receive an official PNQ training completion certificate. To prevent doctors who had not received this official training from ordering product on the phone posing as a doctor who had completed the training, I had each graduation certificate numbered and required Hayashi, Inc. to record the doctor's name together with his/her certificate number. Any doctor calling Hayashi to order PNQ product had to give both their name and correct certificate number.

To help customers interested in finding physicians who were trained and qualified to use PNQ product and who sold bona fide PNQ product, I had Hayashi, Inc. periodically place full page ads in appropriate newspapers and magazines listing all of the names and contact information of doctors who had been properly trained in PNQ products. Newspapers and magazines were the main source of information as the Internet was still not widely used in Japan at that time.

Fortunately, these measures worked and very quickly curtailed the sale and usage of unauthorized product in Japan. It also eliminated the bogus training seminars by physicians who had falsely claimed that they were trained by PNQ's founder.

There was one more major hurdle that PNQ needed to clear before it could commence product sales in Japan's medical channel. It still did not have approval from the Japanese government for its product to be imported and sold there.

When I started working on selecting an appropriate partner for PNQ, one of the criteria I used in evaluating potential distributors was their likelihood to obtain government approval.

I also made the exclusive agreement between PNQ and them contingent upon that company's ability to obtain that approval within six months of signing the sales agreement. Their inability to obtain approval would provide PNQ with the option to terminate the agreement.

It is common for companies to apply for government approval for product importation and sales with the Ministry of Health, Labor and Welfare (MHLW) main office in Tokyo or secondarily in Osaka. Those are the two key MHLW offices in Japan. This is what Suzuki had done and the Tokyo office rejected its approval application. While Hayashi, Inc. maintained its national sales headquarters in Tokyo, its corporate headquarters and factories were located in the outer lying prefecture of Yamagata. It had been the main employer and primary driver of that area's local economy for decades. As a result, it was highly regarded in and a centerpiece of that community.

The Ministry of Health, Labor and Welfare also had an office in Yamagata prefecture, and Hayashi, Inc.'s importance to the area's economic and social life was not lost on the government officials in that office. In the meanwhile, our research into PNQ's active ingredient revealed that while it was not approved for usage in Japan, it was not on the list of banned ingredients either. In other words, it was a gray area. Hayashi, Inc.'s president decided to leverage these two circumstances to appeal to the local Yamagata office of the MHLW for product approval.

Typically, when a product is approved by the MHLW, it is accountable for any problems that arise from the use of that product, not the companies that manufacture or sell the product. The Ministry being responsible for product problems is in part why the government keeps the bar for regulatory approval so very high in Japan—and why obtaining government approval can be such a daunting task in the Japanese market. This is true for both domestic and foreign companies.

Given these circumstances, the president of Hayashi, Inc. took an unorthodox approach in applying for approval for PNQ product. He explained to the MHLW officials in the Yamagata branch office that if the Ministry approved PNQ's active ingredient and products, his company would take responsibility itself for any problems that might arise from using the product. In other words, the Ministry would be off the hook. He further stated that his company would regard MHLW's approval as a special favor to Hayashi, Inc. that it would not forget when deciding how to deal with future downturns in the area's economy.

The Ministry granted approval for PNQ's active ingredient stating that it did so based on the status of Hayashi, Inc. in the community and the company's long-standing contributions to the welfare of the local community. So while the Ministry of Health, Labor and Welfare's main office in Tokyo had previously denied the Suzuki Corporation's product approval application, a local prefectural office of the Ministry granted approval to Hayashi, Inc.'s request.

The MHLW did not decide favorably so it would be off the hook and not be responsible for any product mishaps. It could have simply denied approval again as the Tokyo office had and obtained that same result. What tipped the scales in Hayashi's favor so that the Ministry decided to approve the application highlights the fundamental Japanese notion that a company has a responsibility not only to its shareholders and executives but also to the well-being of its community and society at large. Hayashi, Inc. succeeded in leveraging this obligation to its community's well-being to obtain regulatory approval from its local MHLW office. This Japanese notion that a company has a responsibility to its community and to society is discussed in detail in chapters two and five of this book.

Everything was now in place for PNQ to commence their business in Japan's medical channel. The project unfolded very well. Everything went smoothly for the initial nine months. At that point, PNQ , for reasons unrelated to Japan, put in place a new director of international sales named Ronald Dempsey. PNQ's business results as well as its trajectory for future success nosedived.

In terms of doing business in Japan, Ronald Dempsey was the proverbial bull in a china shop. He very quickly alienated Hayashi, Inc.'s executives as well as the rank and file staff involved in PNQ's business. In addition, he alienated the key spokesperson physicians who had been so successful in endorsing and promoting the product.

PNQ's executives were very surprised to learn of this. Especially since Dempsey had over a decade of experience in doing business in Japan. The problem was that Dempsey's understanding of the medical market was weak and outdated. His previous experience, more than twenty years ago, was as a supplier in the U.S. selling American products to Japanese companies. He was familiar with handling sales to them from America, but he had little understanding of what happened to the product after it was imported into Japan—that is, how the product was actually marketed, distributed, and sold.

Dempsey's previous ten years of experience in Japan gave him great confidence to conduct business in Japan. While one would normally consider that to be a plus, Dempsey was close-minded regarding the way he thought his company should do business with the Japanese. His confidence prevented him from being open-minded enough to understand that the dynamics of engaging in business in Japan are fundamentally different than what he was used to. Instead of being an advantage, Dempsey's previous experience and overconfidence were detrimental to the successful development of PNQ's business in the Japanese market.

B. LESSONS FROM PNQ, INC.'S EXPERIENCE

1. Regulatory Status

Ascertaining the regulatory requirements for a product should be one of the first steps a company takes in preparing to engage in business in Japan or any international market.

The regulatory status of a product will determine which of the following conditions apply for each of the company's products:

- The product is allowed to be sold in Japan as currently manufactured.

- The product requires alteration to meet regulatory requirements.

Once the regulatory status of a company's products is determined, management can then make an informed decision about how best to proceed. If a product needs to be altered, the company will need to consider whether the needed changes for regulatory compliance will make the product prohibitively expensive or, as in PNQ's situation, if the changes would prevent the product from delivering its intended function or benefit.

2. Partner Due Diligence

It is important to thoroughly investigate the reputation of a company before considering partnering with them in any international market. The executives of PNQ, Inc. were shocked to discover that the Suzuki Corporation, a world famous

Japanese pharmaceutical company, had been working to formulate a non-medical, knock off product line behind PNQ's back. In Japan, however, it was common knowledge that Suzuki had a long-standing reputation for being a disreputable company that often did not honor its business agreements, especially with foreign companies. Had PNQ engaged in proper due diligence prior to working with Suzuki, PNQ could have avoided the wasted time, expended effort, and the loss of the $47 million co-investment in their joint venture.

3. The Right Person for Japan

Selecting the right person to lead your business dealings in Japan has a tremendous impact on a company's bottom line. The right people to work in the Japanese market are those who are aware of cultural differences, can respect cultural differences, and are comfortable working with cultural differences. The right person will recognize that their way of doing things is not the only way to do things, and they will be flexible in finding ways to work with, and not alienate, Japanese partners. As business in Japan is relationship driven, the right person will be able to successfully develop and manage your company's relationship with its Japanese partner.

> Ascertaining the regulatory requirements for a product should be one of the first steps a company takes.

III. THE OTF COMPANY

A. THE OTF COMPANY'S EXPERIENCE

The OTF Company is one of the top three multi-level marketing companies in America. It was generating tremendous growth in sales and was on track to reach one billion dollars in sales in its tenth year of doing business when I worked with them in Japan, Korea, and other Asian markets.

International expansion was playing a major role in achieving that success and Japan was the prize international market for the company. The reason for Japan's strategic significance was that it was the world's largest multi-level market at that time, accounting for fifty-six percent of the global multi-level marketing industry's total sales.

I consulted with the company as it prepared to launch in Japan. The company's sales estimate for their first year in Japan was $25 million. They had rented and prepared a corporate headquarters as well as a major warehouse and distribution center in Tokyo for their nationwide business based on that level of expected sales. Upon investigating the company's first year sales potential, however, I calculated that it would be closer to $100 million, not $25 million as OTF executives had forecasted.

In the first year of business, OTF's actual sales topped $125 million in Japan. As the company had prepared its infrastructure in the country for sales of one-fifth that amount ($25 million), preparations proved to be woefully inadequate. The company was overwhelmed by the scale and pace of sales activities from day one.

Distributors calling the company to place orders or for customer support had to wait on hold for two or three hours before getting through. Product, instead of being shipped within twenty-four hours of being paid for by distributors as originally planned, took four or five days to ship. The size of the company's warehouse and inventory in Japan were insufficient and, consequently, core products were regularly out of stock.

As a result of these developments, the most successful

network marketing distributors in Japan who had spent two to three years preparing for OTF's Japan launch concluded that OTF was not a professional company and did not understand how to engage in business in their country. Most of these leaders of Japan's network marketing industry left OTF within the first six weeks of the company's opening, never to return.

Another development that caught OTF by surprise involved multiple distributor registrations. An individual signing up to become a distributor in one group and then subsequently registering to simultaneously become a distributor in another distributor group is one of the greatest headaches for multi-level marketing companies anywhere in the world. That type of multiple registration wreaks havoc on the stability and growth of the distributor groups and the company.

With nine years of business experience behind them by the time the company opened for business in Japan, OTF was accustomed to dealing with multiple registrations. However, the company never anticipated—and consequently was not prepared to deal with—the scale on which this occurred in the Japanese market. In the States and other countries, a distributor might change distributor groups once during their years of involvement with the business. In Japan, such change was rampant with distributors changing groups numerous times and in short order. Why did this unique situation occur in Japan? The answer lies in the greater significance of relationships in Japan's culture.

An individual (distributor A) signs up to become a distributor by being sponsored by an existing distributor (distributor B). When A would subsequently be approached by another existing distributor (distributor C) with whom A had a closer relationship, A would sign up in distributor C's group. This could continue with distributor D, E, and so on. The relationship would obligate distributor A to feel he or she had to work with the distributor with whom they had the closer relationship. The way in which parties are *relationally obligated* to work together is discussed in chapter one of this book.

The power and influence of relationships in Japan is the reason that multi-level marking has always done well there and why Japan has long dominated the global network marketing industry. However, because OTF was not aware of this Japanese cultural trait, instead of it having solely a positive impact, this trait also became a negative factor in the development of the company's business in Japan.

B. Lessons from the OTF Company's Experience

1. Appropriate Launch Preparations

It is imperative that foreign companies have as accurate an understanding as possible of the potential of their business in Japan so they can prepare sufficiently. In OTF's experience, ill preparation caused it to lose the best potential distributors in Japan as well as great numbers of other potential distributors who were put off by the company's shortcomings. Strategically, that unfortunate development hurt OTF's business in two ways:

- **Diminished growth:** Their business could not grow as fast or as large as it would have with the greater number of distributors, including the leaders of Japan's network marketing industry, participating in it.

- **Aided their competition:** As a result of losing interest in OTF, the best distributors in the country went to work with OTF's competitors instead. In addition, OTF's shortcomings hurt its reputation in Japan, as it was deemed to be unprofessional. These further curtailed OTF's business success.

Even though OTF rectified the shortcomings of its preparations within six months of opening in Japan, the leaders of Japan's network marketing industry never returned to give it another try. Japan can be a very unforgiving market, so it is important for foreign companies to do it right the first time.

2. Importance of Relationships

The importance of relationships in Japanese society and business is one of the central themes of this book. Their importance impacts just about every facet of business in that country. In OTF's experience, not understanding the significance of relationships caused major disruption in the stability and growth of their distributor groups when relationships would obligate a distributor to feel he or she had to work with the distributor with whom they had the closer relationship, resulting in repeating multiple registrations. This is yet another example of how different cultural values directly impact the level of success of foreign companies in the Japanese market.

> Japan can be a very unforgiving market, so it is important for foreign companies to do it right the first time.

3. Preparing for & Leveraging Cultural Drivers

If foreign companies take the time to understand and prepare for the relevant cultural traits that drive business in foreign markets, instead of those traits hindering their performance, foreign executives can leverage them to actually advance their business interests. This is a clear example of why it is imperative for foreign executives to fully prepare for Japan's culture-based differences in business practices if they wish to achieve optimal bottom line success in the Japanese market.

IV. THE A.M. CORPORATION

A. THE A.M. CORPORATION'S EXPERIENCE

The A.M. Corporation is a leader in the health and wellness industry. Through its groundbreaking research and products, it pioneered numerous new treatment modalities and products that have benefited millions around the world. When this U.S. company expanded its business abroad, it was very successful in Europe and North America. In Japan, however, it was not able to make significant inroads.

The company's first major product was a chocolate flavored meal replacement bar. Beyond just providing nutrition helpful in keeping up one's energy levels, the patented technologies and ingredients used to produce this bar curbed hunger in the consumer. It was the first product of its kind in the world and sold very well in North America and Europe.

Despite its success in so many other markets, this bar did not sell well in Japan. Unlike many other countries, meal replacement bars were not commonly used in Japan when the A.M. Corporation launched there. Another challenge was that the only chocolate bars in Japan at that time were candy bars. Japanese consumers equated the A.M. Corporation's health bar with chocolate candy bars. They could not accept the product as a health food but only as another chocolate candy bar.

In short, A.M.'s product was too far ahead of the curve in the Japanese market and, as a result, there was no market demand for the product. This is one of those ironic consequences of being the pioneer of a new product or technology—if it is so advanced, there is no demand for it. As the old truism in business says: Timing is everything.

It would take another decade before the notion of meal replacement bars would become accepted in Japanese society and a market for those products developed. At that time, I introduced to the A.M. Corporation a Japanese company that understood the product concept and was strongly committed to selling the product throughout Japan. We successfully negotiated a sales agreement in four months and we were excited to commence sales of the product.

This manufacturer and sales company, NSJ, Inc., put in place a strong marketing plan for achieving its goal of multi million dollar sales in Japan in the first year of sales. It targeted several sales channels, including pharmacies, health food stores, TV shopping, direct marketing, and direct mail. Plus NSJ exhibited the product at all the major, relevant trade shows. It allocated $2 million a month to promote the product and its underlying concept. At that time, the primary sales channel selling meal replacement bars was the pharmacy channel. To optimize the success of products sales in that channel, NSJ entered into a sales agreement with the number one wholesale distributor to the pharmacy industry in Japan. With this arrangement, NSJ had access to over ninety percent of all of the pharmacies in the country. We were ready for significant product sales and market domination.

To jump-start sales of the product and at the same time quickly get word out about the product, NSJ launched product sales through a major TV shopping campaign. As is true in the U.S., TV shopping is a major sales channel in Japan, so their strategy to launch product sales through that channel held great promise. And we were not disappointed.

From the very first installment on TV shopping, the product was well received. It sold over a million dollars a day. Unfortunately, the success was short lived.

As discussed in chapter four, Japan has very high humidity conditions that have a great impact on so many categories of products sold there, including perishable items such as food. Chocolate products in Japan are susceptible to melting. Well aware of this condition, executives at NSJ raised this concern with the A.M. Corporation several times during the negotiating process. Given that their bar was chocolate covered, A.M. had anticipated melting as a potential problem even in America. Accordingly, they formulated the chocolate coating to include the very best anti-melting ingredients available in America and there had been no incidents of product melting in the States. Based on this ten-year track record in America and other countries, A.M. was understandably confident that their bar was melt proof and they assured NSJ executives of this.

> While often necessary, efforts at product localization are not always successful.

Upon commencing product importation and sales in Japan, however, it quickly became apparent that in the conditions of Japan's high humidity, the bar did melt. Not only did the bar melt, sometimes the contents would leak through the bar's foil wrapper. This was a first for both A.M. and NSJ. As a result, sales of the product derailed.

To deal with product melting, executives of NSJ convinced the A.M. Corporation to allow the bar to be manufactured in Japan by the country's leading confectionery maker—the NT Company. Given NT's near one hundred years of experience in successfully producing chocolate products that do not melt in Japan, this seemed to be a sensible solution. NT's bars proved to be melt proof. However, given the requirements of A.M.'s unique proprietary technology used in the bar, NT could not produce the bars with the requisite moisture content. As a result, the bars were too hard to be eaten. Sales of those products ceased and A.M. returned to trying to sell its U.S.-made bar.

B. Lessons from the A.M. Corporation's Experience

1. Market Trends & Timing

Products sell for one of two reasons:

- When the timing of a product's entry or presence in a country is in line with existing market trends, demand for the product exists.

- When the product is so new, different, or advanced that product demand does not yet exist, the manufacturer must be able to create demand for the product. For example, Apple Inc. did this with its iPod and iPhone as did the Sony Corporation earlier with the Walkman.

Foreign companies need to clearly understand the market and product demand for their products in Japan to know in which of these two categories their product falls. Each category requires a different strategy, approach, and allocation of corporate resources for succeeding in the Japanese market.

2. Market Condition Appropriate Products

The A.M. Corporation's experience is an example of the importance, and sometimes difficulty, of ensuring that products are appropriate for the conditions found in Japan, in this case its high humidity challenge. While it is common for products to need to be altered to meet the conditions and requirements for different markets, it is important to remember that in some cases efforts at product localization do not always lead to successful sales. As the founder and CEO of the A.M. Corporation stated: "It's like trying to put a round peg in a square hole."

通訳者

CHAPTER 7

Critical Role Of The Translator
& Cultural Facilitator

Translation is not a matter of words only: it is a matter of making intelligible a whole culture. — **Anthony Burgess, prominent English literary figure of the late twentieth century.**

Gunilla Anderman and Margaret Rogers, *Word, Text, Translation: Liber Amicorum for Peter Newmark* (Clevedon: Multilingual Matters Ltd, 1999), p. 124.

The translator's role in doing business in Japan is a significant but unfortunately often overlooked one. It should be a priority for any company that wants to maximize its success while minimizing its risk in the Japanese market. This chapter will explain the intricacies and importance of this role.

Despite its importance, it is common practice on the part of foreign companies to give little—if any—consideration to the translator's role or significance. I can not tell you how many times the need to prepare a translator for meetings with Japanese companies was not even discussed by or placed on the preparation check list of U.S. companies going to Japan. Foreign companies pay a tremendous price in terms of time, effort, expense, and results and put themselves at a severe strategic and tactical disadvantage vis-à-vis Japanese companies even before they depart their home offices for Japan if they do not have an appropriate translator on their team.

> **Not having their own translator puts foreign executives at a severe strategic and tactical disadvantage.**

American companies frequently assume that someone in the Japanese company they meet with will speak English. After all, English has been the world's international language since it replaced French after World War II. Or if no one in the Japanese company speaks English, then the thinking goes that surely the Japanese company will arrange for a translator with the assumption that it is the responsibility of those who need help conducting business in English to arrange for a translator. Such is the common attitude regarding the translator.

It is important to realize that the potential role and contribution of the translator goes well beyond translating the words in the discussion at business meetings. As this chapter explains, the role of the translator should be central in a foreign company's efforts to succeed in the Japanese market. There are several major reasons for this.

I. LOST IN CULTURAL TRANSLATION: THE NEED FOR CULTURAL FLUENCY & INTERPRETATION

A. IMPACT OF CULTURE

To be effective, a translator must be fluent in both the English and Japanese languages and equally fluent and comfortable with the cultures of both countries. No matter how fluent translators may be in the languages, they will never be able to convey fully and accurately what both sides are attempting to communicate if they do not also understand the cultures of each country.

Why is this cultural understanding so important? Without the cultural understanding, a translator at best can only provide literal translations of what is being said. While literal translations may be "word for word" correct renditions, such translations often do not convey the whole meaning of the message. Worse yet, these literal translations may not deliver the intended message given the communication dynamics of the Japanese language and culture. Literal translations often fail to capture the cultural connotations and nuances—that is, the actual meaning—of what is being said. A translator can only convey the cultural connotations and nuances of the speaker if they (the translator) know the connotations and nuances of both cultures equally well. This point is discussed further in this book's chapter on communication.

Let's look at some examples. The phrase *kentou shimasu* (検討します) is a common response in the Japanese language. It is used by the party that is listening to an idea or proposal (for instance, a Japanese company) in responding to the party that is presenting that idea or proposal (for instance, an American company). This phrase is invariably translated into English as: "That is worth our consideration." In an American cultural context, that is taken as a somewhat positive response.

While that is the correct literal translation of that phrase, what usually does not get translated into English is the actual Japanese cultural meaning, which is "We are not interested." So while that phrase is taken as a favorable response by the foreign company, in reality, the Japanese party is conveying the exact opposite message. When the translator provides the literal translation without the culturally accurate meaning, the result can be a complete failure in communication.

Voltaire, the great French political philosopher of the eighteenth century, lamented the detrimental consequences of literal translations when he wrote:

> *Woe to the makers of literal translations, who by rendering every word weaken the meaning! It is indeed by so doing that we can say the letter kills and the spirit gives life.* — Carol A. Dingle, *Memorable Quotations: Philosophers of Western Civilization* (San Jose: Writers Club Press, 2000), p. 245.

This type of literal translation miscommunication is common between foreign companies and Japanese companies. This is true not only in the realm of business as we are discussing in this book but also in most areas of interaction, including the political relations between the two countries. The greatest example of this failed communication takes place at the highest level of government—between the U.S. president and the Japanese prime minister as is discussed in the chapters on negotiation and communication. To illustrate an important translation point from this account, here is a synopsis.

When the U.S president hosts the Japanese prime minister for meetings at the White House, he and the prime minister discuss many points. At the conclusion of their meetings, both leaders hold a joint press conference. When he speaks, the president lists the topics agreed to by both parties. When the prime minister speaks, always in Japanese, he reiterates the list of topics the president asked Japan to agree to and then says that Japan will *zenshou shimasu* (善処します). This is translated correctly as "I will do my utmost best for that."

The U.S. government is pleased, concluding that Japan has agreed to its agenda, and reports this agreement in media releases.

The Japanese government is also pleased—but for a very different reason. Upon returning to Japan, the prime minister reports to Japan's domestic media that he replied to American demands with *zenshou shimasu*. In the Japanese cultural context it is clear to his audience that his meaning is that Japan does *not* agree. The reason is that while "I will do my utmost best for that" is the correct literal translation, the actual cultural meaning is "I am not interested." The Japanese media celebrates Japan's prime minister having held his ground in the face of U.S. pressure by not agreeing to America's demands.

> Literal translation miscommunication is common between foreign companies and Japanese companies.

While both sides may be pleased with the perceived result of their own communications, it is yet one more case of failed communication between Japan and America and in this case at the highest level of our governments. As George Bernard Shaw stated: "The single biggest problem in communication is the illusion that it has taken place."

B. The Use of Idioms

The American use of idioms also creates translation confusion and miscommunication. If a translator is not fully familiar with both cultures, then it will be impossible to correctly interpret the many idioms that Americans are fond of using.

To share one example, an American client used the phrase "it's raining cats and dogs" in a meeting with Japanese. In the U.S., the phrase would be understood to indicate a situation is very bad. As the translator was unfamiliar with this idiom, she had no other option but to translate it literally. When translated literally, that idiom leaves Japanese listeners either feeling totally perplexed, wondering if the American executive must still be struggling with jetlag, or peering out the window to look at the sky to see what in the world is going on!

C. Saying No Without Using the Word "No"

There are more than two dozen expressions in Japanese to say no, most of which have a literal meaning that has nothing to do with no. This includes the word yes.

Why does the Japanese language have so many expressions for saying no that have different literal meanings unrelated to no? As we pointed out in previous chapters, the answer comes back to understanding the Japanese culture. In their culture, disagreeing directly is considered impolite. Answering in the negative can create discord which is a potential threat to group harmony. It is culturally correct, and indeed expected, that to maintain harmony a speaker will use words other than saying "no" to indirectly express their lack of agreement or interest. This and other cultural impacts on communication in Japan are discussed in chapter three of this book.

D. DIFFERING BUSINESS CONCEPTS

Miscommunication and misunderstanding occur between foreign and Japanese executives not only because of the different cultural meanings of *words* and *phrases* as we have just discussed but as a result of the different cultural meanings of *business concepts and actions* as well. Allow me to share an example.

Early in my career in the course of setting up and managing an American client's business operations in Japan, my client and I developed a very strong working relationship with one Tokyo company in particular. We shall refer to the U.S. company as DE, Inc. and to the Japanese company as the PL Company. The PL Company became very instrumental in our business in the Japan market. It conducted market research, introduced companies we could partner with, took care of obtaining regulatory approval to import and sell the products in Japan, and more. PL had become an invaluable collaborator.

As the business grew, DE, Inc.'s CEO decided to establish a subsidiary in Tokyo. This would provide a strong market presence and direct, real-time access to all companies that DE was collaborating with in Japan. The U.S. CEO wanted to invite the CEO of the PL Company to become the honorary chairman of DE's Tokyo subsidiary. The reason, he explained, was to demonstrate our appreciation for the very strong business relationship between the two companies.

When I met with Mr. Bunno, PL Company's CEO, and extended DE's invitation to him, his whole countenance changed. He become very concerned and he immediately turned down this invitation. I continued the meeting, discussing other topics. About forty-five minutes later, I again extended the invitation to him. He rejected it for a second time.

In Japan, it is customary to decline three times first and then accept an offer after it is presented the third time. This is especially true with important matters. This cultural dynamic is similar to the American custom of saying no thank you to an offer once or twice and then accepting it saying, "Well, since you twisted my arm." Knowing this, I was confident that he would agree to the invitation after I asked a third time. Right before the meeting was to end, I extended DE's offer again for the third time, but Mr. Bunno's reply was the same. He adamantly rejected the invitation and did not subsequently say yes.

I was perplexed by this. Mr. Bunno was aware that the position was totally symbolic and did not require him to get involved in the affairs of the subsidiary in any way. The position was just a token of appreciation of the good will between the two companies. So why was he saying no? After all, he had previously stated on several occasions how much he enjoyed working with DE and how much he admired DE's CEO.

After our meeting finished, we went to have dinner together. Mr. Bunno loosened his tie after a few drinks. That is usually an excellent sign that a Japanese executive is relaxed and ready to talk more freely. Taking this cultural cue, I told Mr. Bunno that I was perplexed by his lack of interest in serving as honorary chairman of DE's Tokyo subsidiary. I reiterated that the position was totally honorary and that he would not be expected to become involved in the company's business affairs in any way. I added once again that the invitation was purely an expression of the good will and strong business relationship between the two companies.

Mr. Bunno looked away in silence for a few moments and then asked me how much DE's CEO wanted. I had no idea what he meant. He repeated, "How much does DE want?" When I still did not understand, Mr. Bunno went on to explain that in Japan asking someone to serve as an honorary executive is merely a polite way to ask that person to be become one of the major investors in that company.

So while in America inviting someone to serve as an honorary executive is a gesture of good will, that very same business concept and action in Japan is a polite way of asking for capital. This is a clear example of how a business concept and action can be interpreted very differently across two cultures.

> A business concept and action can be interpreted very differently across two cultures.

From these examples, it becomes apparent that it takes a translator who has fluency in both the cultures and languages of the two countries to communicate the actual meaning, intentions, and strategic implications of both parties.

II. TRANSLATOR AS TEAM MEMBER

Given the importance of a translator having cultural and language fluency for both countries, how can Americans know if the Japanese national who is translating for them understands the American culture sufficiently to communicate intended messages between both parties? This is an especially critical question since foreign executives usually only meet the Japanese company's designated translator once the meeting begins. Typically the Americans do not have anyone on their team to confirm the accuracy of translation, leaving them in a precarious position and at a tactical disadvantage. This is another reason why American companies need to have their own translator on their team.

If the goal of a business discussion or negotiation is to advance a company's business interests, then they should want everyone representing and speaking for them to be in a position to understand and advance their corporate interests. During meetings, literally who speaks more than the translator?

The fact of the matter is that in a business meeting that lasts two hours, assuming that the American and Japanese companies speak for equal amounts of time—let's say thirty minutes each—the remaining hour is the time the translator is speaking to translate for both parties. From my own experience, I can report that the translator always speaks more than anyone else in a meeting! And on those occasions when a meeting takes place over a meal—such as a working lunch—the translator is kept busy during the whole lunch because he is constantly translating the conversational exchange.

Not only does the translator have the most "talk time" during a meeting but also, whether intended or not, the translator often becomes the face and voice of the foreign executives to their Japanese counterparts.

It is quite common for Japanese executives to look at the translator off to the side when they speak, even though the executives are having the discussion with the foreigners sitting directly across the table. There are two cultural factors that drive this Japanese communication dynamic:

- It is common for Japanese to feel uncomfortable speaking with foreigners so they naturally gravitate toward addressing the Japanese translator when talking and listening to foreigners. This offers them a greater level of comfort.

I cannot recount the all too numerous occasions when,

both in and outside of business situations, I would ask a question in proper Japanese and the Japanese person would look at and reply not to me but to the Japanese person who happened to be with me. This stems from a lack of comfort interacting with non-Japanese, the consequence of being a homogenous society living on an island country isolated from the rest of the world throughout much of its history.

- In formal communication in Japanese culture, it is not polite to maintain continuous eye contact with the other party as we do in America. More information can be found on this in the chapter on communication.

Interestingly enough, it is also common for American executives to look at the translator while addressing the Japanese. However, they do so for the exact opposite cultural reason.

In American culture, it is polite to maintain continuous eye contact with the person with whom you are speaking. So American executives look at the translator as they are speaking and then look at the Japanese while their words are being translated. As a result, it often turns out that when the Americans are talking and looking at the translator, the Japanese are listening and looking at the Americans. Then when the Japanese are talking and looking at the translator, Americans are looking at the Japanese. The result is significantly less eye contact than if both parties were communicating in the same language. Not only is there less direct eye contact as a consequence of this dynamic, there is also a missed opportunity to build a stronger mutual relationship.

If the goal of the meeting is to advance your corporate interests, then it is vital that the translator be a member of your team. For only if he or she is on your team can the translator:

- know what your business interests are.

- be committed to your corporate interests.

- be in a position to actually promote your interests.

As mentioned already, American executives often meet the translator at the time the meeting with the Japanese company begins. In many cases, the translator is not even introduced to the foreign executives. In this circumstance, how much could the translator possibly know about the American company's business goals for this meeting? Likewise, the translator has no commitment to or even interest in the American company's objectives and is not in any position to advance those business objectives. If the translator is an employee of the Japanese company, then he or she will be interested in advancing the business interests of the Japanese company, not the foreign company.

> Foreign companies need a *facilitator*, not just a translator.

Yet the unfortunate reality is that American companies go to meetings with Japanese and almost never have a translator on their team. In contrast, the Japanese always have a translator on their team. The result is that American companies are at a strategic and tactical disadvantage even before they enter the meeting room.

III. FACILITATOR: GOING BEYOND A TRANSLATOR

So far this chapter has concentrated on the importance of proper cultural and linguistic translation skills as the key factors in finding the right translator. Actually, the role of a good translator is broader. Foreign companies need a *facilitator*, not just a translator.

They need someone who not only will provide translations of dialogue but also who will advance your interests by engaging in relationship building with the Japanese company and working toward your strategic goals in meetings.

In most cases, the translator is either an employee of the Japanese company or is hired from an outside translation service. In the latter case, the translator is a third party to the meeting with no prior knowledge of the content of the discussion and no vested interest in the discussion's outcome. Their sole interest is to provide a literal translation of the dialogue. Corporate goals and strategic interests are unknown to these translators, particularly regarding the foreign company, and they could not care less about them.

> The contextual and strategic significance of what is being stated is usually not conveyed.

Further, translators hired from translation agencies often have no experience in the business world. Consequently, having no actual experience with or firsthand knowledge of what is being discussed, translators usually do not understand either the context or the implications of what is being communicated. This typically limits them to providing very narrow translations of the dialogue; they are unable to convey the larger meaning and intention of what is being discussed because they are not familiar with the topics. The result is that the contextual and strategic significance of what is being stated is usually not conveyed to the other party. The true intent of what the parties are trying to communicate gets quite literally "lost in translation" even though the translator may be fluent in both languages. *One cannot fully and accurately convey what one does not fully and accurately understand.*

Utilizing translators who are employees of the Japanese company or of professional translation agencies does not advance the interests of the foreign company. Actually, it is a disadvantage to have them speak for your company. Instead, your company needs its own *facilitator* who will advance your corporate interests. The most desirable facilitator translator is effective in four distinct and critically important areas:

- **Correct linguistic translation:** having thorough comprehension of both languages

- **Accurate and complete cultural interpretation:** providing the actual cultural meaning and implied expectation of what is being communicated as a part of the translation

- **Effective strategy development:** helping ensure that negotiations and discussions advance and secure corporate interests

- **Relationship building:** ensuring that the level of politeness, tone, content, and flow of the discussion are appropriate and will aid in both establishing and strengthening the relationship with the Japanese partner

In order to fulfill this essential role, the facilitator translator must be:

- a member of the foreign company's team—such as an employee or a consultant.

- familiar with the foreign company's business interests.

- committed to achieving the foreign company's corporate objectives.

- able to effectively speak about and promote the foreign company's interests.

- vested in the outcome of the foreign company's discussions.

- fluent both linguistically and culturally in both American and Japanese culture.

- experienced in relationship building in Japan.

In comparing a traditional translator and a facilitator translator, a translator plays a two dimensional role and contributes little to a foreign company's business success. A translator can actually be an obstacle to a foreign company's corporate goals as discussed above. On the other hand, a facilitator plays a three dimensional role and is in a position to make major contributions to advancing a foreign company's business success.

To express the difference between a translator and a facilitator, I use the analogy that a translator is comparable to a tollbooth clerk who collects tolls on a road while the facilitator is comparable to a traffic cop who directs the flow of traffic on that same road.

A tollbooth clerk has no interest in where your car has come from or where it is going. His only concern is to get your car get from one side of the tollbooth to the other. In the same way, translators have no interest in where a foreign company is coming from strategically, or where the foreign company and the discussions are going; they simply want to get the discussions to go from the start of the meeting to its finish. As a result, a translator allows literal translations to pass between companies from one side of the meeting table to the other. He or she is not concerned about how literal translations impact both parties or how they might react. Furthermore, the translator has no vested interest in how well the meeting goes or in the meeting's outcome. And the translator has no interest in relationship building between the two companies.

In contrast, the traffic cop directs the flow of traffic to help you get where you need to go. If you put on your left turn signal, he will stop the oncoming traffic in the opposite direction so you can make that left turn. When you need to make a right turn, the traffic cop will stop pedestrian traffic so you can make that turn. In this way, the traffic cop knows your intentions and helps you move in the direction you want to go. Likewise, the well-prepared facilitator translator will help a foreign company achieve its corporate objectives by appropriately conducting the flow of the discussion, the direction of the meeting, and the relationship building between both companies.

If a foreign company relies on the Japanese company to bring a translator, that translator will act to facilitate the interests of the Japanese company, not the interests of the foreign company. It makes sense then, for a foreign company to have a facilitator translator on their own team.

Another example of the critical role of the facilitator translator can be seen when using the services of an attorney. When preparing, for example, an international sales agreement, joint venture agreement, or patent agreement, would a company ever have that important document prepared only by the attorney of the other company? Of course not. The company would definitely have their own attorney represent their firm. Their attorney would know what their strategic interests are and would be committed to protecting and advancing them. In the same way, a foreign company should want to have their own facilitator translator who is aware of and committed to their strategic interests.

The executive assistant to the president of a Japanese sales company sent me a description of the added value I contributed as a facilitator translator following a discussion she and I had about translating. I share this full letter with you to show the importance of a facilitator-translator from a Japanese viewpoint.

I really appreciate Mr. Azar's participation since he has facilitated our business process by interpreting our conversation in the way which cultural difference between US and Japan would not become an obstacle between us. Without him our business would have to go through a lot more difficulties due to the cultural differences.

I often translate for the president of my company. So one time I discussed translating with Mr. Azar. I was surprised to hear him say that it is quite important for an interpreter to be acquainted with different cultures and take the cultural difference into consideration. Being acquainted with American, Japanese and other Asian cultures, Mr. Azar does not only interpret our conversation but also adds necessary information if needed so that the true message can be conveyed without misunderstanding.

For example, last month my boss handed a gift to one of our business partners at the beginning of our meeting and said in Japanese tsumaranai-mono desuga (つまらないものですが). A literal translation of these words would be "Though this is a worthless thing..."

I can imagine no one would be pleased by receiving something worthless. This is one of the typical Japanese expressions used very often. As modesty is considered a virtue in Japanese society, Japanese people tend to use expressions which may sound too self-deprecating to non-Japanese if the expression is interpreted literally.

A hidden message of this expression is: "Perhaps this gift is not precious or valuable at all for such a well-off and noble person like you, but I chose the most valuable and beautiful thing I could find hoping that you would like it." At that time Mr. Azar interpreted this expression as the following: "In accord with the Japanese custom, we would like to start today's meeting by offering our humble gift as an expression of our gratitude for this opportunity to work together." I was really impressed by his interpretation.

If he had interpreted the expression literally, our business partner would have wondered why my boss had brought something worthless as a gift. Had he explained the hidden message of this expression, it would have been too long and sounded too self-deprecatory to non-Japanese. However, his interpretation was perfect. He interpreted the phrase "a worthless thing" into "our humble gift" to express the modesty of my boss properly, he also added the information that it is a Japanese custom to give a gift to business partners, and at the end he clearly conveyed the true message of my boss even though it was not mentioned (by my boss) at all.

Grammatically speaking, there was no main clause in the phrase "Though this is a worthless thing… " It was only a subordinate clause. I usually cannot interpret such Japanese sentences into English so I would have asked my boss what the main clause was. Actually the missing main clause was "We give you this gift as an expression of our gratitude (though this is a worthless thing)." The most important message of my boss was "as an expression of our gratitude" though he didn't mention it.

Not only my boss but also most Japanese tend to express their intention with only a few words. This is probably because people can understand each other without explaining everything in an almost homogeneous society where we share the same culture. I am often frustrated by this tendency when I try to translate my boss' words into English. In many cases, subjects, verbs or objectives are omitted from his words. So I need to figure out what the missing words are, find an appropriate expression in English to convey the true intention, and incorporate it to the translation. It requires a lot of time for me. Mr. Azar does the same process instantly at our meetings.

Being familiar with both cultures, he has converted a typical Japanese expression into an appropriate English expression, added the information needed, and most importantly, conveyed its true message. He did all these things at the instant of hearing my boss' words. This is why I greatly admire Mr. Azar as an excellent facilitator of our business. Needless to say, our business partner was delighted with the gift my boss brought, and the meeting went well following the wonderful start in a warm atmosphere. This is all due to his exquisite interpretation. — **Kawahara Emiko, Executive Assistant to the President, Shimizu, Inc.**

Given the critically important role of the facilitator translator, it is truly astonishing how little attention foreign companies give to it. By doing so, they unilaterally give up all of the benefits the facilitator brings and place themselves at a strategic and tactical disadvantage relative to the Japanese who invariably have their own translator.

In light of what a facilitator translator can bring to the table, whether a company is expecting hundreds of millions of dollars or just tens of millions of dollars every year from conducting business in the Japan market, it is evident that the cost of a facilitator is well worth the expense.

There are two ways an American company can have a facilitator translator on their team. One is to hire such an individual as an employee and the other is to retain their services as an outside consultant. As always, it is prudent to execute a non-disclosure agreement with any party your company will be sharing confidential and strategic information with. The greater the individual's understanding of your business, its overall business goals, and your Japan-specific strategic objectives, the more effective the facilitator translator can be. The greater the period of time and the degree of involvement in your business, the more effective the facilitator translator is in a position to be.

IV. HOW FLUENT IS FLUENT

Translators who are on the staff of the Japanese company involved in the meeting as well as those who are employed by professional translation agencies are not the only ones who can be an obstacle to the success of American companies in Japan. Non-native Japanese speakers employed by American companies who present themselves as being fluent in Japanese can be an even greater hindrance to success in the Japanese market.

As we know, it is rare to find Americans who speak Japanese with sufficient proficiency to be able to conduct business in Japanese. Often American business men and women claim they are fluent in Japanese—even going so far as to state that on their resumes—when in fact they are only able to carry on basic social conversation.

I have been reading, writing, and speaking Japanese for thirty-five years and still today always say "no, not really" when Japanese say I am fluent in their language. I have been fortunate to develop a level of language proficiency sufficient to conduct business entirely in Japanese, translate for my clients, and appear on major Japanese TV and radio news programs as a U.S.-Japan business and cultural expert speaking in Japanese. Still, I hesitate to claim that I am fluent in the Japanese language. Instead, I am only comfortable to say that I am functional in the language.

We saw in the experience of GGD, Inc. discussed in this book's chapter "Challenges and Foibles" how detrimental the results can be when a foreigner inaccurately claims to be fluent in Japanese. In the case of GGD, John Allen was hired as the director of international sales at least partly because he claimed to be fluent in Japanese, and the company needed help to bring up bottomline revenue from the Japanese operation to meet corporate expectations. However, it became clear that his spoken Japanese was not up to conducting business in Japanese nor could he read or write the language. This lack of facility brought serious consequences to GGD as John Allen's inability to engage in business in Japan in Japanese cost the company millions of dollars in lost sales, time, and added expenses.

Here are two other circumstances in which the matter of "how fluent is fluent" is relevant to succeeding in communicating with Japanese. The first concerns non-native Japanese speakers who actually are fluent in Japanese. Allow me to share a first hand experience I had early on in my career to illustrate this point.

At that time, I worked on Wall Street in the North American headquarters of Japan's second largest brokerage house—Daiwa Securities, Inc.—located in the World Financial Center. Shortly after joining the firm, it was announced that the company's CEO would be visiting from the corporate headquarters in Osaka. As he did not speak English, I was asked to interpret his speech to all 540 employees. I was honored to do so.

The appointed day arrived and I was on the stage with the CEO. When he started to speak, I quickly realized that he was speaking the Osaka dialect of the Japanese language. I froze and turned as red as a tomato. He noticed this but continued speaking in that dialect. The president of the North American headquarters, recognizing what was happening, immediately ran up on stage to the podium and, smiling at me, said: "Don't worry. I'll take care of this." I was mortified. While I speak standard Japanese, which is Tokyo dialect, I am not conversant in Osaka dialect.

UK English and American English are much the same but do have notable differences and in the U.S. there are small colloquial differences across the country. However, the differences between dialects in Japan are much greater. Let's look at a quick example of a difference between standard Japanese (Tokyo dialect) and Osaka dialect for the greeting "How are you?"

- In standard Japanese, the phrase is *ogenki desuka* (お元気ですか) and the literal meaning is "Are you well?"

- In Osaka dialect, the phrase is *mokari makka* (もかりまっか) and the literal meaning is "Are you making money?"

Two entirely different phrases with very different literal meanings have the same cultural meaning within their respective dialects.

While most Japanese speak standard Japanese, local dialects are still used and can be problematic for non-native speakers of Japanese.

A second case regarding "how fluent is fluent" involves native speakers of Japanese. While a translator might be fluent in English and Japanese, there are times when they are not familiar with the specialized terminology that often comes up in business meetings and presentations. They need to be familiar with the specialized terminology in both languages to translate accurately.

The parallel situation that we commonly experience in America is when a doctor discusses a medical condition in medical terms. The patient and their family who are hearing the information for the first time often need to ask the doctor to explain what was said in lay terms. While the specialized terminology is obviously part of their native language, the patient and family are not likely to understand what the medical terms mean without special training.

This potential terminology risk is especially true in the case of translators hired from professional translation agencies. If it is necessary to hire them, American executives need to confirm that both the translation agency and the individual translator(s) that the American company hires are experienced in the company's field of specialization. For presentations, give the translation agency the presentation at least two weeks in advance of the meeting date so they can make sure they know all of the specialized terminology.

Another client experience occurred when I was establishing a business in Japan for an American maker of specialty medical skin care products. We had selected the Japanese company we wanted to partner with and they were engaging in a due diligence review of the product ingredients. The head of their regulatory affairs department, Ms. Tanaka, also happened to be their medical skin care product expert. She had over twenty years of experience and was exceptionally talented at what she did.

One of the product ingredients was ornithine, an amino

acid that produces powerful anti-aging benefits. The problem was that the word ornithine was not in any of the dictionaries Ms. Tanaka consulted—neither standard dictionaries nor scientific ones. The closest word in any of the Japanese dictionaries was ornithology—the study of birds. As a result, Ms. Tanaka's team mistakenly concluded that the ingredient was a derivative of bird dung. You can imagine the surprise my client's president and I had when we received a fax from the president of the Japanese sales company saying they would not be able to obtain Japanese government approval for our products because they contained bird poop!

This experience reinforces the need for American companies to have their own in-house language expert who is in a position to determine the correct translations for specialized terminology and ingredients.

As this chapter makes clear, any American company that is serious about succeeding in the Japanese market must have their own in-house facilitator translator.

成功の鍵

CHAPTER 8

Additional Strategies For

Succeeding In Japan

In the first seven chapters of this book we have covered a great deal of material that will influence the success or failure of a foreign business in the Japanese market.

So far we have

- looked at a multiplicity of specific challenges across a broad range of business practices that culture-based differences present to foreign companies operating in Japan—from communicating to negotiating, management to human resources, product development to sales and marketing and on to distribution and relationship building to conflict resolution.

- identified those challenges in detail, showing how they hinder foreign companies' relationships with Japanese and their bottom line performance in the Japanese market.

- explained the cultural underpinnings of those business challenges.

- provided concrete measures for foreign executives to deal effectively with the obstacles presented by Japan's different business culture. Those methods provide specific means for doing it right in the Japanese market.

These previous chapters dealt more with recognizing the challenges and dealing one by one with specific culture-based differences in individual areas of business—that is, *micro level* challenges and solutions. In this chapter, we will step back and explore *macro level* management approaches and strategies for foreign companies to utilize to optimize their success in the Japanese market.

I. THE RIGHT PRODUCTS

Foreign businesses often adopt a cookie-cutter approach

regarding which products to sell when expanding into one foreign market after another. However, that one-size-fits-all approach is not appropriate for every international market a company enters. It is common for foreign executives to think that their current best-selling product will be a best seller in the Japanese market. While this is often true, it is not *always* true. In my experience, numerous times a client's best-selling product in America or Europe did not achieve that status in Japan—indeed, sometimes that product hardly sold at all.

So, which products should a company chose to enter into the Japanese market for best sales results? This is a critical decision that needs to be carefully considered by foreign executives as they formulate both their market entry and long-term business strategies for Japan. There are several market conditions and cultural factors that should go into determining which products to sell in Japan. These include the following eight specific factors:

A. Regulatory Considerations

The time and the cost for applying for regulatory approval from Japan's government to import and sell foreign products varies from industry to industry. The time to clarify the regulatory circumstances of products and decide on a regulatory strategy is at the outset of the process of entering into the Japanese market. A well-qualified partner in Japan or an industry consultant will be able to assist a foreign company to best navigate Japan's regulatory environment. Failure to effectively manage Japan's regulatory issues up front can cost foreign companies millions of dollars and create serious delays as we saw earlier. Regulatory considerations should be among the first items foreign executives take care of—this point cannot be emphasized enough.

An additional concern here is that regulatory approval may

require product redesign, reformulation, or reconstitution. Such changes may have a negative impact on the product's effectiveness or even result in a completely different product that may or may not meet market expectations.

There are instances where a best-selling foreign product might require considerably more time and cost to earn approval than a company's less popular product. Executives need to weigh whether it makes sense to start with those secondary products while the company's best-selling products are still undergoing government approval for sale in the future.

B. Market Demand for Multiple Product Categories

When foreign manufacturers have more than one product category, demand for their best-selling product category may not necessarily be as strong in Japan as in other markets. There are occasions where one of a company's secondary product categories experiences greater demand in Japan than its primary product category. In that case, foreign executives need to decide whether or not it would make sense to make their secondary category products the main products for Japan.

C. Selecting Products From Within the Best-Selling Category

It is common for foreign companies to research the competitive standing of their best-selling products in Japan to understand how those products might fare in that market. However, rather than taking it for granted that those leading products in its best-selling category will be the company's best performers in Japan, the company should also analyze their other products in that same best-selling product category to see how they would fare.

It could turn out that a lower or even much lower ranking product in the States is a more appealing product in Japan than that best-seller from the American market. The Adams Corporation case study reflected this experience when selling their dermatological lasers in Japan as we saw in chapter four.

D. STRENGTHS OF YOUR JAPAN PARTNER

Potential Japanese business partners will have their own different strengths and weaknesses. A foreign company will need to analyze both when assessing potential Japanese partner companies. Japanese companies are often better suited to sell certain products of the foreign company's product line than others. As a result, partner selection can impact which products a foreign company focuses on in the Japanese market. There are occasions where those products are not the ones foreign executives originally planned to focus on to enter Japan.

E. INFLUENCE OF SALES CHANNELS

Like most major markets, Japan has numerous sales channels. The major sales channels in Japan include:

- Traditional retail channel—retail stores

- Discount sales channel

- Medical channel

- Pharmacy channel

- Direct marketing sales channel—advertisements with toll free telephone numbers in newspapers and magazines, inserts, pamphlets, etc.

- Internet sales

- Television shopping

- Network marketing

Product sales volumes vary depending on the sales channels where they are sold. Products may end up needing to be sold in one channel as opposed to another as a result of the foreign company's preference, regulatory guidelines, market requirements, pricing, or the experience of your Japanese partner and that will greatly influence product selection strategy as well as sales channel strategy.

In the event a foreign company's products can be sold in more than one sales channel, foreign executives may not want to automatically select the channel likely to result in the greatest sales volume at the outset. Succeeding in certain sales channels with lower sales volume potential can yield greater total sales volume in the long term by establishing a foreign company's corporate identity, brand image, and market leadership in the Japanese market. Once established, these strengths are easily transferred to other sales channels with greater sales volumes than otherwise would have been possible.

For example, if products can be sold in both the medical and retail channels, it is usually better to commence sales in Japan in the medical channel even though it initially seems to have smaller sales potential. Success in the medical channel establishes a high level of credibility for a company, its brand, and its product, which cannot be attained in retail channels. Once branding and credibility are attained in the medical channel, that credibility and market leadership can be transferred to other sales channels, typically resulting in even greater sales volume than would have been seen entering those non-medical sales channels first. With appropriate products, this approach strengthens a foreign company's market share over the long term.

Conversely, products that succeed in the retail channel first and then are launched in the medical channel generally do not do as well in either channel. The primary reason for this is that physicians are skeptical of the clinical efficacy of products that become famous as retail products. Products categorized as medical products require a manufacturer to provide proof of a significantly greater level of clinical results than is necessary for retail channel products. A medical industry manufacturer will, of course, produce and lead with medical grade products. In Japan, manufacturers that lead with retail channel products tend to be retail industry companies, not medical industry manufacturers. Therefore, physicians and the public do not view as favorably the clinical efficacy of products made by retail product makers.

F. CONSUMER PREFERENCES

In addition to regulatory requirements, foreign products often need to be modified to meet consumer preferences in the Japanese market. This area was discussed earlier, but here is a recap of three major product preferences.

- **Product size:** Japanese prefer products that are sized smaller than for most other countries. There are two major reasons for this:

  o Japanese are well known for their penchant for miniaturization—think of their centuries' old tradition of creating sculpted dwarf bonsai trees or how they revolutionized electronics, IT, and so many other industries by miniaturizing vacuum tubes into transistors, allowing small size TV's, radios, computers, and so many other products.

o Another reason for their preference for small-scaled products is the practical consideration that Japan is significantly space constrained. A very mountainous area smaller than the state of California is home to Japan's population of 127 million people—a population equal to about forty percent of America's population.

Many foreign products such as cars, furniture, and refrigerators are simply too big for Japan. In addition, cultural differences and preferences once again come into play. For example, Japanese prefer to buy their family's food fresh everyday so they buy in very small quantities and have no need for large American refrigerators.

- **Product features:** Consumer demands and expectations for a product's performance will dictate what features a product must have, from steering wheel placement to chocolate that does not melt in Japan's humidity. Product features must meet Japanese market needs.

- **Fragrance:** Unlike consumers in the West who enjoy fragranced products, Japanese prefer fragrance neutral (fragrance free) products.

G. SHARPSHOOTER APPROACH

In the event a foreign company has a large product line, it is advisable to enter the Japanese market with a select few products initially, rather than the entire product line at once, and then add more products over time. Taking this sharpshooter rather than shotgun approach in determining which products to start sales with in Japan allows foreign executives and their Japanese partners to focus on, monitor, manage, and maximize their product sales with greater effectiveness.

This sharpshooter product selection approach generally yields yet another important benefit. Launching in the Japanese market with fewer rather than a greater number of product SKUs and then adding products as the first products become established typically results in greater success in establishing a foreign company's corporate image and brand in Japan over the long term.

H. Cultural Translatability

In order to succeed in an international market, the names of a foreign company and its products need to translate well culturally in that foreign market. The experience of the company Best Buy in China is perhaps the best illustration of this problem in intercultural sales.

The company name "Best Buy" in Chinese is *bai si mai* (百思买). Meaning "to buy after thinking 100 times," this name tells potential customers that they must work very hard to decide what to buy in that store—not the most inviting name to draw in customers to shop.

Checking the cultural translatability of the name of a company and its products is not enough, however. Foreign companies must also check the Japanese translation of the names of staff who will be involved in their Japan business.

For example, one of my clients had a sales director named Joe Dunn. While a common name in the States, the name in Japanese has the same pronunciation as the word for "joke"—*jou-dan* (冗談). Japanese would often laugh upon hearing his name for the first time and joke about it again and again over time. A foreign company being represented by a senior executive—in this case, the sales director—who introduces himself by saying "Hello, I'm a joke" is probably not the image you want your company to project when trying to succeed in a foreign market. At least not if you want your company and its products to be taken seriously!

II. THE RIGHT PEOPLE

A. SELECTING A COMPANY TO WORK WITH

1. Identifying Potential Business Partners

A company's decision concerning which Japanese partner to work with to sell products and services in Japan is equally critical to determining which products to launch. There are several resources available that American companies can call upon to find a partner company in Japan. The first are government resources:

- o U.S. Commerce Department in Washington, DC

- o Commercial Officer at the U.S. Embassy in Tokyo

- o State-owned business development offices in Japan hosted by different U.S. states

- o Japan External Trade Organization (JETRO)—Tokyo-based government organization promoting business between America and Japan through its offices in New York City and throughout the States

The second resource is international business consultants and attorneys who specialize in the Japanese market. While their services typically cost more than government-related resources, the value they provide is usually worth the cost. Specifically, they bring to the table a track record of hands-on experience in negotiating, building, and managing businesses in Japan. It is common for those working in the government resources offices not have meaningful, firsthand experience putting together and actually running business operations in Japan. Many have no business experience at all. Consequently, while they possess *theoretical* knowledge of what needs to be done and a list of Japanese companies in the given industry, they often have little *experiential* understanding of business execution. Furthermore, they are usually unaware of the many unexpected challenges and pitfalls that confront foreign companies in the Japanese market that only become known to industry participants from experience (and sometimes not even then).

The third resource for finding a partner company in Japan is in-country conferences and trade shows. As is true in the States, the major companies and organizations in an industry usually exhibit at that industry's major conferences and trade shows. The companies that exhibit are those that are active in that industry—those looking to develop their business and advance their standing in their industry. In other words, they are the players seeking to make something happen in the industry.

How can foreign executives identify which of the many companies exhibiting at a conference or trade show they should talk with—the real players, the movers and shakers? One indicator is the size of an exhibitor's booth—the larger the booth, generally the greater the prominence of the company in their industry. Booth location in the exhibit hall is another indicator. The major players in an industry usually rent the booths located right by the main entrance to the exhibit hall. As the main entrance tends to be in the middle of the exhibit hall, the major players likewise tend to be in the middle of the exhibit hall. Companies out on the periphery of the exhibit hall floor are usually the smaller, second- and third-tier entities in the industry.

A fourth resource is parties from your list of existing contacts who can provide an introduction to a Japanese company. Those could be contacts you may already have in Japan or companies in the U.S. that you either know or do business with that have connections in Japan. As you now know, business in Japan is relationship driven, so leveraging relevant contacts can be a viable method for locating a business partner there.

> Foreign companies need to make careful decisions to get it right the first time when selecting their business partner in the Japanese market.

Identifying and being introduced to a potential partner company in Japan, however, only is only the first step to a foreign company's commencing business in that market. The next step is for foreign companies to effectively screen all potential business partners and then select the most appropriate Japanese company with whom to partner.

2. Screening & Selecting a Partner Company

Under normal circumstances, Japanese companies do not look favorably on foreign companies changing business partners in Japan. In their view, changing business partners means a relationship breakdown occurred and that indicates the foreign company did not appropriately manage and value the relationship with its Japanese partner. It further demonstrates the foreign company did not give sufficient consideration to Japan's business ways—namely, that business is relationship driven and that both companies should compromise for the sake of that relationship. Consequently, foreign companies need to make careful decisions to get it right the first time when selecting their business partner in the Japanese market.

How, then, can foreign companies most effectively screen, evaluate, and select the most appropriate Japanese business partner, and what criteria should foreign executives use in that effort? Here are fifteen significant criteria that should be considered:

(1) **The history of the Japanese company:** It's important to research the company's track record. How long has the company been in business and how successful have they been in meeting their goals?

(2) **Experience and capabilities:** Regardless of how long a company has been operating, it is necessary to study the company's length, depth, and breadth of experience in the foreign company's particular industry, sales channel, and product category in Japan. For example, one former client was thrilled that a major Japanese company with over a hundred and fifty year history was pursuing them. It was quite sobering when I informed the client that while the Japanese company did have such a long history, they were a newcomer to my client's industry with less than three years of experience and no meaningful track record yet in their industry.

It's important to determine a potential partner's actual capabilities and possible weaknesses. For example, does a Japanese company sell directly to the end-users of a foreign company's product or do they need to go through intermediaries? Obviously, selling directly to product end-users is most favorable. Depending on the particulars, a Japanese company's selling to end-users through one intermediary sales company can be acceptable, but generally speaking a potential partner company's need for multiple intermediaries is not desirable and should be viewed by foreign executives as a potential red flag.

(3) **Financial performance:** Review the company's track record for sales and profitability over the years. What is the company's overall financial condition?

(4) **Corporate culture & management strategy:** Every company has its own corporate culture and management priorities. A foreign company should determine to what degree the prospective partner's culture and priorities align with their own.

For instance, if a foreign company's strategic objectives for the Japanese market include establishing the company, brand, and product as an industry leader there, is the potential Japanese partner likewise interested in that goal? Is the potential partner experienced in achieving that goal? Or, in contrast, are they a "flavor of the month" type of company solely interested in selling as many units of a partner's product as they can for as long as sales are strong, but then moving on to other business projects?

(5) **Industry standing:** Whenever possible seek out top tier prospects for potential partnerships. What is the company's standing in their industry? Obviously, the greater a company's standing in their industry, the stronger a partner they are likely to be. While there can be exceptions, as a general rule it is not advisable to work with a company that is not in the top tier of their industry.

(6) **Industry reputation:** While industry standing is a

measurable level of a company's achievement in areas such as sales revenues or market share, industry reputation is how a company is perceived and thought of by others in the industry and society at large. For example, how is the company regarded by fellow professionals in that industry? Does the company have a reputation for conducting business in a professional, legal, and ethical manner or are they known for cutting corners, engaging in questionable business practices, and stealing the intellectual property of foreign firms? The American firm PNQ, Inc. initially partnered with a company known in Japan for the latter style of business and encountered major problems as described in the chapter titled "Challenges & Foibles."

(7) **Spokesperson collaboration:** In the event that sales of a foreign company's products can be enhanced by utilizing a spokesperson such as a physician or celebrity, foreign executives need to ascertain if a potential Japanese partner has a track record of attracting and working with the right spokespersons.

 If the leading spokespersons do not work with a Japanese company, that is definitely a red flag. Likewise, the caliber of the spokespersons who do work with a Japanese company is indicative of that company's standing and reputation in the Japanese market. For example, if a company's spokesperson for a medical product is not a first tier, recognized authority physician, that is a red flag.

(8) **Sufficient financial resources:** A potential Japanese partner company should possess sufficient financial resources to market, sell, and provide after-sales customer care and maintenance to the level of a foreign company's satisfaction. Equally important to *possessing* sufficient financial resources,

are they *committed* to allocating the requisite financial resources?

(9) **Appropriate sales plan:** Consider how likely a potential Japanese partner's business plans are to attain your desired goals for the Japan market. Are their plans likely to achieve the expected level of sales in Japan? Are their plans likely to advance a foreign company's standing and reputation in the Japanese market? Furthermore, does the Japanese company have successful experience executing the sales activities included in its business plan for your company?

(10) **Corporate commitment:** While capital is a major factor, it is not the only commitment factor to consider when assessing their commitment to the partnership. A more complete list would include:

- Number of employees they are committing to the business

- Number of company departments or divisions that will be involved

- Number of affiliates in the case of large corporations; in the case of small- and medium-sized firms, the number of cooperating companies

- Number of years in the Japanese company's internal plan for the business project: Twelve months? Three years? Five years? As we have discussed, a medium- or long-term time horizon in Japan is three to five years. While sales projections and marketing activities included in a sales agreement may be for the first two or three years of the project, interest in years four and five is an indication of strong, long-term commitment. Foreign executives need to determine the level of long-term interest of potential Japanese partner.

(11) **Exclusive or non-exclusive business agreement:** A Japanese company's insistence on having exclusive rights in its business agreement with a foreign company is a major indicator of how serious their interest is. A major industry player and strong candidate partner company will always insist on exclusive rights. If they are going to make a major commitment to a business project, they want to make sure only their company reaps the benefits and not their competitors. If they do not clamor for exclusive rights, that is a major red flag, and foreign executives should remove that company from consideration.

> If a Japanese company does not clamor for exclusive rights...foreign executives should remove that company from consideration.

(12) **Project launch:** The scale of the project launch the Japanese company is proposing to officially commence the business in Japan reflects their commitment, financial involvement, and corporate capabilities. Determine where the company proposes to conduct the launch, whom they are planning to invite, and the length of the event.

For example, is it a ninety-minute ceremony inside the

Japanese company and only employees are invited? Is it a half-day affair that takes place in the grand ballroom of one of the major hotels in Tokyo or Osaka with leaders from government, business, the media, and the community invited and involved? Will they have only one launch program or launch events in several major cities? The greater the project launch planned, the greater the Japanese company's commitment and expectations are for the business.

(13) **Manufacturer or sales company:** It's important to know if the prospective Japanese partner is a manufacturer or if they are a sales company only. With potential partner companies that are manufacturers, there is always the inherent risk that they will incorporate knowledge of foreign products into their own product line and eventually sell products that will compete—if not directly, then indirectly through affiliates or companies where they have "cooperative relationships." PNQ, Inc. experienced this with the pharmaceutical company they originally partnered with (see the "Challenges & Foibles" chapter). Companies that are sales companies only are safer in that regard.

(14) **Banks:** All company profiles in Japan list the bank(s) with whom the Japanese company does business. The rank of those banks is indicative of the company's financial strength and reputation. Japan's better banks work with Japan's better companies. The country's top three money center banks are Mitsubishi UFJ Financial Group, Mizuho Financial Group, and Sumitomo Mitsui Financial.

(15) **Motivation:** Potential partner companies in international markets have any number of motivations for wanting

to work with an American company in their market, including gaining the opportunity to work with a leading foreign company to enlarge their market share, expand sales and profit, and increase their standing in their domestic industry. These, of course, are desirable motivations foreign executives seek in partner companies overseas. However, there are several other reasons why companies in foreign markets want to work with American firms and those reasons are not at all in the interests of foreign companies. I have seen several over the years, but the following are some of the more noteworthy:

o   Obtaining and benefitting from the proprietary technology or intellectual property belonging to a foreign company

o   Securing a business agreement with a prominent foreign company as a source of great pride. Becoming the partner of a leading foreign company provides a Japanese company with bragging rights among their peers in their industry. I call these "trophy rights" since the Japanese company is motivated more by the prestige of saying they are working with such and such a foreign company than in actually developing the business project. Such companies collect business agreements on their mantel as if they were trophies.

o   Securing the business rights to a well-known foreign company's products to help establish the Japanese company as the market leader among their domestic competitors

o   Tying up the foreign company to *keep it out* of the Japanese market

In these cases, often the Japanese company is planning on launching or is already selling a similar product line either themselves or through a related company so they drag their feet during the negotiations, during the process to obtain government approval to import and sell the foreign product in Japan, and during the roll out and sales of the foreign product. The Japanese company engages only in minimal marketing and sales efforts on behalf of the foreign product. Foreign companies can lose several years of investment, opportunity, market share, and profit as a result of these motivations.

Clearly these four motivations are not in the interests of foreign companies. Foreign executives need to be extra diligent in ascertaining the motivation of companies they are screening. Here again with most of the above-mentioned criteria for screening companies in Japan, international business consultants, lawyers, and other industry experts are in a position to provide invaluable assistance to foreign executives while government-related entities tend not to be in that position.

Partner selection is perhaps the most important decision foreign executives must make in doing business in Japan. When foreign companies work with the wrong partner company, they can pay a huge cost in terms of time, capital, energy, corporate image, competitiveness, momentum, and lost sales and profit. Foreign executives need to work very closely with industry experts in evaluating and selecting their partner for the Japanese market.

3. Seek a Partner, Not a Distributor

Foreign companies tend to frame their search for a company to work with in a foreign market in terms of finding a good sales company or distributor in that overseas market. However, that is a strategic misstep as foreign companies rarely achieve their maximum success potential by working with a sales company or distributor in international markets. The key to maximizing success in Japan and other overseas markets is to work with a partner.

What is the difference between a distributor and a partner? A distributor is solely interested in selling as many units of a given product as possible during the life of the sales cycle. While product sales represent the entirety of interest for a distributor, sales are but one part of the interest of a partner. Product sales are equally important to a partner; however, a partner also focuses on the strategic dimensions of what is needed to maximize a foreign company's success in the Japanese market. That means establishing the foreign company's corporate image, company brand, and product line as a leader in its industry segment for the long term.

> A partner focuses on the strategic dimensions of what is needed to succeed in the Japanese market.

Furthermore, when initial sales levels begin to drop off, a distributor shifts some, if not all, of its interest and efforts to selling other products that sell better. A distributor's level of commitment to selling a product is tied to that product's level of sales. As sales diminish, so does distributor commitment, focus, investment, and attention. In contrast, a partner is committed to both product sales and the mutual relationship with the foreign company. The two provide buoyance for each other, so if sales slow down, relational commitment keeps a partner focused on the business project. This is a powerful difference between a partner and a distributor in Japan and a significant benefit that a partner brings to foreign executives.

The following are seven additional major aspects that a partner provides to a foreign company that a distributor does not:

- A partner values your product concept, not just profiting from the sale of your product.

- A partner values the uniqueness, competitive advantage, and long-term sales potential of your product along with its underlying concept and technology. As a result, they formulate and commit their corporate resources to a business plan for your product line in Japan that promotes not only your product but also its underlying product concept and technology, and they do so for the long term.

- Your company's total success in the Japanese market is a major priority for a partner company. This is evidenced in

  o the number and quality of management and staff they assign to your project.

  o the amount of capital they commit to promoting your business.

  o the level and frequency of promotional activities they engage in for your project.

- A partner ensures that your product and its underlying concept are properly understood in the market. They achieve that objective by engaging in appropriate marketing and educational activities on a regular basis throughout the market, including product usage workshops designed for both those selling the products and for product end-users.

- A partner respects and vigorously helps you defend your intellectual property. That means they take the lead in identifying and going after companies that infringe on your intellectual property.

- A partner actively updates you on competitive developments in their market that impact your business and proactively seeks new strategies and solutions to best deal with them in real time.

- A partner will go out of their way to find ways for you to improve your product so it can have greater appeal— and sales—in their market.

When a foreign company selects a distributor to work with in Japan, it is equivalent to the American firm starting its business in Japan in the batter's box trying to get a hit and get on first base. When a foreign company has a partner company in Japan that is fully committed to going to bat for the American company, the U.S. firm starts its business in the Japanese market on second base.

The significance Japanese place on relationship in business is discussed in numerous contexts and examples throughout this book. The center of that approach is that business in Japan is relationship based and driven. As discussed, this dimension of Japanese business brings with it additional expectations and requirements, including the need to be committed to the mutual business relationship and business project for the long term.

I strongly recommend that American executives put to work that unique requirement of Japan's business culture to further secure and advance their business interests by selecting a company to work with in Japan that is a full-fledged partner and not just a distributor. By doing so, American executives can benefit from the requirements of Japan's business culture by leveraging them for their own business interests instead of having those requirements be a burden or work against their interests. By being aware of and strategically navigating Japan's business culture, foreign executives can better ensure their optimal and long-term success in the Japanese market.

B. SELECTING THE RIGHT EMPLOYEES

A foreign company's finding the right people for its business venture in Japan applies not only to finding the most suitable in-country company to work with there but also to selecting the employees within its own company who are likely to do well working in the Japanese market. Having the right members for the company's Japan team is critical; it will directly impact just about every facet of business in the Japanese market including:

- How smoothly a foreign company's overall experience of doing business in Japan proceeds

- How productive the relationship is between the foreign company and its Japanese partner

- How effective communication is between the company and its partner in Japan

- How strong and long term the Japanese partner's commitment to the business is over time

- Whether the foreign company achieves maximum success, limited success, minimal success, or outright fails in the Japanese market

What are the right types of employees foreign companies need to have on their team for Japan? Contrary to what foreign executives often believe, the employees who get the best results in the Japanese market are not necessarily the company's best performers in the domestic U.S. market. In fact, the best performing employees in the States often turn out to be the ones who have the hardest time in Japan and cause the greatest harm to the business interests of American companies there.

The ideal candidates for a foreign company's Japan team have the following characteristics. They are aware of—and accepting of—other cultures. They are flexible, and realize that there is more than one way to engage in a task or achieve a goal. While they possess confidence, they are not insistent on their own way of doing things but rather are patient with and open-minded regarding different approaches and styles of communication. They realize that just as there is more than one train to take them to a destination, there can be more than one way things are done in any market. The proverbial bull in the china shop is precisely the person you do *not* want involved in your Japan business.

At least one member of your Japan team needs to be experienced in the Japanese market. If a potential member of your Japan team has had previous experience working in Japan, make sure that experience is not out of date. As we saw in the "Challenges & Foibles" chapter in this book, PNQ, Inc. hired Ronald Dempsey as their new head of international sales because he had a decade of experience working in Japan. However, his experience was more than twenty years old, and he was unaware of the current conditions in the industry. Consequently, his way of conducting business was unsuccessful and even detrimental. Experience needs to be qualified in terms of how recent and relevant it is to your company's specific needs and objectives.

It was emphasized in the previous chapter and it is worth repeating: foreign executives should not rely on their Japanese counterparts to provide the translator for meetings. Doing so is a major strategic and tactical error that puts foreign companies at a significant disadvantage.

American companies need to have on their team their own *facilitator* who can provide accurate cultural interpretation as well as linguistic translation. This person can advance corporate goals and business interests by bridging the cultural differences between America and Japan. He or she can ensure that the American company successfully navigates Japan's culture-based differences in business practices so that instead of those differences hindering a foreign firm's results, the company can intentionally and strategically leverage those differences to enhance its success in the Japanese market.

Having meaningful Japanese market business experience and U.S.-Japan cultural fluency is a powerful catalyst that American executives need to have on their Japan team. When a foreign company has these, it is comparable to having both the correct address in Japan and a GPS system to take you where you want to go; the company knows its destination and has the right tool to get it there without taking detours, getting lost, going down dead end streets, or having misspent expenses. Foreign executives who do not have these assets on their company team only have an address; they know where they want to go in Japan, but have no idea how to get there and no idea of the obstacles that await along the way.

III. RELATIONSHIP BUILDING

Once a foreign company has determined the products, sales partner, and the members of its Japan team, the next major task is building and managing their relationship with their Japanese partner. Remember that business in Japan is relationship oriented and relationship driven. The relationship is necessary for a Japanese company to decide to work with another company and, once started, the relationship enables the business project to continue for the long term. As a result, building and managing that relationship must remain an on-going priority for a foreign company. Some practical steps American executives can implement to maximize their success in this area of relationship building and relationship management include the following twelve actions:

1. Keeping up close communication with the Japanese partner on a regular basis, including face-to-face meetings several times a year

2. Providing a safe harbor environment within which Japanese feel comfortable to discuss in a thorough and timely fashion challenges that arise in the joint business and mutual relationship

3. Being proactive in identifying challenges the Japanese partner confronts in promoting your business and in offering your assistance for best resolving them

4. Articulating and demonstrating that your company's commitment to the Japanese partner and the Japanese market is long term

5. Providing the partner with advance notice of developments that are related to the joint project

6. Celebrating with your Japanese partner milestone achievements in the mutual business

7. Congratulating the Japanese partner on their major business successes that are unrelated to your joint project

8. Updating your partner on new developments and breakthroughs at your company, even those unrelated to the joint business

9. Making opportunities to spend time together outside of official meetings by enjoying meals, after hour drinks, golf, and weekend activities

10. Expressing appreciation for the opportunity to work together with your Japanese partner

11. Sending New Year's greetings by the fourth business day of each year

12. Remaining polite, professional, timely, and dependable at all times, in all ways, in all matters, even with things that seem trivial from an American perspective

IV. SALES & MARKETING

A. PRODUCT LOCALIZATION

For foreign products that are sold to retail end-users on a business-to-consumer basis as opposed to those sold business-to-business, product localization is a powerful measure for increasing sales in the Japanese market. Customizing the product to indigenous cultural preferences can significantly increase the appeal of foreign products to Japanese consumers.

By way of example, McDonald's first started business in Japan with basically the same menu it has in the United States. It became successful and appealed to those who enjoyed a foreign culinary experience—something different. However, when the company added Japanese style items such as "Tonkatsu Mac Burger," "Ebi Fry," and "Teriyaki Mac Burger" to its menu, it added a whole new category of customers, namely consumers who enjoy traditional Japanese cuisine. These menu items present traditional

Japanese entrees in the burger form that McDonald's is known for.

The Tonkatsu Mac Burger, for example, is a McDonald's burger that uses traditional Japanese *tonkatsu* (fried pork) in place of a beef patty. Ebi Fry is McDonald's variation of Japan's traditional fried shrimp. The Teriyaki Mac Burger is a McDonald's beef hamburger seasoned with Japan's traditional teriyaki sauce. By including in its product line items that were localized to suit traditional cultural preferences, McDonald's was able to expand its customer base beyond those who enjoyed foreign food to include those who were attracted by these new styles of traditional Japanese foods. This is an excellent example of a foreign company increasing its bottom line in Japan by adapting its products to traditional cultural preferences.

B. Refreshing Products

The four seasons play an important part of life in Japanese society. Beyond impacting just fashion, the idea of living in harmony with the four seasons impacts product marketing in Japan in a substantial way. For example, many consumer products need to have packaging that reflects each season. Seasonal food products and flavors also are emphasized according to each season of the year.

> Product localization is a powerful measure for increasing sales in the Japanese market.

Major Japanese beer manufacturers such as Asahi, Sappori, and Kirin, for example, all regularly produce and market beer with seasonal themes. Certain beers are sold for the winter season. Different brews are sold in the summer. Yet even more flavors are available in the fall and spring. In addition to the brew, the can or bottle is designed with themes for each specific season. While some American companies lately have started to engage in seasonal marketing by producing different beers for different seasons, this practice is long established in Japan and is common in numerous industries. Keeping this cultural understanding and market preference in mind, foreign companies should be prepared to refresh product offerings more often in Japan than they currently do in America. Consumers expect it. Competition demands it.

C. PRODUCT SPOKESPERSON

If applicable for a product, the use of a spokesperson is another tool for elevating sales volumes and brand building in the Japanese market. Physicians, celebrities, and sports figures are the most common ones. Foreign companies can access a product spokesperson either through their sales partner, an industry consultant, or talent agencies.

The importance of the product spokesperson cannot be emphasized enough. Having the right sales company selling a company's products in overseas markets is only half the formula for success. Having key, opinion-leading physicians or celebrities on board promoting these products is the other. Sales companies promote products from the *bottom up* through their marketing efforts. An effective product spokesperson provides *top-down* market penetration and product leadership. The two approaches combined provide a one-two punch that yields significantly greater sales results.

D. PRODUCT TRAINING

Given the Japanese penchant for details and doing things right, training in product usage and maintenance should be conducted with greater frequency and in greater depth in Japan than in America. Depending on the product, training needs to be given not only to a foreign company's sales partner in Japan but also to the product's end-users. For example, if the Japanese sales partner company sells a product to hospitals and clinics, in-depth training must be provided to both the partner company as well as the physicians or technicians using the product at the medical establishments.

Product training needs to be given both before and after product sales commence in Japan. A greater number of trainings are needed initially than are needed later. While the frequency varies from product to product and industry to industry, a good general rule of thumb would be to have trainings quarterly during the first two years after launching the product; three trainings each in years three and four; and finally two trainings annually beginning year five.

D. MAKE YOUR PRODUCT EXCLUSIVE

Whenever possible, launch a product by making it exclusive, available to only a select few. For example, when I launched America's leading prescription skin care product line in Japan, I initially invited only Japan's top twelve physicians to be product users. That made these elite doctors members of the exclusive club of first product users in their country. I also established the policy that in order to purchase and use the products, a physician must first attend a full day training course on the product's concept, usage protocols, and troubleshooting.

Not being able to readily obtain the products caused the rest of the physicians in the market to want to buy the products even more. Not being able to be members of the group of trained physicians who were qualified to purchase and use the product only made other doctors more interested in being part of that group. This significantly contributed to the manufacturer's corporate image and brand in the Japanese market.

This exclusivity marketing approach for a product is a way to leverage the strong group orientation and emphasis on relationships in Japan for maximizing not only the sales of the product but also for maximizing their status and cachet.

CONCLUSION

This book has demonstrated how capitalism in Japan is practiced based on fundamentally different approaches and methods when compared to the West. The majority of the practices found in management and other facets of business in Japan differ due to the different cultural framework within which commerce takes place in that country. While these culture-based differences in business practices are ever-present, they are generally unknown to foreign executives. Consequently, these culture-based differences present major challenges and obstacles to foreign companies' success in the Japanese market.

The focus of this book has been three-fold:

- To clearly identify culture-based differences in business practices in Japan—what they are, how they inform the manner in which business is conducted differently in Japan, and how they are problematic for foreign companies

- To explain the cultural roots of those differences in Japan's business practices so they may be understood in their correct cultural context

- To provide practical, proven methods for successfully dealing with Japan's culture-based differences in business practices

During the past thirty-five years of working with American and European companies in Asian markets, I have seen their executives deal with these differences in one of two ways. In the first way, foreign executives are disinterested in these differences and choose not to take them into consideration when formulating and implementing their business strategy for the Japanese market. The result invariably has been that their success in Japan is curtailed or outright precluded.

In contrast, other foreign executives, once being informed of them, have pro-actively prepared for Japan's culture-based differences in business practices. Doing so has enabled those foreign companies to successfully deal with these differences and, in many instances, even leverage them so that they enhance rather than hinder the foreign company's business interests in Japan.

The recognition of, insights into, and methods for dealing with these culture-based differences in business practices contained in this book were gained by my slugging it out in the trenches of U.S.-Asia business for three-and-a-half decades. It is my hope that this book will serve as a practical guide to help companies succeed in the Japanese market by providing foreign executives with the strategic insights to effectively navigate Japan's culture-based differences in business practices, thereby promoting prosperity and cultural understanding between our two countries.

BIBLIOGRAPHY

ABOUT THE AUTHOR

WHAT CLIENTS
ARE SAYING

BIBLIOGRAPHY

Anderman, Gunilla and Rogers, Margaret. *Word, Text, Translation: Liber Amicorum for Peter Newmark*. Clevedon: Multilingual Matters Ltd, 1999.

Dingle, Carol A. *Memorable Quotations: Philosophers of Western Civilization*. New York: Writers Club Press, 2000.

Drucker, Peter F. *Management Challenges for the 21st Century*. New York: Harper Business, 1999.

Drucker, Peter F. *The Essential Drucker*. New York: Harper Collins, 2001.

Fridenson, Patrick and Kikkawa, Takeo. *Gurobaru Shihonshugi no Naka no Shibusawa Eiichi: Gappon Kyapitarizumu to Moraru* (グローバル資本主義の中の渋沢栄一:合本キャピタリズムとモラル *Gappon Capitalism: The Economic and Moral Ideology of Shibusawa Eiichi in Global Perspective*). Tokyo: Toyo Keizai Shimpousha, 2014.

Government of Japan. *We are Tomodachi* (*We are Friends*). Tokyo: Spring/Summer 2014.

Ikeda, Kazutaka, translator. *Fukuzawa Yukichi no Nihon Koushitu-ron Gendai-yaku* (福沢諭吉の日本皇室論現代語訳 *Fukuzawa Yukichi's Concept of Japan's Imperial Household*). Tokyo: Shimazu Shobou, 2008.

Inamori, Kazuo. *A Compass to Fulfillment: Passion and Spirituality in Life and Business*. New York: McGraw Hill, 2010.

Inamori, Kazuo. *Amoeba Management*. Boca Raton, Florida: CRC Press, 2013.

Inamori, Kazuo. *Seiko no Youtei* (成功の要諦 *Essence of Success*). Tokyo: Chichi Shuppansha, 2014.

Kambayashi, Norio; Morita, Masaya; and Okabe, Yoko. *Management Education in Japan*. Oxford, England: Chandos Publishing Limited, 2008.

Kitagawa, Joseph M. *Religion in Japanese History*. New York: Columbia University Press, 1966.

Matsumura, Jeremy. "Shibusawa Eiichi: Japan's Great Industrialist Guided by Confucian Morals." *The East* Vol. 39, No. 3 September-October 2003.

Matsushita, Konosuke. *Not for Bread Alone: A Business Ethos, A Management Ethic*. Tokyo: PHP Institute, Inc., 1984.

Matsushita, Konosuke. *Quest for Prosperity: The Life of a Japanese Industrialist*. Tokyo: PHP Institute, Inc., 1988.

Matsushita, Konosuke. *The Path*. New York: McGraw Hill, 1968.

Meigen Ijin "Quotes of Inamori Kazuo."
http://www.meigen-ijin.com/inamorikazuo.

Morita, Akio. *Made In Japan*. New York: E.P. Dutton, 1986.

The NHK Group. *Good Mileage: The High-Performance Business Philosophy of Shoichiro Honda*. Tokyo: NHK Publishing, 1996.

Nitobe, Inazo. *Bushido: The Soul of Japan—A Classic Essay on Samurai Ethics*. New York: Kondansha USA, Inc., 2012.

Obata, Kyugoro. *An Interpretation of the Life of Viscount Shibusawa*. Tokyo: Tokyo Printing Company, 1937.

Ono, Sokyo. *Shinto: The Kami Way*. Rutland, Vermont: Charles E. Tuttle Company, 1979.

PHP Institute, Inc. *Konosuke Matsushita: His Life and Management Philosophy*. Tokyo: PHP Institute, Inc., 2002.

PHP Institute, Inc. *Matsushita Konosuke (1894–1989): His Life & Legacy*. Tokyo: PHP Institute, Inc., 1994.

QuotesWise: Soichiro Honda.
http://www.quoteswise.com/soichiro-honda-quotes-3.html.

Shibusawa, Eiichi. *Kokufu-ron: Jitsugyou to Koueki* (国富論:実業と公益 *Theory of National Wealth: Business and Social Benefit*. Tokyo: Kokusho Kankokai, Inc., 2010.

Shibusawa, Eiichi. *Rongo To Soroban: Gendai Goyaku* (論語と算盤現代訳 *Analects and Abacus: Modern Translation*). Tokyo: Chikumashobo, 2010.

Shibusawa, Eiichi. *The Autobiography of Shibusawa Eiichi*. Tokyo: Tokyo University Press, 1994.

Taguchi, Yoshifumi. *The Managerial Ideas from the East*. Honolulu: Babel Press U.S.A., 2012.

Taguchi, Yoshifumi. *Tao Management: Japanese Management Philosophy Based on an Interpretation of the Tao Te Ching*. Norwalk, Connecticut: EastBridge, 2006.

Tsukakoshi, Hiroshi. *Tree-Ring Management: Take the Long View and Grow Your Business Slowly*. Tokyo: Japan Publishing Industry Foundation for Culture, 2015.

Yamagake, Motohisa. *Shinto no Ikikata* (神道の生き方 *Shinto's Way of Life*). Tokyo: Gakken Publishing Co., 2010.

Yamagake, Motohisa. *Shinto no Shimpi: Kou-Shinto no Shisou to Gyouhou* (神道の神秘:古神道の思想と行法 *The Mysteries of Shinto: Thought and Action in Ancient Shinto*). Tokyo: Shunjusha, 2008.

Yamamoto, Tsunetomo. *Hagakure: The Book of the Samurai*. Boston: Shambhala Publications, Inc., 2012.

About The Author

Robert
Charles
Azar

Robert Azar is a U.S.-Asia business and cultural expert with thirty-five years of executive level success. As a strategy advisor, he specializes in achieving excellence in global business development, problem resolution, and intercultural management.

At this writing, Mr. Azar is one of only 1,000 consultants in the U.S. to have earned the Certified Management Consultant (CMC) designation, the management consulting industry's preeminent recognition for demonstrated achievements and excellence in client satisfaction, professional standards, and ethical business practices.

R. Azar lived in the Far East for seven years, worked in Japanese corporations for ten years, and developed and managed U.S. businesses in Asian markets for twenty-five years. He reads, writes, and speaks Japanese fluently and is familiar with the Korean language.

He was honored to attend the White House's welcome ceremony for Japanese Prime Minister Shinzo Abe for U.S.-Japan trade discussions on April 28, 2015. He was one of four hundred leaders in U.S.-Asian affairs to attend President Clinton's major policy speech before his summit meeting with then-Chinese President Jiang Zemin in Washington, D.C. on October 24, 1997.

Prior to commencing his career in international business and intercultural management, Mr. Azar completed a decade of formal academic training and field research in Asian culture. His double major BA degree in International Relations and East Asian Studies from New York University led to completing an MA degree in East Asian political, economic, and cultural affairs at Columbia University. He then studied international marketing, global management, and business law at Harvard University. *Navigating Japan's Business Culture* is his second book. He also is the published author of numerous articles and reports on U.S.-Asian business, economics, foreign policy, and culture, published both in America and Japan, in English and in Japanese.

As an expert on Asia, Mr. Azar has been interviewed frequently by major international media for more than thirty years. He has been a guest on CNN, CNBC, the Financial News Network (FNN), and the Wall Street Journal Report as well as on local cable television and radio shows in the United States. In Japan, he has appeared, speaking in Japanese, on Television Tokyo's "World Business Satellite" (Japan's foremost business news program), NHK, Nippon Television, Fuji Television, and numerous radio shows. He has also been featured in several interviews in leading American and Asian news publications, including *The New York Times*, *Business Week*, *Crain's BtoB*, and *Kenko Sangyo Shimbun* (Health Industry News).

His international career spans numerous industries and several fields of global business, including strategic planning, negotiating, management, finance, intercultural mediation, global business development, international sales and marketing, market research, international trade, product development, human resources, trouble shooting, turn around services, and political and economic analysis—in both the for-profit and the non-profit sectors.

Mr. Azar has extensive experience in advising companies seeking to succeed in Asian markets. He is often called upon to speak, present, and teach on U.S.-Asian business and culture matters to corporate, government, academic, and cultural entities.

He has served as a member of the board of directors for numerous organizations, including the North Carolina Japan Center, United Arts Council of Wake County, the World Trade Council, Institute of Management Consultants, American Cancer Society, and the Japanese Center for Quality of Life Studies.

R. Azar has logged over one million flight miles traveling to, from, and within Asia. He is a collector of Asian art and antique ceramics and paints Japanese calligraphy.

He currently serves as president of Asia Strategic Advisors LLC™, a company that teaches and advises U.S. businesses, government agencies, cultural institutions, and non-profit organizations on achieving optimal success doing business with Asian companies operating either in Asia or America. See AsiaStrategicAdvisors.com for further information.

What Clients Are Saying

"With your assistance, we were able to increase our sales by 70 percent last year! A good percentage of our growth is attributed to your efforts in Asia. We anticipate, with your help, to continue to expand these markets and increase our sales even further."

Marty Davidson
President & CEO, Excel Cosmeceuticals, Inc.
Bloomfield Hills, Minnesota, U.S.A.

"Koken Co., Ltd. has had the opportunity to work closely with Mr. Robert C. Azar over the past two years. We have found him to be an individual of utmost integrity and professionalism. Mr. Azar's knowledge of the Japanese health and skin care market is unsurpassed, even by our own executives.

In addition to impeccable Japanese language skills, his ability to resolve difficulties encountered in doing business internationally is outstanding. It is without hesitation that I unconditionally recommend Robert Azar."

Teruo Miyata, Ph.D.
President, Koken Co., Ltd.
Tokyo, Japan

"These sales (in Asia) are really good news. Thanks for believing in us.... You are a true hero! Congrats!"

Arnd Kensy, President
Ulrich Tobies, Director of International Sales, Human Med AG
Berlin, Germany

"I have known Robert Azar for several years now, and worked closely with him when he was engaged to provide services to Obagi Medical Products. Robert is highly skilled in launching brands globally and building an international presence.

In one particular project, I worked with Robert to bring the Obagi brand to Japan. In the process of completing that project, it was very clear that Robert had extensive knowledge of the medical channels in Japan, who the key opinion leaders are, what companies had the largest market share, the best reputation and/or the highest growth rates, as well as who the best potential distribution partners would be for Obagi. Further, the key opinion leaders and industry players in Japan knew Robert, and it became clear that he has garnered excellent relationships throughout that country and many others.

One of my existing contacts in Japan noted, after speaking with Robert, that he was very surprised that Robert was not Japanese - which is a testament to Robert's absolutely flawless command of the Japanese language and his natural understanding/competency with cultural norms and subtleties. Finding someone with these skills is rare - but adding those skills to his sharp business acumen and industry knowledge sets Robert even further apart. Top qualities: great results, expertise, high integrity.

In short, Robert is a proven professional who delivered on all of the projects that we engaged him on and I would welcome the opportunity to work with Robert again, anywhere in the world."

Curtis Cluff
Former CFO, Obagi Medical Products, Inc.
Long Beach, California, U.S.A.

"I had the sincere pleasure of working with Robert Azar for many years at Obagi Medical. He was a life-saver.

Robert assisted me in breaking into many Asian Markets—Japan and Korea notably. His understanding of the physician channel, those companies/ distributers who had the largest market-share in that channel and the key opinion leaders within those markets provided Obagi quick access and success.

Robert's command of the Japanese language, his ability to understand the objectives of his clients, and his superior knowledge of the international market, makes him one of the best all-round professionals that I have met in the industry to date. I would welcome, and look forward to, the opportunity of working with Robert again."

Kathleen LaGrave
Former Director, International Sales
Obagi Medical Products, Inc.
Long Beach, California, U.S.A.

"Having worked with Robert Azar for over two-and-a-half years, I must say that he is very much involved in helping grow markets for American Companies wishing to add sales outlets in Asia and Europe.

Mr. Robert Azar is fluent in Japanese, which is very rare for an American, and I have found that to be an invaluable asset in promoting product sales in Japan. He also has very good contacts in Korea, China and other parts of Asia, and excellent relationships with sub-distributors throughout the area. He has a vast knowledge of International Markets in general and a specific knowledge of various Asian cultures. And his focus on strategic sales is both unique and beneficial.

I would definitely recommend Mr. Azar to anyone wanting to enter the International Market."

William Kelley
Director of International Sales, Sciton Inc.
Palo Alto, California, U.S.A.

"I have known Robert Azar for a couple of years now. I worked very closely with him when he successfully introduced Brava AFT System in the Japanese market. His quick progress into the Japanese market proved us correct in trusting Robert with this delicate operation. Robert is highly skilled in finding the best strategy for your medical device in the Japanese market. He has vast knowledge of medical device industry in Japan, from manufacturers to distributors and end users. His understanding of the language and the culture along with his business experience in Japan makes him one of the best in launching products in this market. Robert has been a trustworthy business partner. I am pleased to recommend Robert to anyone looking to expand their business success in Japan."

Ercan Dilsen
VP Operations, Brava, LLC
Miami, Florida, U.S.A.